vest addition to our internationally acclaimed
ople / Incredible Stories. These riveting thrillers
en who perform extraordinary deeds against
t for justice, track down elusive killers, protect the
ne wrongly accused. Their stories, told in their own
id drama and anguish behind the headlines of those
ities and find the resiliency to fight back...

r and Greed, bail bond agent Pam Phree and bounty
side" Beakley are a match made in heaven, only not for
d thugs prowling the streets. Their stories of working
down some of the most dangerous fugitives on the lam
ne time, fighting the corruption in their own business reads
 put to paper. This true story is loaded with intense gunfights,
ase scenes and near-death experiences. Any fan of both true
tion cinema will certainly find *Betrayal, Murder and Greed* a
id intriguing read, one that takes you right into the harrowing
 these brave purveyors of truth deal with on an everyday basis in
er-ending quest to bring criminals to justice.

ext time you want to read a crackling, suspenseful page-turner,
 is also a true account of a real-life hero illustrating the resiliency of
numan spirit, look for the New Horizon Press logo.

ncerely,

Dr. Joan S. Dunphy
Publisher & Editor-in-Chief
Real People / Incredible Stories

Betray

Betrayal, Murder and Greed

The True Story of a
a Bounty Hunter and a Bail Bond Agent

By Pam Phree and Mike "Darkside" Beakley

New Horizon Press
Far Hills, New Jersey

New Horizon Press
P.O. Box 669
Far Hills, NJ 07931

Phree, Pam and Beakley, Mike
Betrayal, Murder and Greed: The True Story of a Bounty Hunter and a Bail Bond Agent
Cover design: Robert Aulicino
Interior design: Susan Sanderson

Library of Congress Control Number: 209922798

ISBN 13: 978-0-88282-313-3
New Horizon Press

Manufactured in the U.S.A.

2014 2013 2012 2011 2010 / 5 4 3 2 1

Dedication

Sandy Straub: Your untimely death shocked all of us. You were one of the most beautiful people we've ever met, inside and out. You are loved by more people than you would have ever guessed and you are missed.

Authors' Note

This book is based on our actual experiences and reflects our perceptions of the past, present and future. The personalities, events, actions and conversations portrayed within the story have been reconstructed from our memories and the memories of participants. In an effort to safeguard individual privacy, most names with a few exceptions have been changed and, in some cases, we have altered otherwise identifying characteristics. Some characters, companies and situations are composites.

Events involving the characters happened as described; only minor details have been changed. The arrests of the fugitives and the investigations leading to those arrests are accurate, but references to the bail companies, employees and individuals are composites and do not refer to any one person or company.

Contents

Prologue

"Mike's been involved in a shooting and paramedics are performing aggressive CPR."

When Pam heard those words, the world stopped revolving. The sun froze in the sky. All the usual office noises like phones ringing and the clatter of fingers on keyboards came to a screeching halt as Pam's mind tried to grasp the enormity of that message.

Mike's been shot? she thought.

The first thing the human brain does is automatically reject what it cannot fathom. *That's impossible. Mike **can't** be hurt. Mike **isn't** hurt.* Pam's hand shook as she grasped the phone.

"Pam," Mike's wife, Dawn, said breathlessly. "My brother just called me. He's a police officer. He just got a call from one of his cop buddies who heard it on the police scanner that Mike's been involved in a shooting and paramedics are performing aggressive CPR."

Much as Pam never wanted to hear those words in her entire life, here they were—blaring in her ear. She often socialized with her long-time bounty hunter, Mike, and his wife, but his wife rarely called at work. Dawn is a calm, cool, collected woman who has her feet planted firmly on the ground. She's not one for hysterics or exaggeration. Pam knew immediately what she was saying was true. Mike might have been shot and might possibly be gravely wounded or dying. Pam felt like she'd been kicked in the stomach.

Finally Pam found her voice: "Mike's hurt?"

"The information is just coming in. All we know for sure is that Mike's involved. I tried to call Mike on his cell phone, but he didn't answer."

"Dawn, I know he's been chasing Roberto. I'll make a few calls, see what I can find out and if I hear anything, I'll call you back. If you hear something before I do, please call me."

Pam called Mike on his cell phone. No answer. Then she called Mike's partner, Byron, who didn't answer either. In all the years she'd known them, they'd *always* answered their cell phones—day and night. Something was wrong. *Very wrong*.

Earlier that afternoon, Mike and Pam had been in the middle of discussing one of Pam's forfeitures when Mike received a call on his cell phone. Pam had heard the urgency in his voice.

"I gotta go." He grabbed his jacket from the back of the chair. "Gary and Savant heard from a reliable informant that Roberto has his car at a local garage for repairs. They've been staking out the place twenty-four/seven waiting for Roberto to pick up his car. The car just left the garage. Gary just called me. He and Savant are following him. Byron and I have to intercept."

Pam nodded.

"Roberto is a really bad guy," Mike had told Pam a few days earlier. "He shot up a couple of his customers' houses in a drive-by. He jumped bail on Gary's bonding company to the tune of $150,000. He had a missile in his living room. Gary and his bounty hunter, Savant, arrested Roberto once before and turned him over to the police who, after they learned about the missile, turned him over to the FBI. Roberto agreed to snitch on who gave him drugs and the missile and to give information on organized crime in exchange for his freedom, so they let him go. Since he hadn't been jailed, he wasn't produced in court and Von Wahlde, a prosecutor who gives bonding companies such a hard time, refused to let Gary off the hook. We view Von Wahlde as a 'by the book' kind of guy. There are no shades of gray with him. He sees only black and white. According to him, the bondsman has to produce the defendant in court or book him into jail to get off the bond. Since Roberto wasn't produced, Von Wahlde gave Gary a choice: either pay the $150K or go get him again.

"Gary thinks that's bullshit. So do I! I feel it's messed up that the prosecutor won't let him off the bond. They did their job. They arrested him. It wasn't their fault the police let him go. Roberto's back on the street and he's running hard. Since he's armed and dangerous, Gary asked me to assist him and Savant in rearresting Roberto. Because *PHREE* is slow right now and all our forfeitures look okay, I agreed to help. Byron and I have been nosing around and learned Roberto is moving around from one place to another, never staying in one place. Finding him won't be easy. According to Roberto's wife, he's heavily armed. She told Byron, 'Roberto will shoot you. He'll die before he goes back to jail and he'll take the bounty hunters who are chasing him down with him.'

"Word on the street is Roberto's whacked out on meth. He goes days without sleeping. You know what that stuff does to your brain. It makes you crazy. Roberto got mad at some people the other night and shot up their house in a drive-by."

"Mike!" Pam had looked at him, worried.

"Don't worry," he had smiled confidently. "We'll get him. It's only a matter of time."

Pam's mind spun. If Mike was involved in a shooting, it *had* to have been with Roberto. But who was shot? Mike, Byron, Gary or Gary's bounty hunter, Savant?

Pam did what she always did when she was agitated: she paced the floor.

*Mike shot? Mike. . .**dead**?*

Introduction

A Brief History of
Bail Bonding and Bounty Hunters

If prostitution is the oldest profession in the world, then the job of a bail agent is the second. Although the word *bail* is not found in the Bible, the word *surety* is mentioned numerous times and since bail agents are sureties, their meanings are synonymous.

Surety means a person who accepts responsibility for another's debts or obligations. In Biblical times, when one wanted to obtain a loan, sometimes it was necessary for a third party to step in—the surety—who guaranteed that the loan would be repaid in full by the first party. As proof, the surety gave his personal cloak as collateral. If the first party defaulted, the surety could repay the debt or his cloak would be sold. If the sale didn't cover the debt, the debtor and/or his children could be sold into slavery or thrown in prison. If the first party disappeared and wasn't around to suffer these consequences, the surety was forced to suffer the same punishment as the debtor. In some cases, it's rumored the surety was put to death in the place of the accused.

1

English Development of the Bail Concept

Bail and sureties played the same roles in England during the Norman Conquest (approximately 1066-1072). According to Bob Burton, bounty hunter and author of *Bail Enforcer,* during this era "sureties for the accused were compared to his jailers." As in Biblical times, courts maintained that punishment of the surety, should the accused avoid it, was sufficient because the accused and his or her surety "were said to be bound 'body for body.'"[1]

In twelfth century medieval England, the local sheriffs, deemed representatives of the Crown, "possessed sovereign authority to release or hold suspects," according to the Professional Bail Agents of the United States (PBUS). Each sheriff determined on his own terms which defendants to detain or release and, of those he released, the conditions of the bail. Not surprisingly, "some sheriffs exploited the bail system for their own gain."[2]

Because the system was so corrupt, in 1275 the Statute of Westminster was born. For the first time, "bailable and non-bailable offenses were specifically listed."[3] However, the sheriffs still had the power to set the bail amount, which meant corruption in the system was still rampant. Sheriffs could name a bail of any amount for any reason whatsoever and if the prisoner was unable to "make bail," he or she would still be detained.

Several centuries later, the way in which bail was enacted underwent another major change. In the early seventeenth century, after obtaining no funds from Parliament, King Charles I ordered noblemen to lend him money, imprisoning without bail those who refused. A group of imprisoned knights argued the King's actions and filed a habeas corpus petition demanding the King allow trial or bail. The King refused to set bail or inform the knights of the charges against them.

Parliament stepped in on the side of the knights and passed the Petition of Right of 1628. This petition stated that "no freeman may be taken or imprisoned...but by the lawful judgment of his peers...

[or] without being brought to answer by due process of law"[4] and that all prisoners have a right to be informed of the charges against them. To circumvent this ruling, the King, courts and sheriffs invented procedural delays in "due process of law" citing such delays as the case was "outside term" or not calendared.[5]

In 1679, Parliament passed the Habeas Corpus Act to thwart the ongoing procedural delays. Parliament decreed that a magistrate "shall discharge the said prisoner from his imprisonment taking his or her recognizance, *with one or more Surety or Sureties,* in any sum, according to their discretion, having regard to the quality of the prisoner and nature of the offense for his or their appearance in the court of the King's bench...unless it shall appear...that the party is committed... for such matters or offenses for which by the law the prisoner is not bailable."[6]

Bail laws were improved with the Habeas Corpus Act, but there was still nothing to prevent excessive bail. Note the Habeas Corpus Act specifically states bail could be set "in any sum." Many defendants imprisoned on charges entitled to bail were unable to pay the exorbitant amounts demanded. Suspects were detained because they simply could not or would not pay the excessive bails. Finally in 1689, Parliament issued the Bill of Rights, which reads, in part, "that excessive bail ought not to be required."[7]

Bail in the United States
Colonial America followed the English bail laws. After seceding from England, the states "enacted their own versions of bail law."[8] Part of Virginia's constitution modeled the English Bill of Rights, stating "excessive bail ought not to be required." When the Bill of Rights was introduced in 1789, the Eighth Amendment was derived from this simple statement of the Virginia Constitution.[9] Additionally, part of the Sixth Amendment reflects the Habeas Corpus Act: "the accused shall enjoy the right ... to be informed of the nature and cause of the accusation."[10]

The same year, Congress passed the Judiciary Act defining bailable offenses in addition to limiting judges' boundaries on the bails they set.[11] The act reads, in part, "Upon all arrests in criminal cases, bail shall be admitted, except where punishment may be by death, in which cases, it shall not be admitted but by...a judge...who shall exercise their discretion therein, regarding the nature and circumstance of the offense and of the evidence, the usages of law."[12]

The conception of the bounty hunter figure began forming and the people acting in this capacity gained their authority "from Article 4, section 2 of the U.S. Constitution and the Act of February 12, 1793, which was passed to give effect to it."[13] According to the Constitution of the United States, Article 4, section 2, "A Person charged in any State with Treason, Felony or other Crime, who shall flee from Justice and be found in another State, shall, on Demand of the executive Authority of the State from which he fled, be delivered up, to be removed to the State having Jurisdiction of the Crime."[14]

Several court cases continued to specify the authority of bail agents and bounty hunters. In 1810, a New York court on the case of *Nicolls v. Ingersoll* determined that bondsmen derive their power from their private contractual agreements with defendants, not from the State. The court also emphasized that a bondsman has authority to pursue and arrest a fugitive anywhere in the state or nation and may appoint agents to this task. The 1822 case of *Read v. Case* declared a bondsman must announce himself before entering a defendant's house.[15]

The United States Supreme Court first addressed issues of bondsmen in 1869, *Reese v. United States*. The Supreme Court ruled bondsmen may arrest their forfeitures anywhere in the country and by whatever means necessary. The Court also expanded on the private contractual agreement addressed by *Nicolls*, saying the government would not interfere with this right.[16]

Crime became rampant and many bail agents had to forfeit their bonds when defendants failed to appear in court. In 1872, part of the Supreme Court's ruling in *Taylor v. Taintor* gave sureties "sweeping rights" to recover the accused.[17] It reads:

> When bail is given, the principal is regarded as delivered to the custody of his sureties. Their dominion is a continuance of the original imprisonment. Whenever they choose to do so, they may seize him and deliver him up in their discharge; and if that cannot be done at once, they may imprison him until it can be done. They may exercise their rights in person or by agent. They may pursue him into another state; may arrest him on the Sabbath, and, if necessary, may break and enter his house for that purpose. The seizure is not made by virtue of new process. None is needed. It is likened to the rearrest by the sheriff of an escaping prisoner.[18]

Bounty hunters were exempt from "due process." They didn't need warrants like law enforcement to break and enter. This led to a great deal of corruption. It's rumored that many bounty hunters walked on both sides of the law—a precedent that, in some cases, is still true today.

In the case of "flight risks" in the Old West, if one knew how to live off the land and possessed a fast horse, one could usually avoid being arrested. Often there was not a law enforcement officer for hundreds of miles.

In British Columbia, the bounty hunter had to bring in the criminal alive to get paid. The United States had no such restrictions, but the bounty was half if the prisoner died before making it to jail.

Bounty hunters remained anonymous for their own protection. None of their names were ever recorded.

Creation of the Modern Bail Bond Business

The modern business of bail bonds began in San Francisco in 1898 by Peter McDonough and his brother Tom, who created "the system by which a person pays a percentage to a professional bondsman who puts up the cash as a guarantee that the person will appear in court." The McDonoughs "controlled the San Francisco bail bonds business and were friendly with numerous police, public officials, judges and the DA [District Attorney]." Setting the standard for many bondsmen throughout the country over the years, McDonough "was accused of bribery, perjury, suborning witnesses, tampering with judges, bootlegging, corrupting officials and controlling and paying off police."[19]

The first major change in bail laws was enacted by Congress in 1966. The Bail Reform Act provides that a non-capital defendant "be ordered released pending trial on his personal recognizance or upon the execution of an unsecured appearance bond in an amount specified by the judicial officer, unless the officer determines…that such a release will not reasonably assure the appearance of the person as required."[20] However, the act left open a serious loophole that allowed dangerous suspects to receive bail as long as they didn't appear to be flight risks.

The next major revision to United States bail law came with the Bail Reform Act of 1984, which replaced its 1966 predecessor. The new law states that defendants should be held until trial if they are judged as dangerous to the community. The law also established new categories of who could be held without bail—those changed concerning very serious crimes, repeat offenders, the potentially dangerous and those who are considered flight risks.

The *Taylor v Taintor* ruling of 1872 still stands—and is the law by which bounty hunters operate today.

Bail agents and bounty hunters operate in all but four states: Illinois, Kentucky, Oregon and Wisconsin. These states have banned commercial bail bonding, instead allowing defendants to pay 10 percent of the bond in cash, which is usually returned at the conclusion of the case if the defendant does not violate conditions of the bail.[21]

Each state that does allow private bail contractors has its own laws and standards regarding formal training and licensing of bounty hunters. For example, bounty hunters in California "must undergo a background check and complete various courses that satisfy the penal code 1299 requirements. In most states [bounty hunters] are prohibited from carrying firearms without proper permits. Louisiana requires bounty hunters to wear clothing identifying them as such." Bounty hunters must adhere to the regulations of the states they enter "meaning a suspect could temporarily escape re-arrest by entering a state in which the bail agent has limited or no jurisdiction."[22]

Forms of Bail

The forms of bail used in the United States vary among jurisdictions. There are four common forms of bail:

1. **Recognizance**—also known as either an unsecured appearance or release on recognizance (ROR), it consists of the defendant promising to attend all required judicial proceedings and refrain from any illegal and court-prohibited activities.

2. **Surety**—a third party, usually a bail bond agent, agrees to be responsible for the debt of the defendant. The agent pays the bail to the court for release of the defendant. The defendant, in turn, pays the agent 10 percent of the bail, which the agent keeps regardless of whether the defendant appears in court. However, if the defendant fails to appear, the agent will not receive its money back from the court. In areas where bail agents are prohibited, courts often have defendants pay 10 percent of the bail for release. This money is returned to the defendant if he or she does not violate the conditions of the bail.

3. **Cash**—typically known as "cash-only," where the only form of bail that the court will accept is official government-issued currency.

4. **Combinations**—courts often allow defendants to post cash bail and then impose further sanctions—conditions of release or protective order—in order to protect the community or ensure attendance.

• **Conditions of release**—non-monetary conditions and restrictions imposed by a court to ensure that a defendant released will appear in court and not commit more crimes. Common stipulations include mandatory calls to the police, passport retrieval, home detention, electronic monitoring, drug testing, alcohol counseling and the surrendering of firearms.

• **Protective order**—also called an order of protection in where the court orders the defendant to stay away from, have no contact with and/or refrain from criminal activity against the alleged crime victim. A defendant is subject to automatic forfeiture of bail and further fine or imprisonment if he or she violates this order.[23]

The Expanding Industry

The bail bond industry continues to grow. In his *New York Times* article "Illegal Globally, Bail for Profit Remains in the U.S.," Adam Liptak reports that "More than 40 percent of felony defendants released before trial paid a bail bond company in 2004, up from 24 percent a decade earlier."[24] In addition, according to the Professional Bail Agents of the United States, an estimated 14,450 bail agents who comprise the association secure the release of approximately 2.5 million defendants each year.[25] With the FBI Crime Statistics estimating "that law enforcement agencies nationwide made 14,209,365 arrests in 2007, excluding those for traffic offenses,"[26] the numbers of bail agents and their clients are sure to rise.

Bail agencies ensure more than the releases of their clients. The Bureau of Justice Statistics report titled "Pretrial Release of Felony Defendants in State Courts" by Thomas H. Cohen, Ph.D., and Brian

A. Reaves, Ph.D., concludes that "Compared to the overall average, the percentage of absconded defendants who remained a fugitive was lower for surety bond releases (19%)."[27] In addition, of the defendants released on bail, only 23 percent failed to appear in court[28] and 40 percent are either acquitted or have the charges against them dropped.[29]

Bounty hunters continue to pursue those who fail to appear and, according to Rachel Clarke's BBC News article "Above the law: US bounty hunters," they claim "to capture about 90% of the more than 35,000 people who jump bail each year in the US."[30]

This brief chronicle of the second oldest profession conveys, we hope, not only that the professions of bail bond agents and bounty hunters have rich and long historical records, but also are entwined in the democratic legal system and concept of justice.

PART I

PAM

Chapter 1

In the Beginning

Growing up in a small town, I was a good kid. I didn't break the law. I just hung out with my friends at the town park, smoking cigarettes and drinking an occasional (forbidden) beer.

At that time, our town had a curfew. Any individual under the age of eighteen who was out on the street past 10 P.M. could be arrested for "curfew violation." Because we were all wise to this rule, at precisely 9:30 P.M. every weekend a bunch of us jumped in a friend's car and headed to an out-of-town party.

One Friday night, the police pulled up behind us and flashed the patrol car's lights before we could pull the car out of the parking lot. At the time the police officers checked everyone's identification, I looked at my watch and it was 10:10 P.M. Shortly after, I was arrested for curfew violation. I was handcuffed and taken to jail.

The jail cell was very small, maybe eight by ten feet. I could walk only a few steps before running into a wall. It held a smelly toilet, a filthy sink, a cot with a very thin plastic mattress, no blanket or pillow and a dimly-lit overhead light that stayed on day and night, giving the surroundings a strange, eerie glow.

When the steel door slammed shut behind me, I panicked. I was fifteen years old. I'd never seen the inside of a jail before and never knew until that moment that I was claustrophobic. I nearly went out of my mind. All night I paced—and cried.

The next morning, I expected to be released. When the guard opened the door to my jail cell, I thought I was getting out of there. Instead, I was escorted to see the officer on duty.

I knew Officer Tate. He was my one of my friend's cousins and we'd met several times before, at my friend's house.

He greeted me by name. "Pam, you're running with a very bad crowd." He frowned. "The kids you're with have criminal records and have been in and out of jail. You might want to think about your choice of friends before you're in here permanently."

I was terrified of the officer, but was very loyal to my friends. "Whatever they do or don't do is none of my business," I said stubbornly. "They're still my friends and always will be."

"Well," he sighed, "then you give me no other choice. I think you need to think about this a little bit more. Take her back to her cell." He motioned for the guard.

My parents were never called. I never saw a judge. I was never booked or fingerprinted nor did I sign any paperwork.

At that time, Child Protective Services didn't exist and minors had absolutely no rights. I knew what the officer was doing was unfair, but there was no one to complain to. I wasn't even allowed a telephone call.

Many years later, my sister confessed she had been worried about me. Running with "a bad crowd," I smoked an occasional joint, took some psychedelics drugs and occasionally shoplifted a pack of cigarettes from a local grocery store.

"If you didn't turn around, I was afraid someday you'd end up in prison," she commented. "I went to Officer Tate and expressed my concerns. He told me not to worry. He'd take care of it."

He "took care of it" all right. I spent three days in jail. Occasionally, one of the guards opened the little peek hole in the bars and looked in. Other than that, they left me alone.

I understand that now in most jails there is a large room where the inmates congregate. They have regular meals, watch television and are given books to read.

I had nothing. No pillow, no blanket, no human interaction, no television, no books.

They didn't feed me either. For three days, I went without food. Sometimes when the guard looked in, I complained that I was hungry, but he just shook his head and slammed shut the peek hole. For three days I didn't eat or sleep. I paced the jail cell and cried.

By the time the cell door opened on Monday morning and I was escorted out the front door of the police station, I was a new woman.

Jail had changed me. I was bound and determined never to go back, no matter what. I'd *die* first.

I realized at that moment the most precious gift I had was my freedom: to come and go as I wished. To be caged like an animal, trapped behind bars in a very small room was life-changing. From then on I stayed away from the park. I stopped hanging out with my old friends. I babysat my younger brothers and sisters, cleaned the house, went to school and, for the most part, walked the straight and narrow.

Jail had scared the hell out of me.

I vowed to *never* go back.

Chapter 2

Strange New World

Eighteen years later, I was working as a waitress for a hugely popular restaurant chain and had grown tired of it. I worked the graveyard shift and it was my duty to serve the drunks who came in after the bars closed. Most were overly demanding, pinched me on the butt at every opportunity and argued with me endlessly when I refused to serve them yet another drink after the 2 A.M. cutoff. I definitely earned my whopping $2.20 an hour. They usually kept me running all night long with their demands for more food and coffee. Even though I typically waited on at least three dozen "guests" during my shift, I made only twenty dollars or so in tips. Just when my shift was about over, I knew I could expect some dayshift waitress to call in sick from partying too heartily the night before and I'd be forced to work yet another double. This had been going on for about one long year and I was getting older by the minute. I'd scrub toilets, empty garbage cans, shovel hot tar on roads—*anything*—just to get the hell O-U-T.

The only thing that made my life somewhat bearable was Mitchell. He transferred in from another store and now worked in the restaurant. Apart from work, we became friends and gradually started seeing each other.

Recently divorced, I was raising my teenage son and working three part-time jobs seven days a week just to make ends meet. I was tired, so very tired. It seemed like all I did was work. When I wasn't working, I was sleeping, which was paramount to having no life at all.

Mitchell's friend Linda, with whom we went out often, saw my struggle and sympathized. One day she asked me if I'd like to work at the bail bond company where she was employed. At the time, I didn't know what the job entailed, exactly. I knew bond companies bailed people out of jail, but I didn't know the particulars.

I never told Mitchell, Linda or anyone else for that matter about the one time I'd been in jail. In retrospect, I would have given *anyone anything* to get me out of jail. I would have sold my soul in exchange for my freedom. Being able to bail inmates out of jail, to give them back their freedom, instantly appealed to my interest.

Linda offered me a job as a part-time bookkeeper, where I'd learn the business to get my foot in the door. She was certain that after the owner had gotten to know me, I'd be promoted to bail bondsman.

After thinking it over, I gratefully accepted.

Linda pulled a few strings and within a week, I was hired.

Arnie's Bail Bonds was situated in an older building in a run-down part of town. Later, I learned this is a very common location for bail bond offices. To be efficient, they have to be situated as close to the jail and/or courthouse as possible. Since most prestigious firms stay away from that part of town, usually bail bond companies are the only ones showing their bright, friendly faces on streets that are covered with litter and debris.

When I walked in the front door at 9 A.M. on a Sunday morning to begin working my first shift, I was surprised to see the office was busy on a weekend. I didn't know at the time that bail bond companies work seven days a week, twenty-four hours a day. They never close, not even for Thanksgiving or Christmas.

Phones were ringing constantly. The office was full of people running around trying to answer the calls and assist the people waiting at the front counter. Linda motioned me into a chair and handed me the company books I was to audit. Then she ran to answer the ever-ringing phone.

With my calculator and sharpened pencils in hand, I began.

Suddenly I heard a woman's shrill voice and looked up. The woman's hair was blonde, not naturally blonde but that brassy-white blonde that comes from cheap dye jobs. It was teased and piled high on her head. Her face was caked with foundation. Her blue eyes were illuminated with bright green fluorescent eye shadow and her rouge and lipstick were so red that at first I thought it was blood. What shocked me the most was her outfit. She wore the tightest red leather dress I'd ever seen. It was strapless and so low in front it barely covered her nipples. To complete the outfit, she wore red, five-inch spike heels. I couldn't believe a woman could walk normally in those heels. I'd never seen anyone like her before—I was both disgusted and fascinated at the same time.

A handsome, well-dressed man approached her and called her by name. He invited her to sit in one of the chairs near the front door.

When she sat down, I noticed the dress was so short her crotch was visible. I wondered idly if the seams would hold.

"Oh, Arnie," she exclaimed in a shrill voice. "Thanks for getting me out of jail. I know I can always count on you."

"Peaches, what happened?" Arnie asked sympathetically.

"It's that Bobby!" she exclaimed. "Do you know what he did to me? That bastard put me on the street blowing guys for ten bucks a pop. Can you believe that? That sonofabitch! I can get a lot more than ten bucks for what I do. But he *made* me. When I told him I wasn't going to do it anymore, he hit me. See? Can you still see the red mark? Then I got *arrested* for soliciting! That bastard! I swear to God, I'm leaving that sonofabitch, Arnie, for good this time. What a prick!"

Arnie had his hand casually around the back of her chair. I could tell from his expression that he cared about her and sympathized with the situation.

"Bobby called and told me you were in jail, so at least he bailed you," Arnie said softly.

"Well, I wouldn't have been in there if it hadn't have been for that bastard," Peaches proclaimed. "I swear to God, Arnie, I'm leaving him. As soon as I leave here, I'm packing up my stuff and I'm outta there. *Fuck* him!"

Now I was no prude. I had used words like that before, but never in an office and never in mixed company. I looked at Arnie and expected him to show surprise or caution the woman to censor her language, but he just sat there calmly. His expression never changed.

After she left, Arnie remarked to a co-worker, "Poor woman. She's been walking the streets for years. Bobby is her pimp. He's been her man for years and he has her out on the street in the dead of winter and in the hot, blazing sun in the summer. At the end of the day, he collects her profits, leaving her not so much as a dime for a telephone call." Arnie shook his head. "Despite her words, she'll never leave him. She truly loves Bobby even when he beats her. And in his own strange way, Bobby loves her, too."

I couldn't believe what I was hearing! So she was a hooker, a prostitute! The first one I'd ever seen up close. And that language! I couldn't believe she'd talk like that in a public office in front of all those people. But she didn't seem to care. She did it so freely and so easily, I felt it came naturally to her. It was language she probably used every day, I was certain, street language.

I couldn't imagine the men who approached her. How desperate they must be. With her outfit and makeup, she looked clownish and artificial, as if she was a caricature rather than a real person. And to blow strangers for ten bucks a pop? I couldn't imagine it.

I looked over at Linda. She was still on the phone, oblivious to the conversation I just overheard.

As I went back to my bookkeeping chores, I told myself that I didn't think this job was going to work out after all. If this is what it meant to be a bail bondsman, my first impression was that I wanted no part of it. I'd talk to Linda privately later and make some excuse why I couldn't stay on at Arnie's.

I appreciated Linda's offer, but I'd never known a world like this before. Truthfully, I didn't want to know about hookers, beatings or guys like Bobby.

At that moment, I was grateful I was still a waitress. Now those drunks coming in at 2 A.M. demanding more drinks didn't seem so bad after all.

Not compared to *this*!

Chapter 3

The Bail Game

After I got home from work that night, I couldn't stop thinking about Peaches the hooker and her pimp, Bobby. As I lay in bed, the drama rolled around in my head like a bad movie I couldn't stop watching. Finally I decided I would stay at Arnie's after all. Although I was admittedly disgusted, at the same time I was utterly fascinated. My old world seemed pretty tame and unexciting. If nothing else, I was pretty sure my shifts would never be boring. And who knew? Maybe I'd even learn something I could use later on down the road.

Linda let me in on the way the business worked; I quickly learned that the premise of the bail bond industry was quite simple.

"In the old days, when Junior was arrested," Linda explained, "Dad or Grandpa walked down to the jail, talked to the sheriff and had Junior released into his custody. The family considered it a matter of honor to make sure that Junior didn't get into any further trouble and went to court until the case was completed. As our world became more mobile and families moved away, Dad and Grandpa weren't around anymore. The court had to change tactics. Someone a long time ago decided that defendants need an incentive to return to court until their cases are done, so they devised a monetary bail system. Today, when someone's arrested, the jail computer automatically sets a bail based on the charge. Courts rationalized that if defendants had to post their own bails at the jail, which would be returned by the court after the case was completed, defendants would return to court, if nothing else, to get their money back.

"So, today, after arrest, defendants have three choices: They can post their own bails at the jail, they can stay in jail until they see a judge who may release them on personal recognizance, known as a 'PR'—their own promise to return to court—or they can call a bail bond agent, who'll post the money for them for a ten percent fee.

"Your job is to accept all collect calls from the jail," Linda continued. "By asking a series of questions, the bond agent is to determine whether this individual will go to court as instructed. If the defendant goes, at the end of the case the court will return the agency's money in full."

She paused for a moment, shaking her head. "But if the defendant doesn't go, the court will notify us and we'll have thirty days to get the defendant back into court or the court keeps our money.

"If we take in a pittance, but pay out thousands of dollars, a bonding company can easily go broke if it isn't careful of whom it bails," she explained. To make the company money, I was cautioned that I had to bail *wisely* and *carefully*. Linda explained that the average case means at least three court appearances and sometimes cases can run as long as two years.

Bonding companies know they're risking their own assets, so they hedge their bets as much as they can. Each defendant, I was told, required a cosigner. This individual, usually a family member, signs a contract with us guaranteeing they'll monitor the defendant to ensure their appearance in court. If the defendant doesn't go, the cosigner pays us the bail so we won't lose our money.

"The trick," Linda said, "is to secure a good cosigner for each defendant. Then and only then—" Linda shook her finger at me for emphasis "—after the cosigner's signature is on the dotted line, do we post the bond at the jail.

"Don't worry about guilt or innocence," Linda carefully warned me. "All inmates are presumed innocent until proven guilty in a court of law. Don't ask them what happened or why they were arrested. That's none of our business. Those matters are for the judge and jury to decide. Our constitution guarantees everyone the right to bail while their cases are pending. As bondsmen, the only thing we're to concern ourselves with is whether or not they'll go to court."

Linda was careful not to teach me these subtleties at the office. While there, I did my bookkeeping work, totaling figures and creating reports for management. Linda instructed me on bail bonding during our free time, usually when I was at her house with Mitchell. She wanted me to understand the real actualities before I became a bail bond agent. She encouraged me to listen to the other agents to learn their techniques so I could develop them as my own.

It didn't take long before I became extremely bored totaling figures. What I wanted to do more than anything else was to become a bail bond agent like Linda. Since that meant becoming formally licensed with the state, I knew I had to jump through some hoops. However, I saw it as a step up, a real promotion from waitressing. Not only was the money better, I could also give up all three of my part-time jobs to work this one full-time position. I'd be able to switch from working nights to a dayshift and spend more time with my son. And working with Linda really appealed to me. She was someone I truly loved, admired and respected. Under the circumstances, I was motivated. Linda worked tirelessly on my behalf to make sure that happened.

In the meantime, I tried to be content working as a part-time bookkeeper. I vowed to learn as much as I could as fast as possible in anticipation of that promotion. In order to do that, I kept my eyes and ears open.

By doing so, I saw and heard *plenty.*

Chapter 4

Necessary Evil

Gambling on whether or not an individual goes to court is very risky. However, if bonding companies play their cards right, a great deal of money can be made in a short period of time.

Whenever big money's involved, along with it come the usual slime and degenerates.

"You're lucky you weren't working in this business a few years ago," Linda told me one night over cocktails. "Back then, it was awful. The prominent bail bondsman in the area, Carbone, in his quest for power, began effectively eliminating all the competition. It was reported that he had the sheriff, Janovich, in his pocket. Defendants were brought over in a car that pulled up in the alley behind Carbone's bonding company. Bail was arranged before the defendants ever saw a jail cell. As police officers are supposed to book defendants directly into jail and allow them to arrange their own bail, this was highly illegal. It took a long time, but eventually Carbone, his cohorts and Janovich all went to prison for these shady activities.

"After this big shake-up, the state enacted legislation to regulate the bail bond business to prevent such occurrences from happening again. A Bail Bond Association was quickly formed by the bondsmen who were left to help regulate their own.

"After Carbone went to jail," Linda continued, "all the other bail bond companies were carefully scrutinized by the state and Arnie's was found to be above reproach. Even though he'd been investigated quite thoroughly, Arnie was found innocent of any wrongdoing. Arnie's was one of only two bond companies left operating after Carbone went to jail.

You're lucky to be working for Arnie," Linda said proudly. "Since he's been in business for many, many years and has a reputation for excellence, Arnie's is the best—and largest—bail bond company in town."

As Linda's protégé, I worked hard, learned a lot and soon I was promoted to bail bond agent. I was so proud the day I held my state license in my hand. I worked hard to obtain it and I didn't take it for granted. I knew it could easily be taken away from me. In our state, all a bond agent has to do is be arrested for a crime—not necessarily convicted—and he or she can lose his or her license forever. As an adult, I had a clean police record and didn't plan on getting arrested. I thought I was relatively safe. Still, I vowed never to do *anything* that would jeopardize my license, a promise I kept to myself throughout the years though it would cost me dearly later.

From Linda I learned the unvarnished truths about bounty hunters.

"Bounty hunters are a necessary evil in this business," Linda explained. "Once defendants fail to appear in court, we have a limited time to produce them back in court or the court keeps our money. By producing them, I mean either they can come in voluntarily or involuntarily. If they willingly come in, we can help arrange a new court date. If they refuse, if they decide to run, we can *force* them via our firm's bounty hunter, Joey. Joey has wide arrest powers. If he can locate defendants, arrest them and place them back in custody, they'll be produced in court and we won't lose our money."

Linda was proud of Joey and bragged about him constantly. According to her, Joey saved the company hundreds of thousands of dollars each year. "When a defendant is running, the cosigner can hire Joey to pick up the individual to avoid having to pay the court," Linda explicated. "Or if we feel insecure, the company can send Joey to arrest the defendant. In either case, the success of our company depends solely upon good bounty hunters—and Joey is the *best.*"

The day Joey came to the office Linda introduced us and I did a double take. Standing next to him, I came up to his belt. Compared to me at five feet four inches tall, Joey was *huge*. When we shook hands, his hand totally enveloped mine several times over. He was wearing a suit, but I could clearly see his muscles bulging through the fabric. Powerfully built, he was the biggest man I'd ever seen.

Linda told me that years earlier, Joey had killed a man with his bare hands and was sent to prison for it. As Arnie, like most company owners, believed it took a criminal to find one—and the more physically intimidating the better—Joey's size and felony record worked for him. Our company had taken one look at this huge creature and hired him on the spot. Joey had been one of the main bounty hunters ever since.

As we worked together I found that Joey had just one problem: He had a bad, bad temper. If someone failed to appear in court and didn't make it right with Arnie, Joey took it personally. He knocked down doors and knocked heads together until *someone...somewhere...*told him where the defendant was. And if he had to track down that person to return to jail, that individual was going to have to pay the piper. Word on the street was Joey wasn't beyond beating up defendants as he escorted them back to jail; male or female, it didn't matter.

"If they're wise, they'll turn themselves into Arnie rather than face Joey's wrath," Linda nodded knowingly. "And many do just that."

Since it scared me to even look at Joey, I couldn't blame them.

Ironically, Joey's partner, Tim, was a small man who was shy, sincere and timid. It was hard to believe that this nonthreatening guy was Joey's partner. I quickly learned that they used that to their advantage. They often played the good cop/bad cop routine while out on the street searching for defendants. Tim appeared nonthreatening, therefore he was much more approachable than Joey and the one most confided in. Although they looked like the old comic strip cohorts Mutt and Jeff, according to Linda they were an effective team.

I didn't worry about "forfeitures" as we called them—much. That wasn't my department. I was given the task of bailing them, which suited me just fine. Linda was head of the Forfeiture Department and she coordinated Joey and Tim's movements. For that, I was grateful. I liked Tim, but for some reason my gut instinct told me to be leery of Joey.

It didn't take long before I learned why.

Chapter 5

Use and Abuse

One Friday night after work, our entire crew went out for a few drinks. We usually frequented a nearby bar—the owner was a close friend of Arnie's and had bought into the restaurant/bar business a few years earlier.

Prior to working at Arnie's, I hadn't been much of a drinker. As a teenager, I'd occasionally had a few beers with my friends, but I never really liked the taste of the stuff. However, as one of only a handful of women in the bail bond business in the state, I knew I'd have to prove myself. Because everybody at the office socialized together, in order to be truly accepted and fit in, I figured I'd better learn how to be one of the gang—and fast. I was a quick study and went out whenever asked, which meant often.

That night in the bar with Arnie and the crew, I was drinking beer, for which I believed I had a large tolerance and could consume a lot without appearing drunk. However, on this occasion, Arnie began buying me shots of whiskey and laughingly urged me to drink up as he planned on buying me a few more. Soon I staggered into the bathroom and promptly threw up. I retched endlessly. Finally, after it was over, I straightened my clothes, brushed my teeth with my finger and rejoined the group. Upon Arnie's urging, I drank another shot of whiskey he had lined up for me at the bar.

I thought no one suspected a thing but Arnie told me the next morning, "I suppose I shouldn't say anything," he smiled shyly, "but due to the proximity of the crew to the women's bathroom, we all heard you moaning and groaning as you upchucked. You made quite a racket."

I was extremely embarrassed, but Arnie only laughed. We all kept meeting to talk and trade stories; as the business grew, it was one of the few outlets for pressure.

Another Friday night, I was sitting in the bar along with the rest of Arnie's crew as usual when Joey walked in.

Immediately I cringed. I felt as though Joey was an insecure guy who had a chip on his shoulder. If you got in his way, he'd just as soon act in a fistfight as look at you. Even though he never did it in front of Arnie, time and time again I personally witnessed Joey pick fights with innocent bystanders and within moments, Joey had knocked them to the ground—without provocation. I couldn't help feeling sorry for the guys. They hadn't done anything wrong. They just happened to be sitting next to Joey when he was in a bad mood. Since Joey was so big, the poor guys didn't have a prayer. They were hit so hard and so fast, they had no chance to defend themselves.

Joey's reputation for picking bar fights was well known. When he walked into a bar, those who'd seen him in action before quietly moved away to give him lots of room. I'd never seen anything like it in my entire life. It was like the parting of the Red Sea. People darted to the left or right just to get out of his way.

Some didn't take Joey's abuse very well. After a severe pounding, some victims left the bar, walked across the street and called the police. Several times I was present when the police questioned Joey. Since he worked as Arnie's bounty hunter, the police asked him a few questions, Joey justified his actions and the police went away. He was never arrested nor even thoroughly questioned. I think the police only responded because they *had* to. Certainly I felt they never took the victim seriously. Bounty hunters were given wide latitude in our area—especially Arnie's. Therefore, most were tolerated by the police. The victim was never happy since justice was never served—as far as Joey was concerned. As soon as the police left, if the victim happened to walk back into the bar, Joey pounded him again—just for calling the police.

That night, Joey was in an extremely foul mood. Someone told me he had been chasing a huge forfeiture without success. Soon we would be paying the court for this loss and Arnie didn't take too kindly to that. Neither did Linda, for that matter. I assumed he had gotten yelled at by both Arnie and Linda prior to his arrival at the bar. Therefore, he was going to take it out on everybody else. Since Joey made more money than any other employee, he was expected to *earn* his money. If that meant working all day and all night, so be it. Arnie and Linda rode him real hard. Like me, he worked all the time and was probably thoroughly exhausted. Still, I didn't think that gave him the right to be such a jerk. And to my dismay that night Joey made a beeline straight for me.

I hadn't made it a secret that I didn't like Joey. I didn't try to get in his face exactly, but I wasn't scared of him either and I wasn't going to take his temper. Since Linda adored him I tried to be respectful of that fact, but I thought he was nothing more than a big bully.

Joey sat down at our table, ordered a stiff drink and started to pick on me. "I know you don't like me," he said as he sipped his drink. "But if you'll only take the time to get to know me better, I'm sure we'll become great friends."

I didn't want to hear his story. I sipped my drink. What really made him angry was I didn't react. I didn't say anything to him; I just ignored him. He got angrier and angrier until he pulled back his fist to hit me. I didn't flinch. I knew a blow from him could easily kill me, but I didn't care. I wasn't going to cower to him *ever*. Fortunately, my co-worker, fellow bond agent and Joey's close, personal friend caught his arm in mid-air and spoke in soothing tones to calm him down.

A few moments later, a young woman walked into the bar. Joey got up and started running. Before any of us could react, he tackled the woman and pinned her down on the floor. After handcuffing her, he led her to the door then yelled for me to help him.

"Drive my van to the office and park it there," he ordered. "Put the keys in the visor and when I'm through booking her, I'll retrieve it." I nodded okay.

Joey took off with the woman in tow who was screaming and hurling obscenities. The louder she screamed, the tighter Joey tightened the handcuffs. I was fairly certain that by the time she reached the jail, her wrists would be bruised and swollen. Even though she was a failure to appear, I couldn't help feeling sorry for her. I knew those wrists would be in pain for a long time to come.

I drove Joey's van to the office as instructed and placed the keys on the visor. Just as I was exiting the vehicle, I noticed a white object sticking out from under the driver's seat. I don't know why, but I reached down to see what it was. A moment later, I pulled out a huge bag of white powder. My eyes opened wide when I realized it had to be either cocaine or crank. I didn't know how much was there, but it looked like a pound or so to me; certainly enough to get a lot of people stoned if they were so inclined.

I was angry that I'd driven Joey's van to the office. Had I been pulled over—which was likely as I'd been drinking and wasn't all that steady on my feet—I would have been busted with the dope, arrested and would have lost my bonding license. And it wasn't even my dope! I didn't even do the stuff! He knew all along the dope was there. If he'd been trying to set me up, he did a real good job. I was livid to say the least.

I put the bag back under the seat, locked the van and, furious, walked to the bar. I decided I wasn't going to say anything about this to anyone. I decided instead to investigate Joey on my own, to see what else he was up to. Not necessarily to bust him—I had no intention of telling Arnie, Linda or anybody else—I just wanted to satisfy my own curiosity.

The next day, I began nosing around and learned a great deal about Joey—more than I wanted to know.

Over drinks, his girlfriend swore me to secrecy. "He beats me constantly," she whispered. "Almost every day. Most of the time, he comes home from work in a real foul mood—especially after he's been drinking. Several times, I've gone to the hospital with broken ribs and once, a broken nose. I left him a couple of times but somehow, he always found me. I never knew how. I thought I'd covered my tracks pretty well.

"It's always the same scenario," she said with a wide-eyed look on her face. "He finds out where I'm staying. He pounds on the front door, threatening to break it down if I don't let him in. Of course, I don't want my friend's door to be damaged so I open it. He beats my protector into a bloody pulp then drags me home—and beats me again just for leaving him. I don't love him anymore. I hate his guts for what he does to me. But now I'm too afraid to leave. I'm afraid he'll track me down as he always has. And maybe this time, as he's threatened so many times before, kill me."

I'd heard Joey cheated on her at every opportunity, but I didn't tell her that. Some hookers I'd bailed once or twice told me that if one failed to appear in court, as they regularly did, Joey picked them up, handcuffed them and threatened to beat them. Then he offered to let the girls go on two conditions: One, they had to go see Arnie the next morning and make a new court date and two, they had to blow him first or fuck him, depending upon his particular mood at the time. Most, not surprisingly, took both options. The ones who didn't were beaten and taken to jail. According to my sources, most still had the scars to prove it.

I also heard that, while cruising the streets, if Joey found the FTAs (failure to appear) he was looking for, he grabbed the defendants and, after handcuffing them, offered to let them go—but only if they gave him enough cash and/or dope to make it worthwhile. If the goods were forth-coming, Joey released them. Some clients, still FTAs, were shaken down on a regular basis for months. Since they were still producing, Joey never took them to jail. And some of those FTAs I discovered were *paid* forfeitures when Joey had known where they were the entire time.

I wondered why Arnie wasn't told these things or didn't believe or act on them.

I thought of Arnie as a father figure—reliable and trustworthy. I couldn't imagine that Arnie would let Joey get away with all the things he was reported to have done if he knew and took the complaints seriously. Perhaps he didn't because of the sources of the complaints. I honestly didn't know what Arnie was thinking, but I wanted to find out.

Just about that time, a television crew was doing a special on bounty hunters and they decided to profile Joey. Linda was all aflutter, sprucing up the office for the television cameras. On the appointed day, a crew of videographers came in and began filming our activities. They concentrated on Linda and Joey. Neither I nor the other bondsmen appeared on camera.

When the television special aired, it showed Linda at the com-puter explaining a current FTA to Joey. She located a possible address for the defendant, then gave Joey that information along with the necessary arrest paperwork, to which Joey and his partner, Tim, would go on their way to make the arrest.

The camera followed Joey as he drove up and down the street, looking for the targeted female. Joey spotted her driving a car in the opposite direction down the road. He swung his vehicle around in a quick U-turn. After following her for a while, he pulled into the left lane next to her. Pulling slightly ahead of her, as the camera rolled, Joey swung the wheel a hard right and *intentionally* bashed his vehi-cle into hers. When she stopped, he took advantage of her momentary daze by jumping out of the van and handcuffing her. He smiled widely for the camera as Tim led her away.

Though the crew never let on, the original intent was to criticize bounty hunters. Their main intent was to show the general public how bounty hunters abused their gratuitous arrest powers. With Joey bashing the other vehicle, he didn't help the cause any. I was so disgusted I turned off the special before it was over. Linda wasn't too happy either. I had to walk unobtrusively around the office for quite a long time before the unpleasant incident was forgotten.

When I felt I had enough evidence to prove Joey was on the take, I decided to approach an attorney who sometimes worked with our firm. Arnie worked with several, but one in particular I felt I could trust. He'd know what to do.

After explaining the situation in detail, I waited for his response. It took a long time before he said anything.

"So what?" he said, getting up from behind his desk and sitting on the edge of it in front of me. "So what if he's on the take? Do you think he's the only bounty hunter in this town who is? Let me ask you something. Do *you* want to go out and get them? Do you think that job is *easy*? Do you know what it takes? All Arnie cares about is that the bounty hunter gets the job done. If he's on the take, so what? Who cares? If I were you, I'd pretend we never had this conversation. Now go away."

I hadn't expected that response. I sat there with my mouth open for a full minute before I had enough sense to stand up and leave the room.

That led me to wonder, *Is the only thing that matters to anyone that Joey gets the job done, however he accomplishes it? What about the other bondsmen in the office, do they know? Do I not only have to watch out for the clients but also for my co-workers, too?*

I didn't know what to think. All I had were questions and no answers. But I knew one thing; this was far from over. I wasn't going to let it rest.

I continued to investigate and search for answers.

Chapter 6

A Thousand Deaths

Her name was Cindy. In her younger days, she had been a truly beautiful woman. I know, because she showed me a picture of herself from those years once. In the picture, she was smiling with big, beautiful white teeth gleaming at the camera. Her blonde hair with real highlights hung loosely around her shoulders. Her green eyes glowed with the innocence that only seventeen-year-olds have—before life has been given a chance to crush their dreams. And she had a body to die for; most women would pay a fortune to a plastic surgeon to look the way she did naturally.

Looking at the picture of her then versus looking at her standing in front of me, I wouldn't have been able to tell it was the same woman if she hadn't said so. After doping for many, many years, her body looked wasted, thin and scrawny. Her hair was unwashed and uncombed. Her eyes had dark circles under them and were sunk deep within her forehead. The previous time we had met, she looked so bad and was so unsteady on her feet, I wondered if she was going keel over on my desk right there in the office.

I never knew the details. All I knew was that her parents were very rich. "Filthy rich," Cindy explained. "I grew up in an elegant mansion in an elegant part of town with elegant servants. We held elegant dinner parties with elegant guests. It's old money, having been inherited from my grandfather's grandfather who made a fortune doing whatever it was he did. I've led a life of luxury. My parents gave me whatever I wanted—as far as material possessions were concerned."

I don't know what happened to that fresh, young, idealistic girl in the picture. Probably something very bad that would have given me nightmares if I had known, so I purposely didn't ask and she didn't volunteer the information. All I knew was that Cindy had become a heroin addict and a prostitute. Like most prostitutes, having no other place to go after the long day was over, she crawled under a bridge to sleep at night with all the other prostitutes, drunks and homeless people. "With one eye open," she told me dramatically. Since it was never really safe there—or anywhere on the street for that matter—she said she never really did get any sleep.

Arnie's general policy was not to bail prostitutes. Linda told me it wasn't because we made any moral judgments but because they had a tendency not to go to court. Strung out on dope, usually heroin, most didn't pay attention to the days as they rolled past. Most didn't know what day of the week it was or even cared. They never purposely meant to fail to appear. However, due to their lifestyle, they just did. We didn't bail the majority of them, at least not then.

Arnie made an exception for Cindy. She was pretty faithful in honoring her court appearances. Since she had a long history of prostitution, the judge always sentenced her to jail time. She did the time—then, as soon as she got out, she was back on the street and under the bridge. The good thing about Cindy was we always knew where to find her if the occasion demanded it. Sometimes after she failed to appear, she came into the office and turned herself in.

When Linda showed me the forfeiture letter from the court, I wasn't surprised. Cindy had occasionally missed court in the past. It was no big deal. Joey would go get her and that would be that.

"You have to go get her," Linda said softly.

"What?" I asked, looking up from the stack of files piled high on my desk.

"Joey is busy working on another case. You're the bond agent— you bailed her. You go get her and bring her in."

Now, I'm a company woman. I was always the first to come in early and work late. I volunteered for extra work when my desk was clear and the phones weren't ringing. Since my son was fifteen years old and pretty much took care of himself and all the other agents had wives, husbands and young families, I worked nights and every holiday. I worked enough hours that if we'd had a union and I'd been properly compensated my time, I would have been *rich*. But I was not a bounty hunter and never wanted to be one. I helped Joey and Tim from time to time. Though I didn't like to admit it, every time I had gone, I was *scared*. On defendants' territory with all their friends around, I never knew if they or someone else would pull a gun or a knife or if I'd be beaten up by a passerby attempting to help the defendants. I never knew what was going to happen and Joey and Tim's presence was no comfort. I didn't trust them to protect me if something bad occurred. I loved Linda, but in this particular case, I was not going to do what she asked and I said so.

"You're my only hope," Arnie approached my desk and said very quietly. "Joey is working on a large forfeiture and Tim isn't around. I could really use your help on this case. I don't want to ask, but I don't have anybody else to do this for me. You know Cindy. I'm certain she won't be any problem."

Even though he didn't say it, I got the distinct impression my job was on the line. It seemed to me like had no choice, so I went.

Cindy wasn't easy to find this time. I cruised all her usual places, the streets, the bars, under the bridge. Finally, one of her friends called me from jail. Desperate to find Cindy, I wouldn't bail the friend until she told me where Cindy was. Hesitantly, she gave me an address.

I parked down the street from the house. It was very, very old; the paint was cracked and peeling. The door hung by just one hinge. The house seemed as though it was abandoned a long time ago. It looked so decrepit; it also looked like a place Cindy might've frequented.

I sat in my car for a long time, trying to get up enough nerve to get out. I hated doing this part of the job—I truly hated it! Since all the other bond agents were busy, I had no backup. I was alone and unarmed. The only thing I'd brought with me was a spare pair of handcuffs I kept in my desk for emergencies. That was what scared me the most. I didn't own a gun and didn't think I could borrow one, so I didn't ask anyone in the office. Arnie didn't approve of weapons anyway. He truly believed they weren't necessary, but Joey and Tim were the ones actually out on the street and they knew better. They knew most defendants packed heat, so they carried weapons without Arnie knowing it. I may have been a novice, but I certainly saw the need for one now. All I had was my wits. And I sure hoped to God that was enough.

When I knocked on the door, to my great relief, Cindy answered. She knew who I was. I didn't have to say a word. She told me to hang on for a moment, she'd get her coat. I stood there shaking as she slammed the door. I decided to stand off to the side just in case a bullet came whizzing through the door, as I'd heard from Joey and Tim that it sometimes did. A few moments later Cindy came back, opened the door and walked toward me. I could tell right away she was high on drugs. I wondered if she'd shot up while the door was closed to make going to jail and staying there somewhat easier.

I knew the guys always handcuffed the defendants, so I pulled out my cuffs. Though I'd never used them before, I handcuffed her so professionally I was impressed with my own skill.

"Okay, Cindy," I said in the roughest, toughest voice I could muster. "I have to search you before I take you in. Do you have anything in your pockets you need to dispose of before we reach the jail?"

She shook her head no. Though Joey and Tim didn't do it this way, I wanted to give Cindy a break. I knew that if I took her in with drugs on her and the jailer found it while booking her, she would be charged with a felony—UPCS—unlawful possession of a controlled substance. Since it was Cindy, I didn't want to make life harder on her than it already was.

I reached into her coat pocket. Within moments, I pulled out an uncapped hypodermic needle. The needle had been facing straight up and it was only by a miracle I hadn't poked my fingers. I pulled it out and threw the needle on the ground. I was so angry, I nearly hit her.

"Dammit, Cindy!" I yelled at her. "Man, you've been shooting up a long time and might have AIDS or something. Your needle almost got me. Now if I reach into your other pocket, am I going to find another surprise?"

"Pam, I'm sorry," she said softly. "I forgot it was there. I wouldn't hurt you, you know that. No, I don't have anything else. I *swear.*"

Surprises were something I wasn't taking a chance on. I reached into her other pocket and pulled out another uncapped needle that was facing straight up. I threw that on the ground and really lost my temper. I wondered if she'd placed the needles like that on purpose, just so I would poke myself. The thought of that really upset me.

I kept on searching. In her right pants pocket, I found a small baggie with heroin in it and a dirty, blackened spoon. Both joined the needles on the ground.

"Okay, let's go," I said, roughly grabbing her by the cuffed wrists. Now I understood why the guys sometimes beat up defendants on the way to the jail—because they would pull dirty tricks like this. For the first time, I understood bounty hunters' hostility.

As I waited at the jail for the officers on duty to take her from me, several hours had passed. Now I had an idea as to why bounty hunters got paid so much, even though they were not as well-compensated as the company. Bounty hunters are typically paid a small percentage of the forfeited bail or receive a salary, like Joey. I had to admit, even at Joey's salary, considering every time bounty hunters went out to get someone and how they were literally putting their lives on the line, it wasn't enough money. They honestly didn't know if they'd be going home that night or not. Then when they did arrest the defendant, the jailers took their own sweet time taking them from us. I realized bounty hunters were severely underpaid. In my opinion, considering all the risks, no amount of money was worth it.

When I got back to the office and told Linda that Cindy was in custody, I didn't know what to expect; certainly perhaps a pat on the back or a joyous "hurray!" for arresting her alone and without incident. But Linda never said a word. She took the paperwork from me and went back to her computer. Arnie didn't say anything either. It was like this had been expected of me, so no thanks were necessary.

Thoughts flashed through my mind. *Well, I don't give a damn if I lose my job at Arnie's or not. I am never going to arrest crazed druggies again. No matter what they say or do, I am not putting my life on the line like that ever again.* Just the thought of being poked by one or both of the needles made me shake. I vowed to myself that no amount of pleading from Arnie would persuade me otherwise.

Moments later, an elegantly dressed woman walked into the office. She introduced herself as Cindy's mother. Cindy had called her from the jail and she was there to bail her.

Arnie charged her the bounty hunter fee for all the hours I'd worked on the case. Cindy's mom opened her purse and pulled out a huge amount of cash—more than I'd ever seen. She paid not only the bounty hunter fee, but also the new bail bond premium. Smiling,

Arnie filled out the paperwork, Mom signed the papers and, after she left, he took the bond over to the jail. Then he came back to the office and walked over to where I was sitting. He looked down at me.

Suddenly, I hated bond agents. I had no sooner gotten Cindy into jail when they bailed her out again.

"She'll fail to appear down the road and we'll have to go get her again. That doesn't seem right or fair," I protested.

"That's just how all bond agents make their money," Arnie said with a smile. "Repeat business. As long as she paid all the money due, in full, along with the new bail premium, I don't have a problem re-bailing her."

For the first time ever, I really appreciated bounty hunters and what they do.

For the first time ever, though I hated to admit it even to myself, I suddenly understood Joey's perpetual bad mood.

Chapter 7

Hit Man

As the pressure and my duties at Arnie's grew, my boyfriend, Mitchell, found somebody else. By then I was working ten- to twelve-hour days, seven days a week, as was Linda. I was honestly too exhausted to date. Besides, I was still reeling after the long, drawn-out divorce from my husband. I wanted to give myself plenty of time to heal.

Then I met Kurt. He was well-built, blond and really handsome. My teenage son had met him a few weeks before and made it a point to introduce us, thinking we just might make a cute couple. And I had to admit—we did.

It all started out so innocently. We met for coffee at a local restaurant; we talked for hours. He came over to my place; I went over to his. Things were going so well between us, I thought this relationship might go somewhere. Maybe we had a future together if we took it slow and played our cards right.

Soon, I met his friend Robin and his girlfriend, Phoebe, who lived next door to Kurt. Like Kurt, Robin was animated and never failed to make me roar with laughter. His girlfriend was quiet and pert. Both encouraged the relationship between Kurt and me.

"Kurt's been alone a long time," Robin revealed. "It's about time he found someone cute, funny, smart and nice. Kurt's in the construction business and makes good money. Most people don't know this, but he mistrusts banks and has a habit of leaving thousands of dollars lying around his apartment. For most women, I suspect, they're more interested in his money than they are in him. But I can tell already that you don't care about his money. You care about Kurt. He seems to really like you, too. That's why Phoebe and I encourage him to see you every chance he gets."

One evening about a month after we had started going out, I was supposed to meet Kurt at *our place*—the restaurant where we met. I was sipping a Bloody Mary when Robin and his girlfriend walked in. Before I had the chance to say anything, both sat down at my booth.

I've had this lifelong knack of instantly reading vibes from other people. I was always so naturally good at it, I could walk into a room, look around and instantly know what people were feeling. In this case, my senses told me Robin and Phoebe were both in bad moods— quiet and sullen as if something was deeply troubling them.

I ordered them drinks. After a few minutes, Robin took a deep breath and started talking.

"It's a long story," Robin sighed. "There are things about Kurt you don't know. He has a past. One he's kept hidden and one he certainly doesn't want you to know about. But since your relationship with him is getting more serious, Phoebe and I talked it over. We decided you ought to know and deserve to know. Don't tell him I told you any of this. I'm sure Kurt would be furious. If he knew I told you, he might never talk to me again. I don't want that. But I like and respect you. I finally decided to tell you the truth about Kurt, whether you want to hear it or not.

"Several years ago, Kurt's father was dying of cancer," Robin began. "Kurt immediately quit his job and flew home to take care of him. Since his dad was terminal and in great pain, Kurt hired a full-time, live-in nurse to take care of his father's needs. Kurt was truly devastated over his father's illness. With the nurse living at the house with them, it wasn't long before the nurse was taking care of Kurt's needs, too. They had a hot and heavy affair—one that they carefully hid from his father.

"When his father died, Kurt immediately let the nurse go. He didn't need her anymore and he wasn't serious about her. She was just there when he needed her. Other than that, there was no emotional tie. By this time, the nurse was in love with Kurt and didn't take too kindly to being fired. She'd envisioned a future with Kurt and wasn't going to let him go that easily.

"She told Kurt she was pregnant. Kurt had no intention of having children and told her so. When they first began the affair, he had insisted upon her using birth control. She told him she was on the pill. Kurt doesn't know if she stopped taking birth control or never took it to begin with. But when she told him she was pregnant, Kurt didn't want to have anything more to do with her. He felt like she was trying to trap him into marriage and fatherhood and he didn't want either. He hurriedly packed his bags and took a flight out of the state. Since he hadn't left a forwarding address, he hoped that was the end of it. He hoped he would never have to see the nurse again.

"She had the child—a boy—but never got over Kurt," Robin continued. "Painstakingly, she tracked him down. She wrote him letters; she called him; she wanted him to pay child support. Kurt moved from state to state trying to elude her, but somehow she always found his address. Then she actually moved to Washington to be near him. Her continuous letters and phone calls are driving him *crazy*.

"He's trying to hire a hit man to kill her," Robin told me soberly. "She's become such a nuisance following and snooping on him, he just wants it over with. He's trying to have her killed."

Kurt didn't strike me as the type to be so violent and so cold. I sipped my drink, carefully hiding my expression so Robin wouldn't know how deeply shocked I was. I urged him to tell me more.

"Nobody knows this. It's a deep, dark secret, but Kurt works for the mafia," Robin paused to sip his drink. "He doesn't do it often, but often enough to make those thousands of dollars he keeps in the apartment. I'm not sure what he actually does for the mafia; I don't want to know. But obviously it pays very well. Kurt will occasionally take a leave of absence from his construction job, disappear for a week or two, then come back with a suitcase full of cash. I'm sure with his connections Kurt can easily find someone to kill her. As a matter of fact, Kurt's so busy looking for someone, he sent me to tell you he won't be able to meet you as planned. He wants me to tell you he's sorry and he'll call you later tonight."

Robin swore me to secrecy, as he was sure Kurt wouldn't want me to have this information. I swore I wouldn't say a word. He and Phoebe finished their drinks and abruptly left.

I was so disturbed over the things Robin told me, I went home and wrote a diary entry detailing our conversation. I had kept a journal for years, just scribbles of things I wanted to remember or spend some time pondering. And this was certainly something I had to think about. Since Robin had been so serious while talking and Phoebe confirmed the facts, I had no doubt he was telling me the truth. I needed to think about this for a while. Certainly this changed our relationship. I wanted no part of whatever he was doing. This was way too heavy for me. I decided then and there to break up with him. I'd make some excuse and just walk away.

When I saw Kurt again, I couldn't help asking him about his past. I was hoping he'd volunteer the information as I had no intention of breaking Robin's confidence. After a while, Kurt repeated everything Robin had told me—except the part about the hit man or trying to have the woman killed.

"She's a pain in my ass!" Kurt paced the room. "I keep moving from state to state and she always follows me. I can't get away from her. I *hate* her! That kid isn't mine. If she thought she was going to trap me into marriage, she has another thing coming. I'll never marry her and I have no intention of ever seeing that kid either. I'm going to see that she leaves me alone, so I can live my life in *peace.*"

I knew then it was over. Kurt had shown me a side of him I hadn't known existed and truly didn't want to see. It had all been fun, but now it was over. I made some excuse about getting back together with an old boyfriend and quickly left.

Six months later, I opened the newspaper and, to my astonishment, photos of both Kurt and Robin filled the entire front page. Once I got over the initial shock, I carefully read the story. Apparently, a woman had been killed along with her small child, a boy; their throats had been slashed. The woman's young daughter had also been attacked and was in the intensive care unit of the local hospital. According to the article, the perpetrator repeatedly banged the girl's head against a wall in an attempt to kill her. She was currently in a coma and on life support with extensive brain damage, but the doctors expected her to live.

Allegedly, one of the neighbors saw Robin exiting the house in clothes covered in blood. Another witness saw him throwing a bloody knife off a bridge. Within hours of the crime, he was arrested. When questioned by police, Robin pointed the finger at Kurt as having been the one to hire him for the kill. Robin insisted Kurt made him do it. Eventually, while high on crank, Robin did.

Soon after, Kurt was arrested. He maintained he didn't know anything about the murder and had nothing to do with it. He claimed Robin knew Kurt hated this woman—he made no secret about that. However, he made the concession that Robin had acted entirely on his own; perhaps to get into Kurt's good graces, perhaps as a favor to Kurt to please him. Whatever the reason, Kurt swore he hadn't hired Robin. Kurt wouldn't do such a thing. He was innocent.

I theorized that Kurt, unable to hire a hitman, may have used their friendship to finally persuade Robin to do it. Since Robin loved

Kurt and was fanatically loyal to him, it wasn't a stretch to believe Kurt could have talked him into it. According to Robin, Kurt had planned the whole thing—even so far as providing the crank that made him high enough to do it. He'd also instructed the bloody knife should be thrown off that bridge so the murder weapon would never be found. According to the paper, divers quickly found the knife in shallow water with Robin's fingerprints all over it.

The article said that the police were seeking information and anyone who had knowledge of this crime should call the department right away.

I went to work and quickly showed Linda the article. After explaining that I knew these people without giving her any details, I asked her what I should do. She urged me to call the police. As a citizen and bail bond agent,I knew that was the right thing to do.

After work, I called and a detective showed up at my door within the hour. I could tell he was leery. He asked me what I knew about the case and I could tell from his bored expression that he didn't really expect me to know much of anything. Once I began talking, his expression changed and he abruptly stopped me. Pulling a small tape recorder out of his briefcase, he turned it on and asked me to repeat what I'd just said. Wide-eyed, he sat and listened carefully as I explained the entire situation.

"Do you have any proof you know these two?" he asked, turning off the recorder and placing it back in his briefcase.

It took me a minute to remember the picture I'd taken of Kurt shortly after we met. I also had my diary entries. I wondered if he'd want those as well; he sure did. I grabbed the book and the photos and gave them to him. He told me that was going to turn these things over to the prosecutor.

He told me not to leave the area.

"Be careful," he urged. "Don't tell anyone you talked to me."

Since there'd be more questions, he was sure he'd be back. "In the meantime, if you need anything or remember anything more, call me right away."

After he left, I couldn't stop shaking. During a crisis, I can calmly do whatever needs to be done, but after it's over, I fall apart. I cried the entire night. In fact, I cried for *days*. The deaths of that woman and her son haunted me. It never should have happened. I wondered if I had told the police ahead of time that Kurt was trying to hire a hit man, if I had reported it, I wondered if that would have saved their lives.

As a bail bond agent, I know only too well that when we arrest individuals and take them into custody, it isn't personal. We have no ax to grind—no grudge against a specific individual. It's just business, even though some of those clients do take it personally. I'd heard from Joey, Tim and Linda about the ones who eventually get out of jail, only to track down the bond agent to exact revenge. So we were all careful to hide our identities. We use tricks to skip trace someone and we make sure that our information isn't on those files. We don't want anyone finding us. So my address wasn't visible anywhere. But in this particular case, both Kurt and Robin knew where I lived; they had been in my apartment on several occasions. If Kurt did have mafia connections as Robin had claimed, I wouldn't be hard to find. They'd be able to walk right up to my door and easily blow me away.

I made the decision to move as quickly as possible. I had my son live with friends until the threat was over. When I heard from my new neighbors—who were aware of the situation—that someone was nosing around asking questions, I moved again. I had nightmares of someone walking up to my door and killing me and that scared me.

The detective always knew where I was and came back to ask more questions. At one point, he asked me if I wanted police protection since this was a high profile case and they desperately needed me to testify.

I refused. I knew that with cops present, I wouldn't be able to work. I'd probably have to take a leave of absence, which is something I couldn't afford to do. With cops around me, I'd be obvious and wouldn't be able to come and go as quietly as I usually did. No, if I was going to hide, I figured my chances were better alone. At work, there was always someone around who would thwart an assassination attempt. I was pretty sure *they* wouldn't get me at work anyway. With all the people going in and out, there'd be too many witnesses. Chances were better that *they* would pop me at home. The detective warned me to be extremely careful and keep a low profile until this was all over. I promised him that I would.

During the next few months, as the prosecuting and defense attorneys filed and argued their respective motions in front of the judge, I was a nervous wreck. Whenever I heard a strange noise, I jumped and my heart pounded. Before I went out in public, I scanned the street to make sure that no one was waiting for me the moment I walked out the door. When I drove around town, I took frequent left and right turns to lose whoever may have been following me.

One day, as I was getting ready to go to the grocery store, I found myself looking out the front window for shadows that might be lurking in the corners. I decided then and there I wasn't going to be scared like this anymore. I was sick of it. If I had to keep living like this—hiding as if I were a fugitive—then I was dead already. I decided that if *they* were going to get me, I didn't want to know about it. Let *them* shoot me when I least expected it. That way I wouldn't see it coming. Maybe then, I would live a little before I died.

When the case was finally ready for trial, nearly a year had passed (Lady Justice isn't swift in most cases). Robin had decided to plead guilty. I received the summons at work to come in and testify at his sentencing hearing. I was the only one who could prove Kurt was behind the crime, which was apparently Robin's defense. If Robin was going to prison for life or to fry in the electric chair, which was likely, he wasn't going to go alone. He wanted to make damn sure that bastard Kurt was right beside him.

The courthouse was packed with reporters and cameras as I was escorted from work to the courtroom. Once I entered, I was surprised to see the room full to capacity. With no available seats, dozens of people were standing in the back of the room. I saw Robin sitting in the defendant's chair; Kurt was seated right beside him. Feeling intimidated, I took the witness stand.

I testified to all that I knew. I testified to the conversation Robin, Phoebe and I had in that restaurant. I testified to the conversation I had with Kurt shortly before the crime was committed. I testified to the diary entries I made, which were projected onto a large screen directly behind me.

"Why did you decide to come forward?" the defense attorney asked. "Isn't it because you learned Kurt had dumped you for his new girlfriend, the one sitting directly behind him in this court-room, his fiancée? Aren't you testifying, because you didn't want him to break it off? Because you were in love with him and when he broke it off, you were furious with him and now you want your revenge?"

Nothing could have been further from the truth. I didn't know anything about a new girlfriend or a fiancée and I couldn't have cared less. I wasn't in love with Kurt and never had been and I said as much.

"Isn't it true you had sex with the defendant? Isn't it true that you and Kurt and Robin had a threesome? That perhaps you're in love with Robin and now testifying for him to help him out or to exact revenge on Kurt?"

Later I learned that this is a common tactic used by both attorneys in legal matters. Such things are used to discredit the witness. Some try to rattle witnesses to say things they don't mean or to find contradictions in their stories. I knew if the attorney succeeded in rattling me or if I appeared confused, I would be discredited in front of the jury and Kurt would walk. Fortunately, I hadn't been intimate with either Robin or Kurt and I said so.

"Why are you testifying?" the prosecutor asked me. "Why are you here today, in this courtroom?"

I didn't hesitate. "Because a woman and her son died! Somebody had to come forward. That poor woman and that boy. Somebody had to come here and tell the truth about what happened. I owe it to her and to him to tell what I know—the truth."

By this time, I had testified for over eight hours in two days. I was exhausted. Since there were no more questions, I was finally allowed to step off the witness stand and leave the room.

After I left the courtroom, I burst into tears. I cried openly and loudly. I couldn't help myself. I was so sad that the woman had died along with her boy. Though her little daughter lived, follow-up articles in the newspaper said she was little more than a vegetable. The article said the girl was brain damaged and would spend the rest of her life in an institution.

The owner of another bonding company, whom I knew well, happened to be in the courthouse when I left the room. Seeing me in hysterics, he took me protectively into his arms. He shielded my face from all the flashbulbs going off as reporters crowded around me, shoving microphones in my face and shouting questions. He hustled me out of the courthouse. Gratefully, I accepted his offer of a drink and we went to a local bar. By the time I left, I was more composed. I thought maybe somehow I could live with this nightmare. Now that it was over, maybe I could move forward and put it all behind me.

Eventually, Kurt was brought to trial. I wasn't called to testify again; my previous testimony had been admitted into evidence. After a lengthy trial and Kurt's constant protests of innocence, the jury didn't believe his story. They promptly found him guilty of master-minding the murders. Like Robin, he was convicted of manslaughter and sentenced to life in prison without the possibility of parole.

"He was real slick," an attorney I knew and who was familiar with the case theorized to me later over drinks at a local pub. "He might have gotten away with it—if it hadn't been for you."

"What are you talking about?" I asked, sipping my drink.

"Kurt had it all planned out," he said. "He made only one error. One fatal mistake that eventually got him convicted—only one."

"What was that?" I asked softly.

"The only mistake he made was allowing you to live, allowing you to walk away knowing what you knew. Had Kurt gotten rid of you, there would have been no evidence and no way to tie him to the crime. He would have walked, because no one would have believed Robin."

I hadn't thought about it that way before. Immediately, my hands began trembling. When I realized what the attorney said was right, I became *really* afraid. I had been the only one to tie Kurt to the crime. It was *my* testimony that got him convicted.

"I guess I was lucky," I said, attempting a half smile.

"I guess you were," he said softly, ordering us another drink.

Chapter 8

Too Young to Kill

Becky was thirteen years old and in custody at our local jail. According to the newspaper, she had stolen her mother's credit card and had charged several thousand dollars worth of merchandise. When Becky thought the credit card bill was in the mail and her mother would open it and severely punish her, she allegedly paid two friends fifty dollars to kill her—which they did. Some thought Becky had not only planned the murder, but had actually participated in it as well. Whatever the case, it was highly unusual for a girl her age to be in our adult jail. Normally, the inmates had to be eighteen years of age or older. I can only assume she was placed there instead of juvenile detention due to the seriousness of the crime.

"You're going to bail her?" I asked Linda. "When she killed her own mother?"

"Allegedly!" Linda said sharply. "*Allegedly* killed her. You know as well as I do that just because you're charged with a crime doesn't mean you did it. She hasn't been found guilty by a judge or jury so I'm surprised at you, Pam. Always remember, we live in America. They're all innocent until *proven* guilty. And yes, I *am* going to bail her. Do you have a problem with that?"

I didn't. I walked away smarting over her sharp words. I loved Linda and whenever she was stern with me, which happened only on occasion, I knew I had done something to deserve it.

Yes, of course, all inmates are innocent until proven guilty. That's what is so wonderful about America. We have the right to be heard with all the evidence presented before an impartial judge or jury so they can determine our guilt or innocence. It wasn't up to me to decide. I thought I learned that lesson a long time ago.

When Linda reminded me that Becky was innocent until proven guilty, I was rightfully ashamed of myself. I knew better and I vowed not to forget that concept again.

When Becky's cosigner—her aunt—came in, Linda was busy and handed her over to me. As we sat down to complete the paperwork, she said, "She's innocent, you know."

I didn't say anything. I hesitated for a moment, trying to form my words carefully.

"It wasn't her fault. Those boys, it was all the boys' fault. Becky never put them up to it. She couldn't have. I know my niece, and she wouldn't have done that. You'll see. When this goes to court, they'll find her innocent. Because she is."

We continued the paperwork without further conversation and soon the woman left the office.

A few hours later, Becky was at the front counter asking for me.

She did not look like a girl of thirteen. Her long brown hair fell attractively around her slim shoulders. She was wearing a provocative outfit with a V-neck that accentuated her full breasts. Her makeup was heavy but expertly applied. Her eyes were outlined with brown eyeliner that made them appear soft and sultry. Her red lipstick, though smudged, was still very much in place. I would have guessed this was a woman in her early to late twenties. I was certain this sexy young woman was not thirteen! But she was. Her birth date clearly stated on the paperwork confirmed it.

A couple of weeks later, one of the bondsmen told me someone was waiting to see me. When I approached the front counter, I recognized the person as Becky's aunt. She asked if she could talk to me privately for a moment. I quickly invited her over to my desk.

"She *is* guilty," the aunt said as we sat down. "I didn't believe it at first. I didn't want to believe it, but that brat killed my sister."

"What happened?" I asked, shocked.

"Well, all during the funeral, Becky cried and cried and cried," she explained. "She acted so sad, crying and wailing and carrying on. I couldn't help feeling sorry for her. Her father left a long time ago and her mother was dead. Her friends had killed her. I knew she felt terrible. I did everything I could to comfort her."

"And?"

"Well, as you know, I bailed her. I took her home with me. I fixed her up in a nice room. I even brought her things over from my sister's house so she'd feel more comfortable. Becky seemed so appreciative, so sweet. I assured her that I'd stand by her. I didn't give a damn what anybody else thought. She was innocent and they'd prove it in court. I told her not to worry."

"Okay..."

"Well, yesterday I got home from work and heard Becky talking to some friends on the phone. I don't know who they were. She didn't know I was home yet. She didn't know I was listening. To those friends, she started bragging about the fact she killed her mother. She described how she gave those boys a gun and before they could shoot her, she hit her mother over the head with a baseball bat. Can you imagine? Her own mother! I must have made some kind of noise, because just then she turned around and looked at me. And what I saw in her eyes scared the hell out of me. I was afraid for myself then; afraid if she killed my sister, she'd kill me, too. So I ran into my bedroom and locked the door."

"I'm so sorry. That's so sad."

"Yes, it is," she whimpered. "I just can't believe it. All along, I thought she was innocent. Boy, did she have me fooled."

"So, did you talk to her about it?"

"Yes," she nodded, wiping her eyes with a tissue she had pulled out of her purse. "She said she didn't know what I was talking about. She told me she had been talking about something else, that I couldn't have heard her correctly. But I know what I heard." Her eyes narrowed. "I know just exactly what she said."

"Okay, so how can I help?"

"I want you to put her back in jail. Now that I know she killed my sister, I won't have her in my home."

"I'm not sure I can do that," I said, standing up. "Let me talk to my supervisor and see what she thinks. I'll be right back."

I went into Linda's office and outlined the situation to her. Much to my relief, Linda said she would handle it. I brought Becky's aunt into the back room and left the two of them to talk.

It was hours later before things calmed down enough that I could finally ask Linda what happened.

"Well, when we bail defendants out of jail, they're technically in our custody so we can surrender them back into jail if we need to. But it's not that simple. We can't pull a bond because they owe us money or the cosigner is mad at them or even if they admit they're guilty. Courts don't care about all that. The only ethical reason to revoke a bond is because they have no intention of going to court or they've already missed. Even then, Joey has to go get them and the cosigner has to pay the fees; it's not easy, but it can be done."

"So are we going to pick her up?"

Linda shook her head no. "According to the aunt, Becky will go to court. That's not the problem."

"So what did you do?" I asked, sitting down on the edge of her desk.

"I told her the minute Becky fails to appear, we'll go get her. That's the best we can do."

At Linda's suggestion, the aunt had called relatives from Linda's phone and asked them to take Becky. She made some excuse about working so much that she was never home and didn't feel that was good for the girl. Fortunately, one of the other relatives agreed.

A few weeks later, Becky was back in the office. She was getting ready to go to court for her trial. Her makeup was gone. Her long brown hair was in pigtails. She had on an outfit that looked similar to the uniform girls wear in Catholic school: black shoes, white knee socks, checkered green skirt with matching vest and a simple white blouse with a Peter Pan collar. In that outfit, she looked like a very young thirteen.

When she spoke to Linda, I couldn't help noticing how even her voice had changed. Before, it was deep and low, almost a Marlene Dietrich-type voice. Now, she was soft-spoken and had raised her voice a decimal or two. When she smiled, she looked down in such a way that her dimples showed. I wondered how long she had to practice that look in the mirror.

I was sorry the judge and jury couldn't have seen the way she was dressed when I first bailed her. I surmised her defense attorney wanted her to look thirteen, so he probably specified what outfit to wear, what to say and how to say it. I was fairly certain that had she walked into the courtroom in her usual dress, they would have convicted her on the spot. As it was, wearing that outfit, she looked far too young to have committed that serious a crime—and I felt that was the defense's point.

At the end of the trial, there was a hung jury. They couldn't decide whether Becky was guilty or not. Though the prosecutor rarely did this, he retried her with a different judge and a different jury. This time, however, Lady Justice wasn't blind.

Despite all of her tactics, Becky was convicted of murder.

Chapter 9

The Legacy

After working at Arnie's for several years, Linda asked me to help with the forfeitures. That was a rare honor, an unspoken promotion that meant she trusted me with all the inner workings of the company and big money. Since Arnie had page after page of forfeitures, we stood to lose over half a million dollars if we didn't locate those defendants and return them to custody. I knew Linda and Joey were swamped, trying to take care of all the cases themselves. Since all the real action happened in the Forfeiture Room, I was happy to help.

The first thing I did was revamp the system. Previously, when Linda received a forfeiture letter from the court, she immediately dispatched Joey to pick up the defendant. He had dozens of cases he was working at any given time. So many, even working around the clock, it was impossible to arrest them all within the time frame specified by the court. With Linda's permission, I began calling the defendants directly. To my surprise, most didn't know they'd failed to appear. Once I informed them, they agreed to come into our office and arrange a new court date. Linda had me accompany them to the courthouse to appear before the judge to quash the warrant and to set a new date. The judges usually obliged. With our bond taken out of forfeiture, "reinstated and continued" until the case was completed, that was one less forfeiture we had to worry about.

For defendants I couldn't reach by phone, I called those who were legally responsible for the defendants on our paperwork—the cosigners. I gave them an ultimatum: produce the defendants for new court dates, give us information as to their whereabouts so we can arrest them or pay up. There was no negotiating. I heard a lot of bitching and moaning but most cosigners did one of the three, lowering our forfeiture rate even further. I don't know how much money I saved the company but I'd guesstimate it was somewhere in the hundreds of thousands. Using these new procedures, Joey's caseload went down to a manageable level.

Business was going well and Linda was pleased with me. She didn't compliment me often, but I felt great when she did. I loved Linda and went out of my way to please her. A lot of times that meant working late hours and coming in weekends, but I didn't mind.

One Sunday morning, while both of us were quietly working, Linda turned to me and said, "If anything happens to me, I want you to take over the forfeitures."

"What?"

"I mean just that. I've trained you. You know what to do and how to do it. If anything happens to me, I want you to take over my position in the Forfeiture Room. I want you to continue helping those defendants as you have been doing; continue getting them new court dates if possible. Most of these people don't understand the legal system and most don't know what to do when they fail to appear. They need people like you and me to explain it to them. They know we care about them and want to help. Will you do that?"

"Of course I will. I'm already doing that."

"I know you are. You've learned a lot in the years you've been here. You're doing really well."

After a few minutes of silence, I turned to her and said, "Besides, nothing's going to happen to you anyway. You're going to die old and gray at your desk like I am."

"Probably," she laughed. "Promise me one thing, though. Promise me you'll always be honest; that you won't take a bribe or a payoff; that you won't be dirty like so many bond agents are. I'm not going to name names, but there's a lot of dirt in this business. Incredible things, horrible things. If I told you, it'd make your hair stand on end.

"Don't be like them," she warned. "Promise me, Pam, you'll always be fair and honest with these people. No matter what, even if everybody else is dirty, *you* be clean."

"I promise." I crossed my heart with my finger for emphasis.

Nothing more was ever said, but I meant my promise. No matter what, I was going to do right by these people. I was going to do right by Arnie and Linda. I wouldn't—couldn't—do it any other way.

A couple weeks later, Linda called. "I don't know exactly what is wrong with me," she told me. "I just don't feel like myself."

I thought I knew what was wrong. She worked incredible hours. Her work schedule consisted of seven days a week, twelve to sixteen hours at a stretch. Since she'd been carrying that load for years, I figured she was just worn out. I encouraged her to take some time off.

She followed my advice and decided to take a couple of weeks off. But Linda was still Linda. Even when she wasn't officially working, she was working. She never failed to call me from home each morning to instruct me on how to handle certain forfeitures, instructions I carefully followed to the letter.

On Monday morning a few weeks later, I had just walked into the office and sat down at my desk when the phone rang. I looked at my watch. Since I always came to work early, it wasn't time for the office to be officially open. The night bond agent was still on duty, so I figured he'd answer the phone. When he didn't and it kept ringing, I thought it might be Linda so I answered.

Linda's husband was calling. After stammering for a few moments, his voice barely audible, he told me he'd tried to wake Linda at her usual time, 5 A.M. Sobbing, he continued, "She wouldn't wake up. She died sometime during the night in her sleep."

I burst into tears. Linda had been my mentor, my friend, my confidant. She'd been my right arm in times of trouble. We had laughed together and cried together and gotten drunk together. I knew her family and she knew mine. I couldn't imagine life without her. She was my rock, my anchor, my fortress. And now she was gone. I didn't know how I was going to go on without her. I didn't even *want* to.

The day after her funeral, I went into the office and, for the first time, sat down at her desk. I assumed Linda's position. No one ever told me to, I just did it. After all, I was the logical choice. I had been her protégé. As she'd so often told me, she taught me well. I was capable and competent. I had saved the company hundreds of thousands of dollars in forfeitures already. I knew I couldn't fill Linda's shoes; she was truly irreplaceable but I'd do my best.

After Linda died, things quickly changed in the office.

Arnie's general policy was not to bail prostitutes—with few exceptions. I can only surmise someone must have talked Arnie into it, because all of a sudden we were bailing them. A whole slew of prostitutes now regularly walked in and out of our office.

Even though I was technically Joey's boss, having assumed Linda's position, he didn't listen to me. I instructed him to stop chasing certain defendants, as I was going to get them new court dates. He nodded as if he understood, then promptly went out and arrested them, beating them up on the way to jail and removing drugs, jewelry and money from them that he kept for himself. I didn't like it, not at all. When I promised defendants that I'd work with them if they worked with me, they took me at my word. For Joey to go behind my back and treat them as he did made my word worthless on the street. More and more defendants started running; fewer and fewer were voluntarily coming in. As our forfeitures continued to mount, that gave me many, many sleepless nights.

I wanted to complain to Arnie. But after Linda died, he was rarely in the office anymore. He was out promoting and attending bail bond conventions, all those things that owners do, while another employee supervised the crew.

I walked into the office one morning and had just sat down at my desk when one of the employees told me we would have to hire a new bounty hunter. He was informed that Tim had just quit.

"Why?" I asked with a surprised look on my face.

He shrugged.

I truly liked Tim and was sorry to hear that he left Arnie's. He was a good bounty hunter. I vowed to call him as soon as I could, but meanwhile that put me in a dilemma. Every bonding company needs bounty hunters. They can save a bond agent's ass when thousands of dollars are owed to the court. Since the police don't have the time or the manpower to specifically look for and arrest our fugitives, without bounty hunters all bonding companies would quickly go out of business. Though Joey bragged he didn't need anyone to help him, the employee who told me about Tim's departure agreed that Joey needed backup.

For the next few weeks, Joey grabbed anybody he could get to help him. Sometimes someone from Arnie's. Sometimes me. Sometimes his friends or relatives. But Joey constantly complained that nobody worked as well as Tim. Either he couldn't reach the people when he really needed them, they were stupid or they got scared and ran during an arrest. Since bond agents and bounty hunters usually have to know someone in the business to get hired, that made it difficult to hire a replacement for Tim. None of us knew anyone who would be willing and able to undertake the job.

With Joey our main bounty hunter and the forfeitures quickly mounting, we were in desperate need of another. We'd have to find one—even if we had to grab someone off the street—and soon.

Chapter 10

So, We Meet Again

When I first saw Mike, it was a Friday night about 8 P.M. or so. Since I'd worked a little overtime, I was late joining everyone at our favorite bar.

I loved this place, because I never knew what to expect. I rubbed elbows with prostitutes sitting at the tables, busily selling their wares to willing johns, drunks lying in the corner, passed out, heads on tables, snoring loudly, drug addicts in the bathroom, shooting up dope and afterward leaving their dirty needles all over the floor. Joey was always in one fight or another with someone. There was never a dull moment. That's exactly why I went. By watching the action that went down normally, I was thoroughly entertained.

As I sat sipping my drink, a young man ran into the bar and headed for the men's room. Moments later, a group of men rushed in and ran into the men's room after him. Within a few minutes I heard a loud voice, "I can't find the dope!"

"It's got to be there somewhere," another yelled. "Check the back of the toilet."

I heard a lot of banging and shuffling coming from the small room. Then a man came out with the young man in cuffs. Holding a small baggie of dope up in the air, he shook it for emphasis.

"He found it!" someone shouted.

Only as he was exiting the bar did I notice the yellow lettering printed on the back of his black jacket: "Police Officer." I remember thinking that was impossible. With his shoulder-length dark brown hair and attractive face, he was too handsome to be a cop. Cops typically aren't that cute.

The second time I saw him, he was standing in the courthouse in the hallway, his arm in a sling. I recognized him right away as the cop who had busted that junkie in the bar.

According to the newspaper, he was a hero.

The lengthy article I had read relayed that while the police officer was in plainclothes visiting a friend at a local pub one night, a man walked into the bar shortly before closing. With apparent intent to rob the place, the assailant pulled out a gun. In the melee that followed, the police officer was shot but managed to return gunfire, killing the robber. Since the bartender hadn't been injured and the robbery thwarted, the newspaper heralded the cop's actions. The police department gave him a well-deserved and highly publicized commendation for bravery.

That day at the courthouse, the police officer was smiling and shaking hands with passersby who had stopped to congratulate him. There were so many people gathered around him with hands extended, I wondered how he could breathe. I watched for a few minutes as, despite the small mob, he stood there smiling, patiently shaking hands.

Then as I maneuvered around the crowd, I found myself unexpectedly standing right in front of the decorated cop. I was a well-known bail bond agent by that time. I was very visible at the jail and courthouse. In fact, most judges and attorneys knew me by name. I even partied with some of them at the local bars. I even had some of their home telephone numbers. Having gained some notoriety testifying in the Kurt/Robin case, I thought maybe the cop would recognize me. But he had no idea who I was. He looked at me with a blank look on his face. Not knowing what else to do, I extended my hand and thanked him for "being a hero." He graciously shook my hand, smiled and said, "Thank you."

I was just another stranger—one of many faces in the crowd. I realized then how egotistical I'd become in my role as a bail bond agent. I walked away chuckling to myself when I realized I was a legend, all right, but only in my own mind.

A few months later, I was shocked to see the cop—minus the sling—walk in the front door of Arnie's. He was accompanied by one of Arnie's friends, someone we knew well. They disappeared into the back room. I would have given anything to hear the conversation going on between them and Arnie. Unfortunately, I couldn't get away from the incessantly ringing phone long enough to eavesdrop.

Before long, Arnie, his friend and the cop came into the Forfeiture Room and Arnie introduced us. I shook Mike's hand and said, "So, we meet again."

Mike smiled shyly and said, "I beg your pardon?" He didn't remember me. I couldn't blame him. I imagined the cop had met dozens of people since his decoration. It was no wonder my face along with theirs had been instantly forgotten.

Arnie related that our firm had just hired Mike, who retired from the police force after he'd been shot, as our new bounty hunter. After Arnie left the room along with his friend, Mike and I stood there chatting for a few moments.

"Well," I said slowly, "I guess that makes me your new boss. If you'd like, I'll buy you a beer tonight and outline the position. That is, if you're interested."

"That would be great," he said smiling.

That night we met for a drink at the bar. Although I was leery of bounty hunters—most of them braggarts with very little skill—I was impressed with Mike's attitude. From what I could tell, he was straight up, ethical, moral and honest. The true test came when a bar fight broke out right behind us. As a cop, I expected him to immediately jump up from the table and, throwing his weight around, hurriedly break it up. Not Mike. He grabbed his beer protectively and moved out of the way.

"Aren't you going to break the fight up?" I asked, surprised.

"Hell no," Mike laughed. "Let them go at it. As long as they don't spill my beer, they're okay."

I laughed right along with him. We shared the same attitude: Protect the beer at all costs.

As the night progressed, I outlined what bail bondsmen do, our general bonding procedure and what was expected of him. I felt instinctively like I could trust him, so I didn't mince words. I told him about Joey's payoffs, shakedowns and the dope I found in his van. I warned him to be leery of Joey: "You have to watch your back."

As I was walking to my car after last call, I was totally ecstatic about Mike joining Arnie's. To have a former, decorated cop as a bounty hunter was a real coup. To my knowledge, no police officer had ever worked for a bonding company before. He would give respectability to a field that sorely needed it.

To my way of thinking, most bounty hunters were criminals—like Joey—and most did half-assed jobs at their craft. Some arrested the wrong people; some used unnecessary force; some took defendants' money or dope or both. Some carried such a huge arsenal of weapons, it was laughable. We all knew they weren't really needed; they were just for "show." Some created a great deal of mayhem while arresting defendants, unnecessarily disturbing the general public as they went about their business.

A recent case in the newspaper outlined bounty hunters busting into a funeral home during a funeral, tipping over chairs and pushing people out of the way as they arrested a defendant who was calmly sitting in a chair watching the service. We knew they did this because they love attention and the outlet to prove how macho they were—when it was all so totally unnecessary. The defendant could very well have been arrested without fanfare later, while he was alone exiting the cemetery. Some bounty hunters were even arrested when they brought the defendant into jail for having outstanding warrants themselves. For the most part, bounty hunters were illiterate, unprofessional and collectively a true embarrassment to the industry. But being a necessary evil, most were tolerated.

As I drove my car away that night, I smiled to myself. I had a feeling that if Mike came to work with us, he would change all that.

PART II

MIKE

Chapter 11

A Job Like That

Seventeen was a good age to be. I had a job flipping burgers at a fast-food hangout in Tacoma, managing to save up enough money to buy a fire engine red sports car. I had a cute blonde girlfriend, a couple of good buddies and enjoyed a pretty carefree time doing what kids do. However, there was a lurking problem in the back of my mind. In fact, I would have called it more of a lurking monster! The same monster that I believe most young men that age have faced, but never talk about it. The reason they never talk about it is because it seems like they don't have to; just about everybody in their lives has a way of reminding them about it on a daily basis. They are not nagging or bitching about it, but it is always there and it sucks—big time. And worst of all, they know it's true.

What I'm talking about is what every elder says to the youth in some form or another: "You're going to be a man soon, kid. What are you going to do with the rest of your life?"

I got a nauseous feeling in the pit in my stomach. I was seventeen years old and my grades were bad, so there was no hope for college. I didn't have a clue of what I would like to do or, for that matter, what I could do if I wanted to. I observed grown men in this world taking care of their families, driving their cars and trucks, living in houses that they worked and paid for and could not help but think: *I'm screwed!* Now the big question: *What do I do about it?* The answer was easy: call up one of my buddies, jump into my sweet little car and go cruising up on the avenue. *To hell with it—can't fix it, forget about it!*

It was the summer and while cruising, I saw something that changed my life forever. I had seen it before, but never really paid much attention. Most of the other kids sneered, hid or just did their plain best to avoid it, but not me. I was fascinated! I saw a Tacoma police officer in his marked police car keeping an eye on the kids and all that was happening when that police car suddenly sprang to life! The emergency light came on, the siren wailed and the officer disappeared into the night. As the sound of the siren grew faint, I instantly knew what I wanted to do with my life. I wanted to be that cop! Wherever he was going, I wanted to be there. I had to know what was on the other end of that siren! I had always heard sirens in the past and assumed that there had been an accident, but not this time. When I saw that cop take off, I realized that he could be responding to anything, including a confrontation on the last day of his life!

I could not get that siren and that police officer out of my mind. What makes a person want to do a job like that? Why would anyone be willing to charge headlong into a situation that could very well cost someone his or her life? Let's face it: Once you signed up for that program, you could not pick and choose what you responded to. It could be the most heart-wrenching sadness a person should never have to face or the scariest gut-check imaginable. However, the reality was that there was nobody else; it was just you and your buddies right there, right then and you had to fix it! Maybe that alone was part of the lure. Suddenly I knew for sure that I wanted to be one of them, but I had a couple of problems.

First, I was only seventeen years old and, in order to apply to the police academy, you had to be twenty-one. Second, it was still the era of the minimum height requirement. I was five feet six inches and the minimum was five feet eight inches. So there I was, too short, too young and nothing was going on in my life, so I developed a plan: get through my last year of high school, join the military, start working out, drink blenders full of weight gainer and hope I get a growth spurt. With a solid plan like that, how could anybody go wrong?

For the next four years, I served in the Navy. I served on a Polaris Submarine completing four patrols as both a Torpedo Man and a Launch Control Supervisor for the Polaris Missile System. I didn't get to see the world like a lot of other sailors. Most of what I saw was either the inside of the pressure hull of a submarine or the inside of a classroom during the numerous service schools the Navy sent me to. I had not lost the desire to become a cop and, when I left the Navy, I was old enough to start applying with a couple of the local law enforcement agencies.

Since I was born and raised in Tacoma, Washington, I applied for the Pierce County Sheriff's Office and the Tacoma Police Department. So far that rock solid plan of mine had worked. I had grown two inches taller and gained thirty pounds. Nature took care of the two inches in height while protein drinks and beer took care of the weight gain. The workout part of the plan suffered a bit, because there were not a lot of gym facilities on a submarine or in a classroom in those days. And since that's the best excuse I could come up with, I was going to hang on to it.

While waiting for one of the agencies to open up for testing, I got a job at a local ship dismantling yard as a laborer, but a funny thing happened while I was there. I was cutting big pieces of steel into little pieces and sorting them into different piles. After a couple of months, I noticed that I was growing out of all of my shirts and not in the gut. The arms were getting tighter as well as the shoulders, which felt really cool. I was getting stronger and filling out in all the right places. The timing could not have been better. The physical agility exams for the police departments were hopefully just around the corner.

The first call came from the Pierce County Sheriff's Office. I had placed well on the written examination and was called in for the oral board. I had some experience with oral boards. When you earned your Dolphins on a submarine, they sat you down for anywhere from four to eight hours and grilled you on every aspect of the boat. This was how they determined if you were worth anything and it could be grueling, but I enjoyed the challenge. I had gone in prepared and, without sounding corny, it was actually a very rewarding experience. The amount of work and dedication that it takes to become a qualified submariner at a young age gave me the mind-set to never give up on anything the rest of my life.

I was sitting in the hot seat in front of three gentlemen asking me questions about becoming a cop. I had prepared as well as I knew how. I could recite the usual babble that I had memorized to assumed questions such as, "Why do you want to be a cop? What makes you think you would be an asset to this department?" I believe these questions are valid and would help the examiners determine whether or not you can complete a sentence without sounding like a total moron or some crazy "kill them all and let God sort them out" type.

As I sat there, snapping out answers to questions from the other two examiners, I looked at the guy to the far right of me. Suddenly, the goofy jerk threw a ballpoint pen at me. Luckily, I saw it coming and actually managed to catch it. Slowly I set the pen on the table in front of this guy and during the entire time, he was staring at me with this stupid grin on his face, never saying a word. The other two guys in the room looked a little shocked at what had just happened. They didn't know what to say. As we watched the guy with the dopey half grin/half smirk on his face, I looked back at him wondering, *How in the hell did they pick this nitwit to determine if I am stable enough to do the job?* Now I know what some of you are probably thinking: *He was just testing your reactions, dude.* Let me say this: I have been through a lot of oral boards, including the one to get into SWAT, and never before or since have I ever heard or seen anything like this.

I left that interview not knowing how I did and hoping that the pen throwing episode was not the norm. Weeks later, I received a notice in the mail that I had passed all of the requirements and was now number forty-four on a hiring list. I was excited to say the least. So far so good—it looked like this dream might actually happen.

While waiting for Pierce County to open up enough new hires, the Tacoma Police Department had begun their testing process. I decided two possibilities were better than one. The first hurdle was to pass the written exam. I sailed through it and felt very confident that I had passed. And passed I did. The next step was the physical agility test, which I again sailed through. Then I got the call for the oral exam and thought to myself, *Here we go again,* but to my relief, it was all very expected.

During the first part of the exam, I was in a room with several interviewers. Both street officers and higher-ranking officers were involved. A lieutenant was in charge. Going into this, one must not think he or she is going to easily fool these guys. First, they asked a battery of questions involving everything from why I wanted to be a cop to any acts I may not have been very proud of during my short life. Once the interview was over, they marched me down to a small but intimidating room and introduced me to a polygraph examiner. The first thing my mind did was race through all of the questions they just asked and hope I didn't try to be clever with some of my answers.

Through a combination of luck and good parenting, I had never gotten into any trouble and the polygraph was a snap. All of my exams were complete and, at this point, it was just a waiting game.

A few months later, the phone rang and the voice on the other end asked, "Do you still want to be a Tacoma police officer?"

More than anything!

"Yes, I do," I answered in a serious tone.

"Then be at the police department at 8 A.M. Monday morning," he said as he hung up the phone.

I had actually made it to the first step. I jumped around the room like a little kid seeing the present he'd hoped for under the tree on Christmas morning.

My hopes and dreams seemed to have come true. Of course, I didn't know my life would change forever!

Chapter 12

Snitches

Snitches are a dying breed! Snitches get stitches! Snitches end up in ditches! Everybody likes to demonize the snitch. I have adult male friends who are not criminals, but still like to talk about the scary things they would do if somebody snitched on them. First and foremost: Shut up! If your goal is to sound like a fourteen-year-old juvenile delinquent, you've succeeded. You're not a dangerous guy and you don't have a clue about what you're talking about. A lot of people would be a lot better off if they didn't spend so much time trying to convince themselves and others around them that they are something they're really not. The fact is informants are the life-blood of investigations—from reporting on the neighborhood kid breaking windows to providing tips on the most dangerous terrorists or drug cartel leaders in the world. To be honest, I love snitches!

Snitches most often fall into three categories: concerned citizen, revenge addict and mercenary. Sometimes you run across informants who are combinations of all three categories.

My heart goes out to the concerned citizen. Many times these folks are living in areas littered with human scum. They are surrounded by predatory thugs who have no respect for anyone or anything, which is a twisted contradiction in itself. These cowards act like they live by some code that demands respect without the slightest clue that respect is not a birthright or something that is owed to them on account of their friends, their gang or the color of their clothes. Respect is a precious commodity that is earned with time, experience and personal behavior. Like some of the best things in life, it is hard to achieve and very easy to lose. Those who believe that they can victimize entire communities and are willing to kill you because in their demented or hostile minds you showed disrespect by looking at them the wrong way are, to me, simply a waste of oxygen! Make no mistake, these thugs are frightening and they are very dangerous! Those concerned citizens who try to help get the criminals off their streets are risking their lives and I stand in awe of them. They are the heroes who deserve admiration and respect.

Probably the complete opposite side of concerned citizens who are trying to make life safer for the community are revenge snitches. In this case, they are angry and they are angry at you! Revenge snitches will screw up your world any way they can and they will lie to do it. In police work, they can be valuable! They are going to tell all about their targets' dirty little crimes.

Revenge occurs for many reasons. However, the primary reason seems to be love! Mismanaged love, whether perceived or real, has brought a lot of men and women down. Don't get me wrong. Revenge is on all sides of the gender pool, but experience and a long career has me believing that an angry woman is a force of nature that I don't want to tangle with! In police work, revenge is a gold mine and a very effective tool.

Mercenaries trade information for something in return. It's nothing personal for them; it's just business or self-preservation. When I say it's just business, I don't want to give the impression that it is simply for the money. Sure, your down-and-out junkies will snitch out the people closest to them for the twenty bucks that will buy their next hit. But these types of people are not good informants, they are just snitches and they cannot be trusted. They will lie about anything to anyone, including the cops, to get what they want. They would bring you a piece of bunk (fake dope) and swear that they bought it from the Pope if they thought they were going to get paid. True street-level mercenaries are also after something they can't buy—the adrenaline rush. They know that if they get caught by the bad guy, there are a whole lot of bad things that can happen to them. But fear takes a backseat to the thrill of that rush.

The number one problem with informants like these is their presumption that they are smarter than you. They know the people they are buying drugs from better than you do and because they have been living this lifestyle, they think they are streetwise. They assure me that they know everybody and everything—nobody out there would mess with them. What they seem to forget is that the headlines and morgues in this country are full of people like them every single day. The single biggest mistake an informant can make is believing that some seemingly dumb loser is a trusted friend and the informant can tell the person all about his/her really cool job with a really cool undercover cop. So, the first thing you have to do with a new informant is have a very serious talk about the rules of survival. If the informant doesn't get it, you have to cut that person loose. Otherwise you could be responsible for the informant's death— something I'd never want, personally.

The reality of it all is that some of your informants may start out as scum in your life, but when you get to know them, they do turn into real people and you do care for them. It's an odd relationship, but I can honestly say that I have become fond of some of the many informants I have worked with over the years. In fact, I would rather sit down and reminisce with an old informant than a lot of personal friends.

I had begun working narcotics investigations with the Tacoma
Police Department. During this period, crack cocaine was close to
destroying a section of the city known as the Hilltop. We were
learning about a then-rising new street gang called the Crips, who
were coming in from California setting up bases of operation in
Tacoma and the surrounding areas. We were also hearing a lot about
a group known as Marielitos—a term referring to Cubans who
arrived in the United States by boats. Some intelligence suggested
that the Marielitos were the big-time dealers and were, in fact,
supplying the Crips with a lot of cocaine.

At first, the information we were receiving didn't seem believable.
However, it didn't take long to realize that it was all very real and the
powers-that-be had better come up with a plan or the community was
going to be in deep trouble. City leaders and law enforcement had
never seen anything like this phenomenon before and it took a while
to get our bearings. History has shown that when city leaders and law
enforcement are either in denial or don't want to give the city a bad
name by recognizing the problems, it's the citizens who ultimately
suffer.

The Tacoma Police Department soon recognized the threat and
decided to form a special team to deal with it. They pulled current
SWAT team members out of their daily assignments and formed
them into that special team. That's where my buddies and I came in.
We were all original members of the SWAT team that had been
formed some years earlier to deal with the current trend of new
criminals and their heavier firepower. It was a perfect fit.

I don't think we could have had a better group of guys to deal with
the violence going down on the streets of Tacoma. We had the
weaponry, the training and the attitude to deal with these criminals.
In fact, we couldn't wait. The only thing we were lacking was the
knowledge to conduct a complicated narcotic investigation. No one
on the team had ever prepared a search warrant nor did we have

the slightest clue as to the procedure. We had never worked with informants or, for that matter, even knew how to get somebody recognized by the courts as a confidential, reliable informant. The solution was to add an experienced narcotics agent to the team to teach us how to conduct an investigation.

It didn't take long for the bad guys to know who we were and what we were about. They could try to bullshit anyone they wanted, but the fact was they were afraid of us.

In one article in the local newspaper, a reporter interviewed one of the resident gangbangers. According to the report, the gang "owned" a particular block in the neighborhood and nobody, including the police, would come onto their turf. The fact was we had begun rolling up to that corner late at night and often saw twenty to thirty of them standing around doing their dope deals. As soon as they saw us, twenty to thirty gangbangers ran away as fast as they could. We were the light and they were the cockroaches—end of story.

The narcotics investigator and I became fast friends. He liked to teach and I loved to learn. I listened to every word and soaked up his knowledge like a sponge. It didn't take long before I was handling my own informants and pounding out the search warrants. We were a very successful team and had been working this assignment for a year or so when I was approached by a married couple with a fascinating story.

Apparently, Suzie and Rich had come into some money from Suzie's grandmother. When Grandma passed, she left Suzie a six-figure inheritance. The problem was that Suzie and Rich loved their drugs; Suzie favored crack and Rich was into any drug he could get his hands on, mostly crack and/or heroin. These two were not your suburbanite-type drug addicts; they were the got-to-hustle-every-day-for-your-fix drug addicts and when that inheritance money came in, whoa buddy, the party was on!

First order of business for Suzie and Rich was how to let the other drug vermin know that they were the coolest dopers on skid row.

They figured out that the best way to do that was to buy a couple of brand new luxury cars. It's amazing how popular you become when you show up at the local crack house driving his and her luxury cars. Suzie said that they had more friends than she realized. It was like the sidewalks had opened up and regurgitated more of society's waste than they could keep up with.

Within six months, the money, the dope, the cars and the friends were all gone. Once Suzie snapped out of her six-month haze and realized what had happened to her one chance to change her life forever, it sickened her. She was back to the cold reality that she had given everything to addiction and had to hustle every day again for food and dope. Most important, she realized for the first time that other addicts were not her friends! They use and abuse everyone and everything that gets close to them and never look back.

Down and out, Suzie and Rich came up with a new plan: work for the cops. Suzie explained that she had been wronged by the drug world and now she wanted to do something for the community. She was ready to tell the names of all the big players in the drug world and, in fact, would testify in open court.

I didn't care about her intentions. I had to keep reality firmly in my mind. She was probably lying to me and I was simply another way for her to score some money for more dope. That was the world I worked in, but I also knew I would be foolish not to investigate new revelations. Unless you weigh the information and check it out, you may be passing up something really important.

I plunged ahead and, to my surprise, nothing was popping up as false information. We jumped through the usual hoops to get Suzie recognized by the courts as a confidential and reliable informant, but this time it was different. The confidential part was only an issue as far as keeping her alive during the investigation. Once it was wrapped up, Suzie insisted that she would still testify, hoping that she could make a difference.

I was still skeptical; they are all on the hustle, they are all liars and I was worried that as soon as she made a little money from us, she would be on another drug binge. But I decided to wait and watch, telling myself, *Let's see what happens.*

Once things started to happen, they happened fast.

True to Suzie's word, she knew all the big players. She was buying directly from the guys we could not get close enough to and Suzie seemed to love it, taking great pride in her work. She came back after buying crack from these guys very excited and smiling from ear to ear. She had been in the drug world for so long that nobody ever suspected her. Even then, I was always on the lookout for the scam. I had to make sure that she was not simply buying crack from a lower-level dealer and claiming it was from some big player.

The first rule was to not give her any targets and let her pick from whom she would buy. It was important to keep a tight rein on her and verify all information. The investigation went well, resulted in some fifty arrests and caused quite a stir with the drug dealers.

When the investigation wrapped up, the television stations and newspapers broke the story.

During the investigation, we made a lot of drug buys inside a neighborhood tavern. The drug dealers had taken the place over and were running a lot of dope through there. In fact, it was so bad in this tavern that, at one time, a judge found enough cause to give us a search warrant for the establishment itself. We didn't really think much about it. A week or so after the busts went down, we wanted to let the ones who got away know we were still thinking about them, so four or five of us mounted up and paid the tavern a visit. We entered in force as we always did, prepared for anything.

It was a close neighborhood and the tavern was a family hangout. As we entered, the patrons saw us and began clapping their hands, giving us a standing ovation. At first, I was highly suspicious, but as patrons started approaching us and thanking us for cleaning up "their place," the feeling was indescribable. I actually asked a couple of them if they were kidding. They assured us that they weren't. They led me over to a copy of a newspaper they had posted on the wall. It was an article that showed a picture of me taking one of the dealers into the jail. On that picture, they wrote "Good Guy" with an arrow pointing to me and "Bad Guy" with an arrow pointing at the drug dealer. They told us that they had all but given up hope that anyone was going to help them. They were sick of the dealers, but had no way to fight them. They were too scared to say anything and believed that the police department would not accomplish much. The dealers who remained free were on the run. They had no way of knowing if we had warrants for their arrests and didn't want to risk it. Those cheers that day lasted just a few minutes in a very long career, but I will never forget them and I do feel very proud of it.

The dealers were well aware of who I was, but just because this investigation was over didn't mean they got any breathing room. There were more of them left and our team continued a relentless pursuit of them. Relentless enough that we received two separate reports that informants had attended meetings with some of the big boys and my death was discussed at great length. It was serious enough that one of my SWAT buddies, Rod Cook, was assigned to specifically watch my back when we were out on the streets doing our thing.

I already trusted any member of the team with my life—we all did. When you do this kind of work day in and day out, you become very tight with one another. Rodney and I were very close friends outside the job. We were, and still are, hunting and fishing partners. We drink together, ride our motorcycles together and know each other as well as we know ourselves.

When the team was out working the streets, we all had our areas of concern. I was Rodney's area of concern; I never had to look to see if he was there, because I could feel his presence at all times. Anyone who does this type of work or has worked special teams in the military knows exactly what I am talking about.

My life was getting edgy now. With the revelation that I might have not one but possibly two contracts on my life, I was looking at everything in a different light. I would never let my SWAT buddies know I was concerned, but the threat of danger was always there and the guys couldn't always be with me. Things like that tend to make you a lot more aware of your surroundings.

You look at everything and everyone. You look at people's eyes and watch their hands. That is where you will see it coming from. If they are not professionals, their eyes will lock on you and you will know something is wrong. If they are skilled, you might notice a glance that is out of place or an unusual movement that doesn't fit—or you might not.

Then there was the other possibility that the risk might not be as ominous as it seemed. Maybe it was an attempt to get us to back off. Well, that wasn't going to happen. It might have been nerve-wracking, but there was no way in hell some drug dealer was going to intimidate this team or this department. I think the worst part was not knowing if there was going to be an attempt or not or how long the threat would last. How long can one be on edge before it takes its toll? I sweated this hit thing for a couple of months and it was time to take a break. It was hunting season and my bud Rodney and I decided to head to the mountains for a week.

We liked going up into the Gifford Pinchot National Forest during hunting season. We headed up into the high country about thirty miles above Randle, Washington. It can be some rough country out there, but it was always exciting. We were in great shape, loved those hills and when we got back in there far enough, we didn't see a lot of other hunters.

We camped at an area Rodney referred to as "the old Indian campground." It was the regular season in October, but it was cold that year. I found myself standing on a ridge overlooking a large ravine that cut its way through the mountains and worked its way down to Wobbly Lake. The scenery was beautiful and the peace of mind was even better.

Here in the peace and quiet of these mountains, I could think about my life and work some problems out. It felt like I was a million miles away from the filth and misery of the brutality and savagery I dealt with every day. Every day I had to climb into the lives of hopeless, desperate people. Though I loved my job, as do others working in this field, we are not naïve. We know that we will never stop drugs or drug addiction. The problems will never go away and we will never save the world but being there in the serenity of the mountains, I got a different perspective. When I was in the middle of kicking in crack house doors or chasing some junkie through a back alley, it was easy to get the feeling that none of it mattered and I was not really accomplishing anything. Standing on the ridgeline in the mountains, my brain had a chance to clear itself. I suppose it wasn't that different from the addicts I spent some of my days hauling off to jail. They need to get off the dope to get clean and my teammates and I needed to get away from the action to allow our thoughts to get clean.

The snow was falling heavily and everything was incredibly peaceful. Rodney was somewhere else on the mountain and I hadn't seen another person for hours. In this beautiful isolation, I reminded myself that our efforts had reaped rewards.

I was thrilled about the fact that I would be spending a week in the mountains and I could let my guard down, because I knew that if someone was trying to get me, it was not going to happen here.

Chapter 13

Hot Toddy Man

On my first day back from the peacefulness of the mountains, my shift ended at midnight. After clocking out, I headed to a neighborhood bar to which a couple of my fellow officers had introduced me. I went there often and was friendly with the bartender.

I walked through the back door that opened to a narrow hallway about twelve feet long with restrooms on the left, while an ice machine and other equipment occupied the right. The end of the hallway led to the main area. The bar itself ran along the left side of the building with tables and a dance floor on the right. The two were separated with a row of booths running down the center of the room.

This was a working man's bar. The people who lived in the area had been coming here for years and everyone knew one another or they were related. The drinks were free pour and they poured a lot of them. You couldn't tell what color the carpet used to be or what that particular smell was each time you came in. The lighting was dim and the once-white ceiling tiles were now dark brown, stained from nicotine. On the weekends the music was good and you could usually count on watching a fistfight or two. I loved the place!

I was still kind of an outsider in the bar. But if you stayed out of people's business, they wouldn't bother you. This was the east side of Tacoma. It's a diverse neighborhood with a tough reputation. There was a mix of longshoremen, truckers, bikers and anyone else who worked hard for a living and played hard whenever they felt like it. The service was good and the conversation lively. It was the kind of place I liked then and still love to frequent to this day.

I entered as I always did, cautious without trying to appear as though I was paying that much attention. Clearing the hallway, I walked a few steps to the left and stood at the end of the bar. From this position, I could see anybody coming in the front door. Anybody coming in the back door would not be able to see me until the person cleared the hallway. However, at that point, I would be able to see them and hopefully gauge their intentions.

Another guy had entered the back door just seconds behind me. He sat on a barstool near the other end of the bar. There were only three of four other customers hanging out and it was getting close to last call. Not much was going on. It looked like I could let my guard down and relax that night, so I ordered a beer and settled in.

The guy who had come in after I did was asking the bartender her recipe for hot toddies and seemed to be flirting more than really interested in her skills as a mixologist. The other patrons were engaged in small talk and enjoying their evening. It looked like another humdrum winter night drinking at the local neighborhood watering hole.

Around 1:15 A.M., I watched as two guys entered the front door together and then separated. One of them came to the bar side of the room and the other went toward the dance floor side. Immediately I recognized one had been a troublemaker in the past. He had made it obvious on earlier occasions that he knew I was a cop and had a real problem with it. When they separated, it appeared as though they were taking up positions. They both scanned the room, making eye contact with me. Then they went back out the front door together as the bartender and I glanced at each other with a mutual look of concern.

"I'm going to head out the front door and see if I can get a license plate and vehicle description," the bartender said. My only thought was that these guys could circle around the building and come through the back door behind me.

I moved to the far end of the bar. From this position I could see both the front and back doors. The actions of these two guys had me on such high alert that I drew my Model 19 Glock, keeping it concealed under the bar. None of the other customers seemed to have noticed anything was wrong. A short while later the bartender came back inside saying, "One of the guys got into a vehicle and I have the tag number. I didn't see the second guy."

At that moment, the second subject, the one I had recognized as the troublemaker, came through the back door. He looked visibly surprised that I had moved to the other end of the bar. Sitting down on the barstool closest to the end of the hallway, he glanced back and forth between me and the bartender. After a few seconds, he asked the bartender for a drink.

"I've already called last call and we're getting ready to close up," she told him.

"It's too early to close," he muttered back to the bartender, then stared directly at me and said, "I hope I make it home tonight without getting seriously hurt or killed!" A few seconds later, he stormed out the back door. I thought I was on edge when they came in the front door, but after he said that my senses went on high alert.

The customer who had followed me in and had asked about the hot toddy recipe noticed the attitude and comments of the guy who left. He asked me, "Does that guy have it out for you?" I shrugged and acted like I had ignored the situation. I was hoping that the guy was just a disgruntled jerk and had nothing to do with the contract on my life. It didn't seem likely that he would have the horsepower to be involved in something that heavy. Concealed by the bar, I put the Glock back into its holster without anybody noticing.

The hot toddy customer continued flirting with the bartender while my mind kept reeling.

It was about 1:30 A.M. and the bartender had had enough. She began the same old routine of locking the front door and herding the remaining customers out the back door.

The hot toddy guy was nursing his last drink and with all the other customers gone, the bartender asked me to check the bathrooms, making sure they were empty. I did and found myself again standing at the end of the bar closest to the back door. The bartender stood behind the bar to my left, talking to me, when the hot toddy man finished his drink and started to walk toward me and the back door. When he got about three feet from me, he reached under his sweatshirt with his right hand. I couldn't see what he was reaching for. Suddenly a snub nose .357 Magnum came up toward my face. This was it! There was no time to think about levels of response or escalation of force; either my SWAT training kicked in right then or I was dead.

In the next few seconds, we were face-to-face and I was looking straight at that gun! I reached up with my right hand, grabbed the barrel and pushed it to my right, away from my body. We didn't say a word to each other, but as I grabbed the gun, instantly my anger exploded and I yelled, "No!" Holding onto the barrel of his gun, I pulled my Glock out of its holster on my left hip and shoved the barrel into hot toddy man's chest, pulling the trigger. The impact of my bullet hammering its way into his chest made him jerk backwards. When he pulled back, I lost my grip on his gun.

Quickly taking a couple of steps around a small partition wall at the end of the booths, I desperately hoped that my first round put the guy down, as I didn't want to get shot. As I stepped around the small wall keeping my weapon up, standing sideways with my left arm fully extended toward my assailant, I heard a loud bang. My left arm went completely limp. I had been hit and hit hard! The .357 bullet had found its way between the sleeve of my leather jacket and my wrist.

My left arm fell to my side. With no control over my arm, I dove to the dance floor keeping the row of booths between me and the bad guy. Trying to get my bearings as I lay on the floor, I realized the hot toddy man was still shooting at me; rounds were going through the booths and over my head. Then, within seconds, the shooting stopped and I struggled to get my gun from my left hand to my still good right hand while at the same time trying to figure out where this guy was going to come at me from next.

A deathly quiet filled the bar, giving this neighborhood establishment a very eerie feel. The lights were already dim; the smell of gunpowder and smoky haze filled the room. I was bleeding profusely as I slowly started to get to my feet trying to locate the suspect. Peering over the top of the booths, I noticed the bartender had risen from her hiding place behind the bar. She made eye contact with me and pointed to a table on the other side of the booths. I stepped up on one of the seats and saw the suspect draped over a table. He had been walking on the other side of the booths paralleling my movements, trying to shoot me. Then he had turned and started toward the dance floor collapsing.

I didn't know if this guy was dead or alive. What I did know was that there could be two more people coming through that back door to help him out and that meant my back would be to this guy. From my vantage point standing on the seat, I fired four more rounds at my assailant with my right hand. I saw his body jerk twice and was satisfied that I could now pay attention to any other threats without getting shot in the back.

Immediately I took up a cover position so nobody could come through that back door without my being able to deal with them while the bartender called 911. I didn't know what damage the bullet had done to my arm yet. I had a leather jacket on and couldn't see where I had been hit. I did know that my arm was useless and I was oozing a lot of blood. A few seconds later the bartender had the 911 operator on the phone, but she was very upset and having trouble clearly telling the operator what happened.

"She wants to talk to you," the bartender told me.

Leaving my position of cover, I joined the bartender behind the bar. While holding my gun in my right hand and my left arm dangling at my side, the bartender held the phone to my ear so I could talk to the operator and keep my gun trained on the end of the hallway at the same time. As I was talking to the operator, the sirens screamed louder and louder as they got closer.

I was struck by the irony of the moment. As a teenage boy, the sound of police sirens often mesmerized me as they faded off into the darkness—the same siren sounds that urged me to pursue this career were now coming for me! Those same sirens could very well mean the end of the career they had started.

Suddenly the streets around the bar area came to life. Prowl cars screeched to a halt with emergency lights flashing and the sirens gave a final yelp as they wound down. Blue uniforms started to fill the bar as thoughts of what was to come raced through my mind.

The first thing I realized was that it was over! My fellow officers were there and they would take care of everything. One of my buddies came to me and gently removed the Glock from my hand saying, "Don't worry, we got it. Now let's take care of you."

We walked to the front door where paramedics greeted me. They took my leather jacket off to see where I had been hit. As I looked down at my left arm, I saw that the underside of my forearm had been ripped wide open. The bloodshot muscle and flesh that was normally inside my arm was protruding out along the full length of my arm, which looked more like a fillet salmon than an arm. I looked at the paramedic and told him, "I've seen enough. Let me sit down while you do what you can with this mess." They sat me on the floor and began to work on my arm.

Bad as my arm looked, I realized how incredible lucky I was. If that bullet had been only a quarter of an inch lower, it would have missed my sleeve, striking me in the armpit then taking out both lungs and my heart. I would have certainly been dead. As fate would have it, I would see this shot again.

Shortly afterward, the ambulance arrived and they loaded me up. They worked on my rather severe wound for a few minutes before rushing me off to the hospital for emergency surgery.

One of my cop buddies came to the back of the ambulance and asked how I was doing. I gave him a thumbs-up. As I was holding my thumb up, he asked if I knew the condition of the bad guy. I rotated my arm, pointing my thumb down.

"The suspect is dead," the cop confirmed.

Chapter 14

Some Say Hero

How did I get here? I asked myself. My left arm was almost blown in half. The .357 Magnum round did quite a job on me. It entered my left arm about three inches past my wrist and dug into the lower part of my forearm. It continued its journey along the length of my arm just below the surface, splitting my arm wide open as it traveled past my elbow and lodged in the side of my bicep. The good news: I was still alive. If it was an eighth of an inch lower, I'd be a goner. Death would have been fast, but I know now from experience that it wouldn't have been instant. An eighth of an inch lower and two people would have been lying dead on the dance floor.

Instead, the other guy—the bad guy, the dead guy—took a nine millimeter round from my Model 19 Glock directly into the heart with my pistol no further than an inch from his chest. It had been a toe-to-toe gun battle and although I shot him first, he was still able to get four rounds off. He pursued me for about fifteen feet then I was able to place four more rounds into him leading to his death. He died trying to kill me, draped facedown over a table still clutching his .357 Magnum.

I'll never know the thoughts going through the mind of the person I killed that night. After my first round hit him, he must have been in total shock. This was not a case of police officer versus bad guy; this was a case of bad guy versus a new set of innocent victims. As far as he was concerned, he was the robber, he was in charge and he could do whatever he wanted with his new prey. I can't imagine the disbelief and horror he must have felt when he first realized that his prey had turned on him and was, in fact, killing him. There is no doubt in my mind that he knew he was dying. Many would have simply lay down with sad resignation and just let go. However, it appeared that he tried to make me pay. After all, who was I to kill him? I was his victim.

But I was already thinking there was no reason I should have been lying on the gurney. I had been on the Tacoma Police SWAT team for almost six years and I had just finished a year and a half of intensive anti-terrorist training.

Standing five feet eight inches and weighing 165 pounds, I was a lean, fast and tough thirty-eight-year-old. Because of my training, I should have been able to put two slugs in the criminal's chest and one in his head while controlling his gun. At one point, I had grabbed the barrel of his revolver, but didn't hang on to it with enough force.

Some will call me a "hero", but inside I was branding myself a *major screwup*. Until now, I have always kept that to myself. That is the easy part to come to grips with and it pales in comparison to my real screwup that night. I had just been in a gun battle in a place I shouldn't have been. Yeah, a lot of people will be saying hero alright. I will be smiling and thanking them on the outside, while thinking *what a stupid asshole I am* on the inside.

The chief of police and the rest of the top brass were already at the hospital when I arrived in the ambulance. The chief stayed in the examining room with me as the doctors and nurses buzzed around. The chief assisted the nurses with getting my clothing off me and getting me dressed in the appropriate gown.

I only had one request. I wanted to personally call my mother and my wife. I did not want them being woken up in the middle of the night by a strange voice telling them that I had been shot. I knew if they heard my voice telling them that I was fine, the news would be much easier to handle.

It was about 2:15 A.M. when my mother answered the phone, but she sounded as if she was wide awake.

"Mom, it's me."

"What's going on?" she asked.

"Well, I'm in the hospital right now. I was shot tonight, but I'm okay. It's just a minor flesh wound and I am absolutely fine."

"Well, that explains that," she said.

"Why? What do you mean, Mom?"

"Well," she began, "I woke up startled at 1:30 this morning and have been pacing the floor ever since. I knew something was wrong, but didn't know what."

"Well, now you know and again, I promise you, I'm fine. I will probably be here a couple of days getting patched up, so you can come down tomorrow and see me. Try to get some sleep, Mom."

"Okay, son. I will see you tomorrow."

My mother's reaction did not surprise me. She has had this strange connection with me all my life. She was only nineteen when I was born and I put her through hell. She endured over fifty hours of labor, only to have her baby be born with a misshapen skull. Over time she massaged my head, constantly working on reshaping it.

Often in my life, I called my mom and she answered the phone knowing it was me before picking it up. She seems to always be tuned into me. Now, mind you, I don't buy into all of that psychic crap but one thing I do know: Mothers have unique powers!

After I talked to my wife I was taken to surgery and the surgeon asked me if I would like to remain awake or be put out. As I slipped out of consciousness I couldn't help but wonder again, *How did I get here and what's next*?

Time seemed to pass quickly although I was out for several hours. My eyes opened and as the light sneaked its way into my brain, the events of the night came flooding back. I've stopped kidding myself. None of the *where am I?* and *what am I doing here?* questions. I knew exactly where I was and felt a great sense of relief. I was in the recovery room looking up at two of my SWAT teammates.

As we met one another's eyes, the realization hit us all that this incident may not have been a simple armed robbery gone bad. There was a very real possibility that this was an attempted contract hit on a police officer.

That first day my hospital room was humming with police personnel and hospital staff. I drifted in and out of consciousness thanks to the effects of the anesthetic, knowing that I could rest easy with my pals watching out for me.

Later that day, my mom tried to visit me. My SWAT guards would not let her enter the room until I identified her.

Up to this point, everything was great. I had just survived a potentially fatal attack; the boys were guarding me and other than this hole in my arm, I was feeling on top of the world. I assured my pals that it appeared to be just a flesh wound and I expected to be back on the job within six weeks. As soon as I saw my mom's face, everything changed. I went from being a hard-assed, highly trained SWAT cop to simply a child whom his mother almost lost.

I asked my buddies to please give us some privacy. It was either that or risk blubbering in front of those guys and we all know that steely-eyed trained cops would never do such a thing.

With a slight sniffle and a crack in her voice, my mom simply said, "So, Rambo does bleed," using the nickname some drug dealers and gangbangers had given me. I knew she was trying to let me know she was alright, but when I looked into her frightened eyes, I knew that this time I had really scared her.

I reassured her and she patiently listened to my bullshit, not believing any of it.

A few days later, I learned that the dead guy had been wearing a wig and had recently robbed another bar in the same manner. He had waited until all of the customers had left before holding the bartender and her boyfriend at gunpoint, searching them and locking them in the cooler.

We will never know what would have happened if I hadn't fought back. What would the criminal have done if he had found my gun and badge? The police had also tracked down the other two suspicious characters who had entered the bar earlier that night. From what I was told, it was pure coincidence that they had entered the bar at the same time. According to the follow-up investigators, the two parties did not know each other. The guy who got into his car and left was looking for a friend. The other guy, the troublemaker, was just being a smart-ass with his comments.

My hunting partner, Rodney, still thinks it was an attempted contract killing. I tend to lean toward an armed robbery gone bad. The only one who knows for sure is dead. As for the guy with the bad attitude, I have never seen him again. I guess being a smart-ass doesn't always work out the way you hope it will.

Several doctor appointments and six months later, the police pension doctor gave me the news. The ulna nerve in my left arm took a severe beating from that bullet. Since I was left-handed, he didn't feel right putting me back on the streets. The good news was, "You can collect your paycheck and go home." The bad news was, "You can collect your paycheck and go home."

A thirty-eight-year-old pensioner with no skills other than police work.

Now what? I asked myself.

Chapter 15

Undercover

After the newspapers broke the story of how I was wounded taking down the bad guy, everywhere I went I was treated like a hero. To be truthful, the limelight was kind of fun. Friends, acquaintances and complete strangers came up to me and shook my hand, thanking me for my service to their community. All of them seemed genuinely concerned for my well-being and wished me a speedy recovery.

Wherever I went, the greetings were warm and the alcohol was free. I couldn't buy a beer in town if I wanted to. To this day, I look back at those times with great fondness. I am truly grateful to all the people who were so appreciative toward me. Some of those strangers became friends of mine and we remain tight to this day.

The partying was fun, but I knew I had to figure out what to do with the rest of my life. Drinking every day was neither an answer nor an option. My arm still had a lot of healing to do. That meant I had to figure out a way to work with my brain.

I hit the books and obtained my real estate license, landing a job at one of the local brokerage houses. For our orientation, the office manager gathered up all of the new agents and gave us a motivational talk, welcoming us aboard. When the office manager told us that real estate could be one of the most exciting jobs we would ever have, I felt like I was hit in the gut with a baseball bat. In a few short months, I had gone from ninety miles an hour to two miles an hour. As I looked at all the upbeat faces surrounding me in that room, all I could think was: *This cannot be all that's left for me!* How long was it going to take to let the drama of the past go and settle into a "normal" life?

Another former Tacoma cop had obtained his real estate license and was working out of the same office. I managed to drag myself to the office every day, meeting up with him. We spent our days telling war stories and planning our free lunches at other brokers' open houses. Life sucked!

I was sitting around wallowing in my misery one afternoon when the phone rang.

"Beak, it's Bruno. What's up, my man?"

Thank God! Bruno is back in town. In some circles, this guy was a legend. He is a retired Special Forces operator who spent over a year training our SWAT team, getting us ready for anti-terrorist threats during the Goodwill Games. *It is going to be nice to talk to somebody who speaks the same language*, I thought to myself.

"Not a thing, Bruno, but it sure is good to hear from you."

"You healed up yet? I heard that bullet ripped your arm."

"Yeah, it's my strong hand. I still have a lot of therapy left."

"That sucks," Bruno said. "Are you well enough to do some real work or are you comfortable being a civilian?"

"Whatcha got cookin'?" I asked.

"Here's the deal, Beak. The little town I'm living in is developing a bit of a drug problem. The cops down here are a bunch of good guys, but they're not geared up for dope investigations. Every dirtbag in town knows who they are and they've never been trained in this crap."

"I don't know what I can do for you, Bruno. You know I left the force on account of my injury and I'm on pension. I have no authority to do anything."

"We've got that worked out," Bruno said. "The chief down here is a good Joe. He's talked to the mayor and they've figured out a way to give you a limited commission. All you have to do is act like you're one of the dealers, drink beer and buy dope. They will take care of the rest."

"Drinkin' beer and buying dope is right up my alley. Do you think this will really happen?"

"Oh, it's definitely going to happen. They're just waiting for the right man and I told them about you. Think you're up to it?"

"I'm up to it alright, but one problem. You live out in the country and it sounds like I'll be on my own. What happens if I get spotted by one of my relocated thugs and I have no way out?"

"No problem. Remember Mongo?"

Hell yeah, I remember Mongo, I thought. He is another retired Special Forces sidekick of Bruno's. He helped Bruno train the SWAT team. These guys are both top notch. I can trust my life to either one of them anywhere, anytime.

"Of course I remember Mongo. I'd go anywhere with that guy."

"Good," Bruno said. "Mongo is aware of the operation and has already volunteered to protect you. Any more questions?"

"Count me in, pal. I'd like to see what's going on in your little slice of heaven."

How could I refuse? In fact, I couldn't wait to get started.

We met with the chief and got our game plan in order. The city supplied me and my backup with false Washington State driver's licenses. We came up with our cover story and the department came up with a van that another department had seized in an earlier drug bust in a different city.

We'd already talked about the basics. My bud and I would go into town a couple nights a week, spending our time drinking beer and buying drugs from the bad boys. The rest of the plan was that afterward, we would meet the sergeant in the woods outside of town, turning over the drugs that I had already field tested and documented for evidence. The sergeant would give us more money and we would start over again.

We worked for four or five months and ended up with around fifteen arrests.

Halfway through the undercover investigation, I was hanging out at my favorite bar, the one I got shot at, when an older gentleman approached me, introducing himself as Marty. He said he'd heard about how I'd gotten wounded, wanted to shake my hand, buy me a beer and see how I was doing.

We visited for awhile and he asked what I was doing with myself. I told him I had my real estate license, but was bored to tears selling houses.

"How would you like to get into something a little bit more interesting?" he asked.

"Like what?"

"Arnie's Bail Bonds has been in this town for quite awhile."

"I've heard of him. Why?"

"Have you heard of his bounty hunter, Big Joey?"

"Sure. I worked the paddy wagon downtown for a couple of years and had plenty of run-ins with Joey."

"Here's what going on," Marty explained. "Joey has been getting in a lot of trouble lately, more than Arnie can put up with."

"What's that got to do with me?"

"Arnie had to let Joey go. He has nobody to chase down his bail skips so how would you like to be a bounty hunter?"

"I don't know," I said. "Besides, I'm not a 'Joey.' Most of those guys have reputations of being worse criminals than the people they arrest!"

"That's the problem! Arnie needs a guy who is honest with a good reputation. The cops and the courts are tired of the antics of guys like Big Joey."

"I don't know, Marty. I do have a good reputation. I don't need all my police buddies thinking I've lost it and gone to the other side. That's not me."

"Maybe you could bring a little bit of credibility to the bail bond industry," he pressed.

I shook my head. "That would be difficult. You've got to understand that the cops have had their share of guys like Joey. One day Joey will be giving the cops a hard time or beating some poor slob and the next day, he'll be arresting somebody and putting them in jail. Cops hate that stuff and so do I. Remember, Marty, I'm still a cop through and through. Some things don't change and the fact is I wouldn't have the slightest idea of how to even get started. Hunting down the bad guys is one thing, but doing it as a civilian? I don't know. . ."

"Tell you what, Mike. I have to go to Arnie's tomorrow. I'm going to run my idea by him and see what he thinks. In the meantime, think about it, okay?"

"Okay. I'll think about it, but don't count on me."

A few days went by and I blew off what Marty and I had talked about. I figured it was just bar talk and that was the end of that. Then Marty showed up again.

"I talked to Arnie about you. Arnie thought your coming to work for him would be a great idea. He told me to tell you to come in and talk to him."

"I'll think about it some more. I'm still not sure this is a good idea."

"Okay," Marty nodded. "But call and set up an appointment."

My mind was reeling now. Could this be an opportunity or could it be a disaster? Cops didn't think very highly of bond agents or their bounty hunters. We spent a lot of time putting crooks in jail and the bond companies spent a lot of time getting them right back out. I knew it was part of the system, but it still didn't sit well. If this was the real deal, it would be a good way to get back onto the streets and do what I like to do. Maybe I would call this Arnie guy after all, just to see what's up. I did and he asked me to come in.

Arnie met me at the front door of the bail bond company. He was a tall, well-dressed, distinguished looking gentleman. His handshake was firm and he escorted me to an office. We spoke for some time about the bail bond business and the role it played in the criminal justice system. Arnie cleared up a lot of my preconceived prejudices about bond agents. I was intrigued and asked about having a partner to work with. Obviously, this job could be extremely dangerous and to do it alone would be just plain foolish.

"You're on your own with that one," Arnie paused. "I had to fire my last bounty hunter, but I don't want to go into it."

Arnie could sense that I wasn't convinced yet.

"Tell you what. Let me introduce you to Pam. She is in charge of the Forfeiture Department. If you decide to take the job, you would be working under her direction."

"Fair enough."

Arnie and I walked into the front office.

"Pam," Arnie said, "I want you to meet Mike. He is considering doing fugitive recovery for us."

"Great," Pam looked closely at me. "And it's nice to meet you again."

"I'm sorry, I don't remember. . ."

"There was a crowd of people and the press around you at the time thanking you for taking down that bad guy." I flushed, but smiled. She continued, "It would be a nice change to have a former police officer as our bounty hunter. I'd like to talk more to you about it, but I'm inundated with work and deadlines. Could you possibly meet me after work for a beer and we'll talk about what you're getting yourself into?"

"Getting myself into," I repeated. "I haven't committed to that one. I'm just a little intrigued."

Standing there talking to Pam, I scanned the office. When cops retire, their badges may get put on the shelf. However, their instincts do not. I had the feeling that Pam had something more on her mind than a job interview. One thing I knew for sure, she didn't want to talk in front of the other employees.

Pam asked if I knew of this little bar not too far from the office.

"Of course I do. My buddy and I have tipped more than a few there."

The bar was a small, cozy place that could comfortably hold about twenty people. Rodney and I stopped there sometimes after working a swing shift. Because of the location, among the customers were some employees from the nearby hospital and the local newspaper. An occasional thug or drug dealer also wandered through the place. Rodney and I liked this bar, because it was close to the station and didn't have last call a half-hour before closing.

The bartender usually served us until it was time to lock the doors. Sometimes, if she was in a good mood, she locked up and let us stay. Then we had a couple of drinks and told her war stories while she cleaned up and told us about the recent beating she had received from her boyfriend. I didn't know it then, but her boyfriend and I would soon get to know each other a whole lot better. It turned out that it was Joey, Arnie's old bounty hunter.

As Pam and I started to sip our beers we were making small talk, just trying to feel each other out. Then Pam started to tell me about the job Arnie wanted me to do. It wasn't the flowery, "You're going to love this job!" speech I expected. Instead, it was a story of extortion, beatings, sexual favors for freedom and every other kind of corruption that was available in the bail bond business. She told me that she loved the business, but she wanted to do it right. She hated the dark side of the industry and all that came with it. She was excited that a former cop might be getting involved and hoped I would help her change the business for the better. She looked straight into my eyes, "Will you help me do this job the right way?"

I was impressed.

When Pam leveled with me in that candid, sincere way about ethics, corruption and honesty in an industry that was beginning to look to me like it had the potential to be very seedy, I thought, *I can work with somebody like this.*

"Okay. How do I get started?"

Chapter 16

Bounty Hunting

Pam and I were now going to be working together. In the office, there was a small room called the Fugitive Recovery Office. Pam had a computer for her use, but the bounty hunters did not. Pam showed me two small boxes full of three-by-five-inch cards. Each card had the name of a fugitive on it.

Quickly she handed the boxes to me. "We need to have these people arrested," she said.

"What do I do with them after I arrest them?"

"Book them into the jail we bailed them out of," she explained.

"How do I know which jail to put them in?" I asked.

"When you grab one, call me. I'll find out where he or she goes and let you know. Most of them will be going to jails in Pierce or King County. Others will be going to other county jails throughout Washington State."

I peered inside the boxes. "This is insane!" I told her. "There must be two hundred names in here!"

"Yep. Joey hasn't been around for awhile, so they've been backing up. Have fun."

This is turning into a nightmare, I told myself. *Oh well, just try to make the best of it and see where it goes. One thing's for sure, I am going to need some help.*

I called one of my retired Special Forces buddies and asked if he would like to give it a shot. He agreed and went out on a couple of arrests with me, but wound up not liking the job. I was running around town with a pager and a pocket full of quarters for the phone booths. When I got a hot lead, I called him, needing him to drop what he was doing and meet me in five minutes. The problem was, at least half the time the hot lead was bullshit and ended up being a big waste of my friend's time. After a while, he told me I was on my own.

Quickly I began realizing that I might be in over my head. Every jail and court jurisdiction had their own rules and procedures when it came to bail bond surrenders and I didn't know any of them. Hunting down fugitives and arresting them was a piece of cake compared to dealing with the courts, cops and jailers. I had been under the impression that my fellow brothers and sisters in blue would be happy to see me back on the streets arresting the bad guys and that the jailers would greet me with open arms when I brought in the desperados. Well, nothing could have been further from the truth.

I had a meeting with Arnie and explained my dilemma.

"Do you know anybody out there who might like to get back into the business?" I asked him.

"I have been approached by one guy," he said, "but you're not going to like the candidate."

"Who?"

"Before you say anything, just hear me out," Arnie said. "Joey has been asking me for his job back. He said that he knows he screwed up and wants another chance."

"Do you think that's a good idea? That guy is a walking liability."

"I know, I know," Arnie said. "But Joey's apologizing for all the shenanigans he's been causing and promises to fly straight. I told him that you are on board now and you are the boss. No exceptions!"

"What happens if he starts screwing up again? What authority do I have to deal with him?"

"I told Joey that you have full control. If he doesn't do as you say, you can fire him at any time," Arnie stated. "Look, let's sit down with Joey and put everything on the table, then decide what you want to do."

This will be a joke, I thought. *Of course Joey will agree to anything. He can't find another job but right now I have no other options.*

"Okay. I'll talk to him."

The meeting went as expected. Joey agreed to anything and everything I said. He just wanted to get back to work and would have promised the world to do so.

"Alright," I told Joey. "We'll give this a shot, but everything 'by the book.' If somebody gives us a hard time, we use enough force to get the person under control and that's the end of it. No extra shot to the ribs because they pissed you off. Another thing: nothing illegal—and I do mean nothing!"

I knew that taking Joey on was going to be a lot like dancing on quicksand. If I didn't watch my step, he could cause me a lot of grief. Another problem would be the perceptions of many of my police friends. Every cop who knew Joey thought he belonged behind bars for the rest of his life. Now they were going to see me running the streets with him, dragging people off to jail.

Standing next to Joey I realized he was a lot bigger and heavier than I was. He had been bounty hunting around Tacoma for years and had a fearsome reputation. He was known for being heavy-handed and very tough. I knew I'd have to show him I could stand my ground.

At first when Joey and I started hunting people down, it went well. Nobody wanted to cross Joey and once we got on the person's trail or had the person cornered, he or she gave up rather than risk Joey's wrath. We were cleaning up a lot of cases fast and I was learning the system.

It almost seemed too easy at first. However, the fact remains that if you are putting your hands on another human being with the intent of taking his or her freedom away, he or she will not appreciate it.

It was an October night that was colder than usual. Joey and I decided to take my four-by-four pickup truck bounty hunting due to the icy conditions. Heading out to the Lakewood area just southwest of Tacoma, we had to apprehend a fugitive. We had gotten a tip that he was staying in a small camping trailer on a family member's property.

We located the trailer in a dark corner of the property. We could see lights on in the trailer and decided to try and make contact. As we approached the trailer, we were surprised by three dogs that were chained just out of reach of the front door. All three were obviously vicious, but they could only get within a couple of feet from the trailer. With these dogs barking and snapping at us, we knocked on the door. The door opened and there stood our fugitive.

He was startled to see us standing in front of him and instantly bolted. It happened so fast that he managed to slip through both of us as we both grabbed at him. He ran straight for the dogs. I tried to follow, but the closest dog was trying to attack me. Taking out my mace, I sprayed the dog with a steady stream aimed directly at his nose. The dog opened his mouth and began lapping and biting at the mace as though I was squirting him with a water hose! For a few seconds, I was mesmerized by his response. I kept spraying and he kept lapping away—the mace not bothering him one bit. Shaking my head, I knew it was time to shift to plan B.

Meanwhile, the fugitive was disappearing into a small grove of trees. I ran around the left side of the dogs and Joey ran around the right side. As I entered the grove from the left, the suspect ran straight at me. I grabbed him and the fight was on. Joey approached the scene from the right side and he jumped into the fight. Then Joey grabbed the guy and we all fell to the ground. Suddenly I heard Joey howl in pain. I knew something had to be very wrong. Joey was hanging on to the man as well as he could, but he was in obvious agony and the fugitive was fighting like hell. Joey was starting to lose his grip. I had to end this encounter and quickly. We were still in a big pile on the ground when I took out my heavy metal flashlight and cracked it across the back of the guy's skull a couple of times. I hit him hard enough to slow him down and get the handcuffs on him. While the suspect was still struggling, I noticed my partner's lower right leg was bleeding profusely. The fugitive had at least two gaping wounds in his head and was bleeding pretty badly. Meanwhile, not only were the dogs barking, but also family members were starting to come out of the main house and neighbors were yelling that the police were coming.

We had no way of knowing what this guy's family members might have in mind or, for that matter, how many neighbors might be friends of the fugitive. Joey struggled to his feet and we noticed that someone had cut down the small trees, making them look more like spears sticking out of the ground rather than stumps. One of those pointed stumps had punctured Joey's leg just above the ankle and ripped a large ten-inch gash along the length of his shin bone. We grabbed our prisoner and struggled toward the truck amidst the cacophony of people yelling and dogs barking.

When we reached the truck, Joey grabbed our prisoner around the waist and, using all of his strength, lifted the suspect off the ground and threw him into the bed of the truck. He pulled himself into the bed of the truck and yelled, "Let's go!" I jumped into the cab and we got out of there, heading for downtown Tacoma and the nearest emergency room.

It was bitterly cold and they were freezing in the bed of that pickup. The only thing I could do was open the sliding window leading to the back of the truck and turn the heat up full blast. I pointed all of the vents toward the open window. Joey and the suspect huddled as close to the window as they could.

As we headed out of Lakewood, we passed two deputy cars with lights and sirens on. It was obvious that they were going to where we had just left.

Once I was at the hospital, I called Arnie and quickly outlined the situation. Arnie met us at the emergency room and we told him the rest of our story as he surveyed the damage. After he heard the gruesome details, he agreed to cover the medical bills for Joey. The doctors put a couple of stitches into our captured fugitive and I ran him down to the jailhouse.

Joey spent several hours in the emergency room getting his leg cleaned and sewn up. His leg was in bad shape and looked awful. From the looks of it, I would be without a partner for several weeks. Problem was, the case load wasn't going to slow down. But when I showed up for work the next morning, there was Joey—dragging his wounded leg behind him.

"I'm okay," he growled. "Let's get to work!" That's when I knew that Joey wasn't just big and mean; he was also tough.

Over the next several months, Joey and I arrested a lot more people and were very successful. I heard a lot of rumors about Joey, but when we worked together, I didn't see or hear him doing anything illegal. Although he was a little rough, he never crossed the line I had established when we became partners.

I'm sure that part of his model behavior was due to the fact that he knew I wouldn't cover anything up for him. I thought that this part-time criminal, part-time bounty hunter and I had actually become friends. Well, it turns out that some people just can't play it straight.

One day, Arnie called me in to his office and told me that Joey had been constantly telling him that I didn't know what I was doing, that Arnie should get rid of me and put him back in charge of the Recovery Department.

I called Joey and promptly fired him.

Arnie backed me up.

Chapter 17

A Real Partner

It was inevitable that Joey had to go. However, working with him gave me a chance to get to know the system as it applied to bounty hunting. I was learning the only thing bounty hunting has in common with being a police officer was arresting wanted criminals. After that, it was an entirely different world.

Finding someone to work with was easy. Finding a qualified partner was not. There was a steady parade of goobers walking into our office daily asking to be "one of them thar bounty hunters." For the most part, it was a collection of wannabes and screwballs. The first thing out of their mouths was how they were ready to go out and kick some ass or how big their guns were.

As the weeks went by, the procession of goofs wanting to be bounty hunters never slowed down nor did my ever-growing caseload.

Pam kept nagging me about meeting some bounty hunter she had worked with in the past.

"Mike," Pam said over and over, "you've got to meet Mark. He did a good job for me in the past."

"Come on, Pam," I kept replying. "This Mark guy did one job for you and was pretty effective. But face it—you really don't know anything about him."

"I know I don't know him that well, but I can tell he's one of the good guys."

"Then why haven't you hired him already?" I asked her. "If he is as good as you say he is, why didn't you bring him on board as soon as Arnie fired Joey?"

Pam shook her head. "Arnie kept me in the dark when he fired Joey. I didn't know anything about it until you fired Joey the second time."

"Fine, I'll meet with him," I replied cautiously. "Are you sure you're not just passing this guy off to me, because he's been bugging you every day about coming to work here?"

"No," Pam shyly said. "In fact, I've already asked him to come down for an interview hoping he could meet with you and he declined."

"Why is that?" I asked her.

"Mark told me that he is tired of meeting a bunch of idiots who think they're going to conquer the criminal world. Does that kind of remind you of somebody we know?" she asked teasingly.

"Pam, you're starting to figure out how to work me way too soon," I laughed. "Set it up and I'll be glad to meet with him."

"Good!" Pam smiled. "Now I just have to convince the other prima donna!"

After several phone calls and scheduling conflicts, Pam set up a lunch meeting between me and Mark at one of Tacoma's local restaurants.

Men are a strange breed. It's not our fault—it's just the way it is and it seems to be more prevalent when those men have chosen careers doing society's dirty work. These guys are all alphas and filled with pride. The initial meeting between men reminds me of two neighborhood dogs circling and sniffing each other when first encountering one another. I am grateful that men's circling and sniffing is mental and not literal, but it does happen. Mark and I were no exception.

Mark's a big guy, six feet six inches and about 235 pounds. Since I'm five feet eight inches, I could tell he was not impressed with me. That's okay; I was used to initial weak impressions. I've been dealing with them all my life and it's simply not an issue with me.

Our meeting went well. Mark was working for several different bail bond companies in the Seattle area. We both needed a partner, but our individual caseloads were pretty heavy and Arnie's firm really needed somebody full-time. Mark seemed like a squared away dude and I planned to call him if I needed him in the future.

Meantime, back at the office, I was getting burned out meeting egotistical guys who wanted to be cool. I asked Pam to screen these guys first and if anyone looked like they met our standards to let me know.

When an individual walks into the office and states he or she wants to be a bounty hunter—as thousands have over the years—the first thing Pam asks is, "*Why* do you want to be a bounty hunter?"

Most of the time, the response is, "Man, to kick ass and get paid for it at the same time would be a real cool way to make a living." When Pam hears that response, she answers a few questions and then politely shows the inquirer the door.

The truth is bounty hunting is much more difficult than movies and television portray. One has to enter the profession for all the right reasons. The wrong ones can and do get people killed.

We're not looking for big and bad. We're not interested in someone who's all brawn and no brains. We're looking for smart—and hardworking—people who want to see justice get served.

A good percentage of the job is, in fact, desk work. The bounty hunter has to verify the warrants with the courts, then spend hours on the phone trying to locate defendants' whereabouts. Sometimes the latter can take days, weeks or even months, depending on the situation.

It's also a good idea to be—or become—computer literate. Most bounty hunters use the computer a great deal of the time. If you're Internet savvy, so much the better. Bounty hunters use a wide variety of tools to locate defendants. The more programs and databases they're familiar with, the easier defendants are to find.

I was learning Pam also looks for a certain personality type—a chameleon. She believes very strongly that bounty hunters shouldn't unnecessarily disturb the general public as they go about their business. Bounty hunters shouldn't dress provocatively, act aggressively or stand out from the crowd in any way. During an investigation, bounty hunters should be able to blend in with all walks of life, anytime, anywhere—from a formal black tie affair to hooker alley—without anyone being able to peg them as bounty hunters.

If a prospective bounty hunter is looking to get rich, he or she can forget it. There's not a lot of money in this field. If you divide all the hours spent working on a case with the actual paycheck, sometimes it pays less than minimum wage. Most bounty hunters get paid 10 percent of the forfeited bail and *only* if they make an arrest. That means one can spend a great deal of time trying to locate a defendant without success. So despite all the hours somebody can spend working on a case, if they don't make an arrest, they don't get paid.

It's really not a nine to five job, either. If the bounty hunter is looking for someone, he can get calls from informants at all hours of the day or night with vital information about a case. If a bounty hunter limits his or her working hours, he or she won't obtain the information needed to locate a defendant. Most bounty hunters, out of necessity, sometimes work around the clock on large dollar cases. If they're not willing to devote that much time, maybe they'd better look for work in another profession.

So then, if bounty hunters don't get rich and don't have stable working hours, why do it?

Good question.

Being a bounty hunter doesn't give a person prestige or world renown; a bounty hunter won't have his or her picture in the newspaper nor will he or she be offered a television series. In real life, those things just don't happen.

What it does mean is that the bounty hunter is working on the *right* side of the law.

The bail agent's job is to bail individuals out of jail pending the outcome of their court cases. We don't make any judgments. We can't. We weren't there. We don't know all the facts. What we can do is ensure their appearances in court so judges and juries can decide their guilt or innocence. Right or wrong, good or bad, if Pam bails them, they *have* to go to court. That's the deal.

Sometimes clients don't go to court on purpose. The court issues a warrant for their arrests then gives us a limited time to produce them back in court or we forfeit the bail money. That's where the bounty hunter comes in. The police are too busy to purposely look for these individuals—but we're not. Not only is the firm trying to save itself from losing the bail money, but it's also interested in justice. From personal experience, 95 percent of those who jump bail quickly offend again. Pam doesn't want clients avoiding court and committing new crimes as they're running from the law. If a bounty hunter can find them, arrest them and return them to custody, they'll be produced in court and will be forced to face the consequences of their own actions. In that way, we protect the general public, our communities and society in general. We work with the police to get these dangerous criminals off the streets. In a very real way, we help promote public safety—and that's why we do what we do. The hours are long and the money lousy, but we're needed. We're valuable. We can and do make a difference.

I was sitting at my desk one afternoon when Pam approached me.

"Mike," Pam said, "I think you should take a look at this guy. He's applying to be a bounty hunter."

"Whoopee," I exclaimed sarcastically. "Him and a few hundred other guys. So what?"

"This guy seems different from the usual types. He can actually complete a sentence. And another thing, when I ask him a question, he answers politely saying, 'Yes, ma'am' or 'No, ma'am.' I can tell from talking to him for a minute or two he is intelligent, non-aggressive and hardworking. He's kind of cute, too."

"Pam," I told her jokingly, "you've been dealing with criminals for way too long. Just because a guy walks in here and can count to ten doesn't make him marriage material."

"Okay, okay, very funny, Mr. Perfect," she jabbed back. "But I'm serious. This guy just might work out. He's the first one I've seen who has a decent résumé."

She handed it to me. Quickly I scanned the bio and nodded.

"Fine," I moaned. "Bring him in."

Most company owners hire bounty hunters at their own discretion. Sometimes partnering up two strangers to work together can make a successful team. But in my experience, most do not. I'd run into bounty hunters working for other offices who were not compatible. They bickered and fought and eventually became a major headache to the company owner, their supervisor, the clients and the general public as well. The *last* thing the bonding company needs is two idiots who constantly bump heads. It's not only disruptive and unprofessional, but also downright dangerous for all parties involved.

Fortunately, Arnie allowed me to pick my own partner. That was a rarity, although it only made sense. It's my butt out there on the street and it should be my choice as to whom I trust to protect it if something bad were to go down.

A few minutes later, Pam came into my office followed by a formidable looking young man. He was every bit as big as Joey was— about six feet four inches, 250 pounds and in pretty good shape.

So far, so good; I wouldn't mind having a big guy around to keep an eye on me, I thought.

"Chris," Pam announced, "this is Mike Beakley; Mike, this is Chris Dausch."

"Nice to meet you," Chris extended his hand.

"Same here," I said, shaking his hand. "Go ahead and have a seat. Well, this will be informal. Pam gave me your résumé, but do you have any experience in the bail bond business?"

"No, I don't."

"Do you have any law enforcement experience?"

"No, I don't."

"Do you have any idea at all what the job you're applying for consists of?"

"Nope, not really."

Interesting, I thought. *He's not trying to bullshit his way through.*

"Why are you here?" I asked him.

"I'm interested in learning something about investigations," he explained. "I've been playing with the idea of becoming a private investigator or going into law enforcement in the future. I guess I'm assuming that your job is basically skip tracing."

"What do you know about skip tracing, Chris?"

"That you're trying to locate people who have skipped out."

"That's correct. Do you know what we do when we locate these people or how we get paid?"

"No, not really."

"Chris, I'm going to lay it all out for you. This job is not for everyone. When you hear what's involved either you will be very interested or you won't want to have anything to do with it. What I need from you is an honest answer, okay?"

Chris nodded.

"We do skip trace, but here's the catch. We don't get paid for that. In fact, we're not paid hourly nor are we on salary. If you decide to do this, you will be my partner. You and I will not be working for Arnie's Bail Bonds; we will be working for ourselves. We will be considered independent contractors and the only way we get paid is if we put somebody in jail. Our job is to hunt them down and bring them in. If they won't answer the door, we kick it in and go in after them. If they resist arrest, we overpower them and bring them in. If they use weapons, we must be able to defend ourselves. We have to do all of this with just the two of us. We cannot expect backup from the police or anybody else. There is nobody else to call if we get in a jam. We will be ethical, professional and legal while dealing with some of the biggest jerks you will ever meet, which may include not just criminals but also many people who work in this business. To top it all off, those private investigators and police officers you aspire to be one day will treat you like yesterday's garbage."

As I looked across the desk at Chris, I thought to myself, *I don't have to ask this kid if he is interested. He has a gleam in his eye that I have seen in many of my SWAT buddies. His answer will not be just yes, but hell yes!*

"Well, Chris, what do you think?"

"Yes, sir. I think I would like to give it a shot."

"You do realize that I'm taking a big chance hiring somebody with absolutely no experience, don't you?"

"Yes, I do." Chris responded. "But I will give it my best."

"Sounds good. The most important thing for you to understand is that I am in charge. It's not an ego thing or being a control freak. Simple fact is, I've got the experience and you don't. I'll listen to any ideas you have but final decisions, tactical or otherwise, are mine."

"When do we get started?" he asked, smiling.

PART III

PAM AND MIKE

Chapter 18

Pulling Your Gun First

Now with Mike and Chris on duty, defendants were taken to jail without being beaten up and without being shaken down for money or dope. Whenever a defendant was unexpectedly given a new court date, Mike immediately stopped working the case and returned the file to Pam. Things got more effective. The firm's word, especially Pam's, was once again good on the street.

Mike and Chris were so professional that the firm no longer had to worry about arresting the wrong defendants, which avoided opening the company up for hefty lawsuits. Nor did they have to worry about injuries. Mike minimized the odds of anyone getting hurt by carefully planning how and where to arrest an individual. Most of the time, he staked out the individuals first to get to know their habits. If they left for work at a certain time, Mike planned to arrest them after they left for work, thus saving the family the grief of having to witness the unpleasant ordeal.

After an arrest, Mike asked the defendants if they had any drugs on them. Mike and Chris then told the defendants if they had drugs on them at the time of arrest they'd have the added UPCS (unlawful possession of a controlled substance) felony charge while being booked into the jail. Many times Pam personally witnessed Mike and Chris emptying defendants' pockets of burned spoons, needles, roach clips and pipes. The drug paraphernalia was disposed of in the large garbage can outside the office back door.

Though things were going well, one day Chris walked into the office with a large gun visible in its holster on his hip. Pam knew Arnie was dead set against guns and forbade carrying them. According to Arnie, guns weren't ever necessary. He believed defendants could be arrested and taken to jail without the use of deadly force.

As soon as Pam could get Mike aside, she and he talked over the problem. Mike said he and Arnie had argued over the subject vigorously. Mike absolutely refused to go out on the street without a gun. As a former cop, Mike knew how dangerous some defendants could be. "He who pulls his gun first wins," Mike said emphatically. "Even when we're arresting these guys for a misdemeanor, something like driving with a suspended license, sometimes they have felony charges out of another court we're not even aware of. In those cases, defendants will do anything to avoid going back to jail. All I'm doing by having my gun is evening out the odds. I'd be stupid to go out on the street if they have guns and I don't. And believe me, I'm not stupid."

Arnie insisted that, at the very least, their weapons weren't to be visible in the office. Arnie didn't want the guns to frighten little old ladies when they walked in the front door to bail out their grandchildren.

One day when Pam told Mike she'd again seen Chris's weapon for a moment or two, Mike promised to talk to Chris about it. "I'll make sure our shirts or coats completely cover our weapons before we walk into the office."

Since Mike had taken over bounty hunting for the firm, Arnie's still had a fair amount of forfeitures, certainly enough to keep Mike busy. But the firm's rate of having to pay to the court forfeitures went way down. Now the firm paid only two or three small ones a month. Even so, Mike was diligent. Washington State had the provision that if defendants were returned to custody within one year from the date they failed to appear in court and the bonding company was *directly responsible* for producing them, the court would then refund the firm's money in full. Mike wouldn't rest until fleeing defendants had been arrested and the court refunded the firm's money.

Pam and Mike became a respected team. Pam carried out her part of the operation with enthusiasm and honesty. Mike gave legitimacy to the bounty hunter field. He proved it could be done professionally without fanfare and with minimum fuss. Pam didn't believe that any bounty hunter on the planet had the same credentials and profession- alism. She truly believed, in all honesty, Mike broke new ground. He was an example for others to follow. He set the standard.

Pam knew Linda wouldn't have wanted to see Joey go. Undoubt- edly she would have argued with Arnie over that decision, but Pam truly believed she would have really liked Mike.

Pam was sorry Linda didn't live long enough to meet him and have her faith in the bail bond business vindicated. Meanwhile, Pam and Mike vowed to expose and clean up what they both saw as many of the industry's most dubious practices.

As time went on, Mike began looking more and more like some of the guys he was chasing. His hair grew longer and he'd started getting a little ink on his arms. He knew he must have been looking pretty rough when he got a call from one of his former police partners. The phone rang one day and Jim Young, also known as "Dunna", was on the other end of the line. Mike and Dunna had rode police motor- cycles together. They had also worked SWAT and dope missions together. He knew Mike as well as Mike's hunting and SWAT partner Rodney Cook did.

"Beak," Dunna said. "You're not gonna believe what some of the boys are saying about you."

"What could anybody be saying about me? I'm not in the loop anymore."

"I know, but I've had a bunch of guys asking me if I've seen you lately. They're all saying that you've gone to the dark side. They think you've flipped and you're one of the bad guys now."

"Really? That's kind of funny, Dunna. What do you think?"

"Don't worry, Beak. I laughed at those guys and told them the Beak's the Beak and he'll never change."

"Thanks, Dunna, and just to let you know, I haven't changed one bit. I'm just doing another job now," Mike explained.

"Hell, I know that. I've got you covered on this one."

"I appreciate it, Dunna. Tell those guys to stop being a bunch of rumor mongering old jerks."

"You got it, Beak. Watch yourself out there and I'll talk to you later."

A couple of weeks later, Rodney (whose nickname is "Punisher") called Mike with the same buzz. Well, that's all it took. From that point on, especially to his biker friends, Mike was known as "Darkside."

Chapter 19

On the Streets

Chris had walked in with zero experience. But to his credit, he understood that and didn't try to act like he was a know-it-all. He watched, listened intently and had a strong desire to learn everything he could. It seemed like Mike's instincts about Chris were paying off. Training a bounty hunter who had no bad habits or wasn't corrupted by the system turned out to be a very good thing.

Chris and Mike began pounding out cases and became fast friends. Things in the office, however, seemed to be another story.

Pam sensed from day one that some of the other employees weren't very thrilled about Mike being hired. One guy seemed very nervous when Mike was around. Pam thought he acted sort of like a kid with his hand in the cookie jar.

A few weeks later, Mike and Chris arrested a street prostitute. She had missed a court date, but convinced Mike that she would have a friend come down to the office and post a new bond for her. As soon as Mike and Chris entered the office with her, the employee who always acted strangely around Mike began nervously pacing the floor while the prostitute kept glancing over at him. Mike theorized the employee and the prostitute had a relationship outside the office.

Pam wondered why the firm was bailing out street-level whores. She and Mike felt that it was just plain bad business. Hookers at this rung of the ladder were typically homeless and indigent. Unless they had some sugar daddy on the hook to pay the bail bond, they couldn't afford bail. Once out of jail, they bounced between tricks, pimps and friends, which made them very high-risk clients. Typically they didn't go to court and could be hard to find.

The more bad girls Mike arrested, the more stories they heard. They felt there were other serious problems. Street hookers were usually hardcore drug addicts, had severe emotional problems or quite often had a combination of both tribulations. When the cops found street hookers, they threw them in jail. Talk about being at the bottom, so why make them clients?

Pam and Mike decided to watch and wait to see where this new specialty was going.

A week or two later, another of the local girls was sprung from jail. She had a unique characteristic: a heart-shaped mole on her right cheek.

"Another one," Pam sighed as she handed the file to Mike.

"I don't have a partner available today, but I'll check out the usual places and see if she's around," Mike replied, meeting Pam's glance. "Sometimes these girls don't remember when their court dates were and they're not hiding yet."

Mike had his pickup truck with him that day and headed down to one of the areas the prostitute was known to frequent. It was a sunny afternoon so he brought a box of pending files with him to look at as he waited. He decided to park behind one of the restaurants on the street to go through his cases while waiting to see if he could spot her. He was sitting there with the car windows down enjoying the day, checking out some files, when he spotted a girl about a block away. It looked like she was working the strip and heading in Mike's direction.

He couldn't tell from that distance if she was the right girl or not so he kept reading files. Before he knew it, the girl was standing at his passenger window. "Are you looking for a date?" she asked. Mike looked up and straight at the heart-shaped mole on her cheek.

"Get in," Mike told her. "I would love some company."

She jumped into the truck and started to say something when she spotted Mike's files with her picture on top of the stack.

"Are you...?" she started to ask.

"Yeah, I'm with Arnie's and you're under arrest."

"Damn!" she blurted out. "I can't believe I jumped into your truck. Can't we work this out? I can't go to jail today. I'm sure we can figure something out."

"Sorry, sweetheart, the company has to pay this bond if I don't book you and I'm not one to make deals."

If they were all that easy, the job would be a cakewalk. But they're not and soon Pam and Mike needed an informant who lived on the streets and knew the players. Chris and Mike started actively looking for an informant to recruit. Mike has dealt with a lot of informants both during his police career and bounty hunting, but he was about to meet one he would never forget: Little Lynne.

Little Lynne was a street whore who was under five feet, curvy and worked the skid row areas of downtown. She also liked her drugs and alcohol way too much. To supply her habits, she sold her body.

Mike met Little Lynne while he was looking for another street-walker. He spotted Lynne strolling along the street and started up a conversation with her. He needed information and she needed a bottle of cheap wine.

Mike talked with Lynne at length, first about the harshness of life on the streets and then about the lack of honor some of the street people have. Lynne had her brushes with the law and needed to be bailed out of jail on occasion; she knew of Arnie's. They talked about the fact that the bail bond companies were there for people when they needed them the most and it didn't seem right that defendants turned around and screwed the people who helped them get out of jail. Lynne agreed and they struck up a bounty hunter/hooker-who-needs-a-bottle-of-wine friendship. She told Mike where to find fugitives and Mike gave her a couple bucks after the arrests. Sometimes he saw her walking the streets, having a hard time of it and Mike took her down to the corner store and bought her a bottle. They had talks about not trusting anybody and not talking about her contact with Arnie's to anyone. Mike watched out for her safety.

If Mike needed a street person, Little Lynne was his girl. She had a full head of shoulder-length blonde hair that waved from side to side as she walked and a foul mouth like none other. If she wasn't yelling, "Fuck all these motherfuckers!" she wasn't happy. She was a street person, which meant she had no money and no loved ones. Her clothes were whatever she could find, but she still carried herself as though she was in a better position in life. After all, as Lynne put it, "All these fucking motherfuckers want a piece of my ass!"

Whenever he needed to get hold of her, Mike drove down a particular street she always worked. Lynne would either be standing out on the street trying to pick up dates or she would spot him from one of her hiding places and wave him down.

One afternoon while looking for her, Mike noticed a commotion up under a roadway overpass. It was Little Lynne. She was half walking, half stumbling, surrounded by a big cloud of dirt and dust, making her way down a steep hill from an underpass. Mike couldn't help but laugh. She was quite a sight to see. When she finally reached his vehicle, Mike asked her what the hell she was doing under the overpass. She replied, "The judge gave me permission to live down here, because I'm homeless." As sad as this may sound, it didn't seem to bother her, but Mike still felt obligated to take her to the corner store and buy her a bottle. Once she had her little paws wrapped around it, she gave Mike the information he needed. After the underpass incident, Mike's partner, Chris, started referring to her as "the bridge troll." ·

One night, Lynne called to let Mike know she was having a rough day and she was hungry. She had scored a room at one of the seedier motels in a small town on the edge of Tacoma. Mike bought a couple of burgers and brought them to her room. She had managed to get a trick on the hook by the time he arrived at the room. When Lynne opened the door, the trick was cowering in the corner of the room. He probably thought he was going to get robbed by her pimp. As he was whimpering away, Lynne stayed true to form and instructed him to "shut the fuck up, motherfucker!" Mike handed Lynne the burgers and left.

After the firm made an arrest based on Lynne's information, Mike hunted her down and gave her a few bucks, but she seemed to appreciate the cheap bottle of wine more than the money. It seems the little things in life matter to people.

Pam and Mike always talked over meetings with female informants and, other than the very rarest of occasions, Mike always had a witness with him. The witness was normally Chris or if necessary, Mike dragged a friend along. Friendly relationships or not, things change in addicts' lives. For enough money, addicts will accuse you of any horrific thing they can come up with or, for the right money, set you up for an ambush. You need a witness for some of the things you happen upon, because without having someone there to see it for him or herself, no one will believe you.

One day, Pam and Mike heard that Lynne had died, but they didn't know for sure. Later, on a sunny afternoon, Chris and Mike were cruising Lynne's area, looking for a skip. Then Mike pulled into the parking lot of a local store and there she was, petite and blonde and happy as hell to see him.

Lynne waved frantically at them. She had a huge smile on her face, blonde hair shaking back and forth. Mike noticed she was wearing a pair of red leggings over black spandex with a few holes scattered here and there. A grungy pink blouse that was ripped at the neckline exposed a white shoulder, while a pair of dirty tennis shoes finished off the ensemble. As Mike got closer, he also noticed a large smear of bright red lipstick from the right corner of her mouth halfway to her right ear. It was still early as they greeted her. She proudly announced, "I have already made a hundred dollars so far today." Mike congratulated her on her successful business skills and after some small talk, they parted company. Needless to say, rumors of Lynne's death were greatly exaggerated.

Chapter 20

Undercover Operation

Chris and Mike were pounding the streets hard, clearing up a lot of cases. Most of the cases were small bail, but Mike and Pam were soon handed a larger case.

"Mike, we've got a big one and we don't have much time on it. Arnie is on the hook for $110,000! Everyone in the office has been trying to fix this one without giving it to you guys. Arnie doesn't want to have to pay over ten grand to bounty hunters, but I don't see where we have any other choice. We're out of options."

"Okay, relax," Mike said calmly. "Tell me what you've got."

"The firm bailed out a biker by the name of Stretch. He has some heavy-duty charges and is facing a long time in prison. Arnie is holding titles to some vehicles we took in as collateral on the bond. There's a designer motorcycle that his friends put up for him, but it's not even close to covering the bond even *if* we can find the stuff. Stretch missed court and nobody's talking. Arnie's had everybody in the office calling all our clients trying to get some information on him. We were hoping we could talk him into turning himself in, but nobody's heard from him. We heard he might have left the state."

"How much time do we have?"

"Not much. The court wants the money one week from today and I'm not sure we have it. This could shut us down!"

"Damn! How long have you had the file? How long has he been a skip?"

"Mike, we've known about this for a couple of weeks."

Mike grimaced. "By the time I get the file, everybody has tromped all over it. All the numbers on the application have already been called. All the leads we could have had are now stone cold. Why doesn't Arnie give me the file to begin with so I can work on it? I know he doesn't want to pay $11,000, but it's certainly a lot cheaper than having to pay the court $110,000. Why wait so long? What does Arnie expect us to do on such short notice?"

"I'm sorry, Mike. If it were up to me, as soon as I received the forfeiture notice from the court, I'd give you the file. The only reason he gave you the file now is he's hoping for a miracle on this one. I know if anybody can find him, you will. Here's the file."

As Mike read through the file, he realized that he knew most of the players involved and many of their associates. "It's a rough crowd. They are well-known methamphetamine cooks who have a reputation for violence and moving a lot of weight. I've arrested a few of them in the past and have developed a rapport with some of them. These guys are bikers but they aren't affiliated with any of the clubs I am familiar with." Motorcycle clubs are extremely loyal to one another. If you take on one of them, you take them all on. This particular crew was loose-knit and Mike knew that if he played his cards right, someone would talk.

With only a week to go, Chris and Mike hit the streets hot and heavy, looking everywhere they could think of to find Stretch. About four days into the investigation, Mike and Chris found a source that was part of the background with this crew, one of those benign people to whom nobody pays much attention, but who is actually privy to clandestine phone calls and private conversations.

A couple of days later, Mike got word that Stretch was supposed to be meeting with somebody to take care of some sort of business before splitting town. Mike was also told the make and model of the car Stretch might be driving. Chris and Mike started canvassing the area hoping for a glimpse of him or the vehicle. Finally, they thought they spotted Stretch. He was in the described car with one of his partners in crime named Crash. "We have to follow these guys until they land," he told Pam.

Bounty hunters are not the cops—they don't have lights or a siren so they can't pull people over. Mike also has a strict policy of not employing one of Joey's old tactics of ramming people off the road. The chance of injuring innocent people is substantial and there was at least one occasion when Joey rammed the wrong people because of a mistaken identity.

Mike and Chris followed these two until they parked in a gas station parking lot. Watching them for a few minutes, they tried to verify that it was their guy. After a short time, Stretch got out of the vehicle and was standing around as though he was waiting for someone. This looked like the perfect time.

Mike and Chris pulled up behind their car and jumped out screaming, "B.E.A.! Get on the ground! You're under arrest!"

Stretch went straight to the ground and Mike and Chris took him into custody. Crash remained in the car and didn't seem to want any part of the situation. They cuffed Stretch, threw him in the van and got the hell out of there before any other friends showed up or Crash had a change of heart.

When you take somebody down with a lot of yelling, speed and violence necessary to control the situation, it confuses and shocks the person. It is really very basic stuff when it comes to dealing with potentially dangerous subjects. With Stretch, no violence was needed. Confusion and shock had worked its magic. They were probably a half mile from the scene of the arrest when Stretch got his bearings. Once he settled down, he started looking around the van and glanced over at Mike and Chris. "Who the hell are you guys?" he asked.

"B.E.A.," Mike told him. "Bail Enforcement Agents."

"Damn!" Stretch said angrily. "I thought you said D.E.A., man! I thought you were the feds!"

"Nope. It's just us. We're from Arnie's. You skipped out on over a hundred grand in bail."

"If I knew you were just bounty hunters, you wouldn't have taken me down that easy. You would have had some serious problems."

"That's why we came at you hard. We heard you can take care of yourself and we didn't want anyone to get hurt. Don't take this personal, Stretch. We're just doing our jobs."

"I know you are, but I'm looking at a lot of time in the pen. Look, guys, I was just getting ready to leave town. My car is full of cash, dope and a few guns. If you take me back, I can give you guys $95,000 in cash right now!" Stretch pleaded.

"You've really got that much cash in the car—right now?" Chris asked with mock interest.

"Yeah, I do and you guys can have it. Just get me back there before my buddy leaves."

"Sorry, Stretch," Mike retorted. "Nice offer, but my partner and I don't roll that way. If Arnie had to pay your bond, he would have to shut his doors. Everybody in the office would lose their jobs if that happened."

"I know, but I'm looking at a lot of time in jail. Isn't there something—"

"Sorry, dude," Mike cut him off. "There's nothing we can do."

"Okay. This sucks, but thanks for not being jerks to me on the way in."

"No problem, Stretch. As I said before, this is not personal. We don't have anything against you; we're just taking care of business. Fact is, Stretch, you don't seem like a bad guy. It seems you've just got yourself caught up in some bad stuff. I know you think it's a bunch of crap right now, but this trip to jail may have saved your life. Look me up when you get out and I'll buy you a beer."

"I will," he moaned, "but it might be a long time. . ."

When Mike called Pam to let her know they had booked Stretch into jail, she was ecstatic! The courts were going to demand the money the next day, so the company breathed a collective sigh of relief. Arnie paid Chris and Mike the $11,000 commission. He wasn't happy about it, but he was grateful it didn't go the other way.

Arnie told Mike and Chris, "I got screwed on that case. I paid out a lot of money with nothing coming in. If you guys could collect the collateral on this case, I'll pay you your usual commission on the recovered property."

Chris and Mike both agreed they would give it a shot.

The first thing they had to do was check Stretch's file and see what kind of stuff was up for grabs. Chris and Mike were not repo men. This was going to have to be an undercover operation that would require a little finesse.

One thing was for sure, Mike and Chris would only have one shot at it. They had to go for the most valuable item. As soon as they grabbed one piece of equipment, the rest of the gear would go underground and they would never find it.

Looking over the list, Mike and Chris spotted the target. It was a newer motorcycle. Mike knew that he would have to get close to Stretch's guys if he expected to snag that bike. He also knew that patience would be his strongest weapon.

The fact that he had arrested some of these individuals in the past was not a problem. Mike had a good reputation with all of them. He always treated the people he picked up with respect and never ever used force if it was not necessary.

After Mike had retired from the police department, he had finally bought his own bike. He'd been riding motorcycles since he was fifteen years old. Mike arranged to ride his bike to some of the same functions where these guys were showing up.

Soon, a few of them were hanging out together on different rides. While Mike was riding around having a good time with these guys, he was also mentioning that his buddy was looking for a good deal on a bike. As luck would have it, the gentleman holding the title on the target bike was falling on hard times. After several discussions, Mike managed to convince him that his friend had the cash for the bike and would probably buy it.

"Only problem is my pal is married and has kids," Mike stated. "No offense, but he doesn't want anybody with a shady past coming over to his house." The seller said he understood so they agreed on a time Mike could come over and pick up the bike.

Mike needed a ride to get the bike, because he certainly couldn't leave a vehicle at the seller's house. It wasn't a good idea to bring Chris with him. Stretch's friends all knew Chris and Mike were partners and it would be very suspicious showing up together. Mike decided to give his old undercover buddy Mongo from the force a call. He is a big, barrel-chested, teddy bear-looking guy with a full beard and looked every part the biker. Mike filled him in and he was more then happy to tag along.

When they arrived to pick up the bike, Mike almost felt bad for the guy. He was sweating, washing and polishing every inch of the bike so it would look its best. Mongo stayed in the car while Mike waited for about an hour until the bike was sparkling. Every time Mike looked back at Mongo, he just shook his head, smiling in disbelief. When the bike was looking the best it probably had in years, the guy handed Mike the keys. "I'll be back soon," he said and rode off.

The next day Mike made the call.

"Dude," Mike told the seller. "I've got good news and I've got bad news. Good news is don't worry about your bike. It's fine. Bad news is it now belongs to Arnie."

The cosigner was understandably angry and had a few choice names for Mike before he hung up.

Mike felt bad, but quickly got over it. All these guys knew the rules. To intentionally screw your bondsman was not cool. Sometimes you have to out-con the con.

News about grabbing the motorcycle spread like a brushfire. The rest of the crew hid anything they had on the line. Eventually, one of the guys needed to sell his truck and contacted Mike about getting his title back. They negotiated a price he could live with and Mike sold the title to him. The rest of the stuff disappeared.

Stretch still is in prison, but is due to get out soon.

Mike sincerely hopes he is doing well.

Like he said, it's nothing personal.

Chapter 21

Typhoid Micki

When Micki walked in, Pam couldn't help but stare. Micki was nineteen years old and a real looker. With long black hair that reached her waist and a perfect body, she turned heads wherever she went. Her makeup was perfectly in place and she had on expensive clothing; it was hard to imagine her being a hooker with a drug problem, but Pam had heard that was exactly what was going on with her. She didn't hide the fact she was a heroin addict. After she was bailed, she'd score first before coming into the office.

Since most street prostitutes wore wrinkled clothes and smelled badly, Micki made quite an impression. Pam imagined she did very well on the street—probably a lot better than most.

The manager had left a long detailed note on Pam's desk asking her to throw in the bond when she came into work. According to his note, a cosigner ("a john," he'd written) was expected to come into the office. When he did, Pam was to collect the money, have the guy sign the paperwork and take the bond over to the jail.

Standing there in the front office completing the paperwork, Micki volunteered the information she wasn't a hooker but a call girl.

"There's a difference between the two you know," she said smiling. "I don't work the streets; an agency sends me where I need to go. I charge $500 and up a night and get it most of the time, because I'm good."

Although Pam was usually talkative, she decided not to comment on that. She couldn't think of anything appropriate to say.

A few weeks later, Pam opened the forfeiture letter from the court. Micki had failed to appear. When Pam showed the letter to the manager, he said he was certain he could find Micki. He said he'd bring her in on his own; no need for Mike. Pam nodded okay.

A few days later, the manager brought Micki into the office and asked Pam to go over to the courthouse, get her on the afternoon court docket and get her a new court date.

As Pam and Micki were walking over to the courthouse, Micki started to cry. Her perfect body convulsed with sobs. Pam stopped walking, turned to her and asked, "What's wrong? I'm certain you're not going to jail. I'm going to ask the judge to quash the warrant and you'll walk out of here with a new date."

"It's not that," she waved her arm. "It's just that I never told anyone, but the last time I was in jail they made me take a blood test. They made all of us charged with prostitution do that—something about a new law. Anyway, they tested my blood and told me I have AIDS. They just told me a few days ago and I'm not used to it yet."

"I'm sorry," Pam said softly as she put her arm around Micki's shoulder.

"It's okay," Micki smiled weakly. "I didn't mean to cry."

"I understand, Micki," Pam nodded sympathetically.

Pam and Micki walked the rest of the way in silence.

When Pam and Micki stood before the judge, he quashed the bench warrant and set a new date for the following week. As the two women turned to leave the courtroom, the judge said, "You'll have to change professions, you know."

"Excuse me?" Micki asked, turning around.

"You heard me," he roared from the bench. "With your medical history, which I happen to have right here in front of me, I better not catch you soliciting again. There's a new law in place now. The next time, if there *is* a next time, you could be charged with attempted murder."

The look on Micki's face was indescribable.

After Pam and Micki left the courtroom, Micki ranted and raved. "How dare he judge me! He doesn't know me. He has no idea of what I've been through. Well, *fuck him*. He can kiss my ass!"

When Pam brought Micki back to the office, Pam talked to her about her illness and the necessity of using condoms so she wouldn't infect others. Micki nodded as if she understood the gravity of the matter. "I promise," she said softly, looking away. Another worker offered to drive her home. Pam didn't tell him what the judge had said. Pam figured Micki could volunteer the information if she wanted to. It wasn't Pam's place to say anything. That was Micki's personal business. Pam just hoped the guy wasn't sleeping with her.

Several months later, Pam walked into the office one morning and was surprised to see Micki sitting in a chair near her desk in handcuffs.

"Pam, thank God you're here!" Micki shrieked.

She looked awful wearing filthy jeans and what used to be a white T-shirt. Her long black hair was cropped short, askew and different lengths as if she had cut it herself. She wore no makeup and had large, dark circles under her eyes. She smelled badly too; quite unlike the beautiful, high-class call girl who had walked into the office six months earlier.

"Micki!" Pam exclaimed, surprised. "What happened to you?"

"You've got to let me go." She wiggled in her chair, her eyes wild with fear. "Please, tell him to let me go!"

"Wait a minute. Slow down and tell me what happened."

"You'll never believe this. Remember how you took me to court? Remember what the judge said?"

"Yeah."

"Well, I didn't know what he was talking about. Remember just as we were leaving, he said something about how I'd have to change professions or else?"

"Yeah."

"Well, I got busted again. You weren't here; another guy who works here bailed me out. My lawyer told me this time they're going to charge me with murder!"

"What?" Pam's mouth fell open. "You've got to be kidding me!"

"I wish I was. I swear to God it's true."

"Wait a minute," Pam said slowly. "You can beat that charge."

"Not a chance." Micki stared at the floor. "This time, they caught me red-handed. When the cops walked up, I still had the guy's dick in my mouth."

"Micki!" Pam said, exasperated. "Tell me you made him wear a condom. You know you have AIDS. You can't go around infecting people. We talked about this the last time you were here. You promised me you'd make them wear condoms."

"I tried," she said sheepishly. "But guys don't get off when you're sucking rubber instead of the real thing. They were paying for it, so they always made me take the condoms off."

"And you did?"

"I have to make a living."

"So what happened? Why are you here?"

"I didn't go to court. My lawyer told me they were going to send me to prison, something about a new law. They're going to make an example out of me. Shit, Pam, I don't want to die in jail! You've got to help me! You've got to let me go!"

Pam had had several clients with AIDS and most lived only one or two years after diagnosis. She didn't know how much time Micki had, but from the way she looked that morning, it seemed to Pam that she was indeed dying.

Bounty Hunter Mike "Darkside" Beakley as a member of the SWAT team, kneeling with an M-16 while on standby working with the anti-terrorist unit during the Goodwill Games.

Mike keeping guard of one of the venue sites during the Goodwill Games. Neither the fans nor contestants knew his team was there.

Mike with his SWAT buddy, Rod "Punisher" Cook, aboard a Huey helicopter training to drop in on any terrorist threat.

Mike in his rugged biker attire.

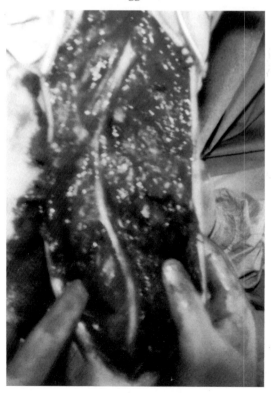

The injury Mike sustained after his shoot-out with the "hot toddy man".

Pam Phree hard at work in the offices of her bail bond agency, Phree Bail Bonds.

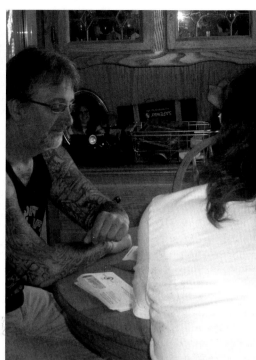

Whether it's on site or at home, Mike and Pam's work is never done.

Mike and Pam celebrate with a beer at their favorite pub after a hard day of catching bad guys.

Mike with his two most loyal work partners: Apollo (left) and Snickers (right).

Mike bringing one of the bad guys to justice.

Mike with his old buddy and fellow police officer Jim "Dunna" Young, who gave Beakley his nickname, "Darkside".

Mike and Pam with Big Chris, a fellow bounty hunter, at Mike's home during his annual Biker Bash.

The bounty hunter-bond agent team, Pam, Mike, Chris (left) and Mark (right), on a case.

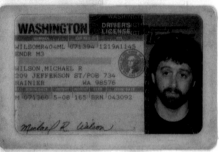

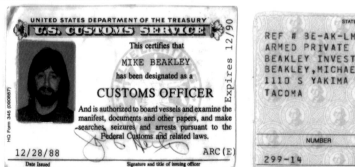

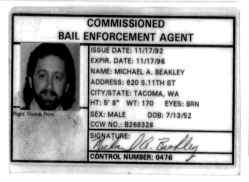

Mike "Darkside" Beakley's many roles in catching criminals.

"Time to go," Mike said softly, entering the room. He unfastened the cuffs and, taking her by the arm, gently lifted Micki to her feet.

"Oh my God!" Micki burst into tears. "Help me, Pam! Let me go! Please!"

Mike looked at Pam. She held up her finger, signaling him to wait a moment. She had to think about this.

Pam could let Micki go; she had the authority. Though they worked closely together, technically Pam was Mike's boss. She could ask him to undo the cuffs and return Micki to wherever he'd picked her up. Pam knew she could explain it to their boss. She'd tell him she just decided to give Micki a little more time. After all, she was dying. They could always pick her up again before it was time to pay the court. Micki wouldn't be hard to find.

After what seemed like an eternity, Pam made her decision.

Wordlessly, she nodded at Mike—and he led Micki away.

When Pam checked with the court later, she learned Micki had been convicted of attempted murder and sentenced to prison for twenty-five years—the first AIDS case prosecuted in the state—which meant she'd die in prison just as she predicted. The saddest part of all: Micki was only twenty. Mike and Pam both knew she wouldn't live past her twenty-second birthday, if even that.

Pam felt that as much as she cared for Micki, she had to do what she had to do. Micki was out there, infecting innocent johns who were unaware of how ill she really was. Unknowingly, they were going home and spreading the disease to their wives and girlfriends. Who knew how many clients Micki had, just how many had already been infected? Mike and Pam shuddered at the thought. Whether they had personal feelings for her, whether they liked it or not, much like Typhoid Mary, Micki *had* to be stopped. . .

Pam was just sorry that she and Mike had to be the ones to do it.

Chapter 22

Hide and Seek

When Pam had introduced Mike to Mark Straub, the bounty hunter she knew, they were working for different companies. But as time went on, Mark and Mike trusted each other working on many of their separate cases. Then when Chris joined Arnie's, the four of them all worked well together. Pam was the first to confess that having the guys knocking on the bail jumpers' doors helped to avoid a lot of potential problems. About 99 percent of the time, you can tell if someone is going to put up a fight before he or she makes a first move. Pam knew with these guys standing in their living rooms, the fugitives would go peacefully unless they were either mentally deranged or just plain stupid.

People won't usually fight, but they will hide. The firm had several methods of knowing whether or not a bail jumper was home. Once the team knew for sure that the fugitive was in the house, he or she never got away. Mark and Chris were good at rooting them out, but Mike felt it was his niche. "Warrant for your arrest! Everybody get down!" he yelled entering a house, getting an adrenaline rush.

However, once you've entered that home, either with or without resistance, and you know your subject has gone into hiding, everything changes. Suddenly, everything becomes very personal.

During Mike's SWAT team days, he had the backup of several guys searching the house together, covering doorways, watching one another's backs and leapfrogging through the building until they located the target. That's not the case with bounty hunting. Usually, there are two bounty hunters, maybe three, if they're lucky. More often than not, other people are in the house with the suspect. In that situation, one partner has to keep an eye on the additional occupants while the other has to search for a hidden fugitive all alone. Often the team members don't know if the fugitive is simply hiding or lying in wait to ambush them, but it's their job to find him.

One summer day, Mark, Chris and Mike hit the house of the fugitive for whom they were searching. It was a family member's home and it took several minutes for someone to answer the door. They'd heard the fugitive was home and had the back covered so the guy couldn't get out of the place. As Chris and Mark began searching the house, Mike talked with the family members. One of them kept looking Mike in the eyes then, without moving his head, moved his eyes straight up toward the ceiling. Mike pointed one of his fingers toward the roof and the guy opened his eyes wider, the only tip-off so the other family members wouldn't know that he snitched.

Casually Mark, Chris and Mike finished their search, ending up at the attic access. They opened the access hatch and Mark, being the tallest, stuck his head through the opening to see what he could see. Immediately Mark dropped to the ground. The suspect in the attic had charged at Mark as soon as he saw him. It was hot outside that day, which meant it was probably about 130 degrees in the attic. Normally, they talked to the fugitive and convinced him to give himself up before he melted, but this guy was different. He had come at Mark hard and they didn't want to take any chances with him, so they decided to empty a can of pepper spray into the attic opening. The combination of the high temperature and the pepper spray drove the guy berserk. He wouldn't come out through the attic access, because he was determined to get away, but he couldn't remain in the attic, which was now an unbearable environment. In his desperation, the guy ripped the vent out of the gable end of the attic and climbed onto the roof. Mark, Chris and Mike ran out into the yard to see the guy stumbling around on the roof trying to find a way down. Problem was, the pepper spray in that heated attic had forced his eyes almost completely closed. He was hacking and spitting wildly, trying to breathe. After several minutes of this, he lost his will to fight. Mike managed to get him off the roof and booked him into jail.

Some clients get very clever when hiding. Mike then begins a methodical search. Starting the search and going deeper into the residence, everything becomes very intimate. The murmur of your partner talking to other people in the next room might be heard; but at the same time, your partner can feel a million miles from anyone else. Senses are peaked. You listen for any telltale sign of another human being in lieu of the fact that all you can hear is your own breathing and heartbeat.

The trick is to slowly open every door then quickly try to observe every minute detail of the area. Every room you enter presents a plethora of new hiding places. Another bed to look under, another closet to clear, more furniture, piles of clothing and other crap to look behind and under. The next door you open leads down a staircase into a dark basement. Now what do you do? Do you turn on the light, illuminating the way, but also exposing yourself to whoever's waiting? There's no right or wrong answer. You've got to use your instincts and follow your gut. Let your senses feel the room. Hope for the best. You know the perp is there somewhere and you know he or she can hear your every move. The suspect knows you are getting closer to him or her, but you don't know how close he or she is. Inch by inch, you look into every nook and cranny, because you know if you make one false move, he or she will end up behind you. As you're slowly looking, you begin to run scenario after scenario through your mind.

Mike has often asked himself during a search, *What if I see a gun barrel? What if he comes out from behind this wall or around that corner, swinging a knife or any other weapon at me? Am I ready to react to anything without overreacting to nothing? Is this guy going to give up when I find him or try to kill me? Am I going home tonight?*

The first thing Mike is certain of is that the fugitive does not want to go to jail, but he knows the only reason Mike is there is to put him in jail. The second fact is whatever's going to happen will happen quickly. Mike knows if it doesn't work out, he won't get to try again. He *has* to win. In this job, second place sucks!

Mike knows people who have been killed in these situations and he still wants to do it. He can't help it. He loves it! Why he loves it, he doesn't have a clue.

After years of digging these guys and gals out of their hidey-holes, Mike learned the typical spots such as in closets and under beds. These are "panic spots." The people are caught by surprise and simply don't have a better plan. Other common panic spots are under stray blankets that are lying around on the floor, behind furniture or simply standing behind a door, hoping you won't look. Another very common spot is underneath piles of dirty laundry. Mike has probably found a dozen people hiding under someone else's nasty, old wet bath towels and dirty underwear. A lot of targets have hidden in attics, kitchen and bathroom cabinets, between mattresses and even in clothes dryers. Mike has even seen them go so far as to bury themselves under the insulation between the rafters.

One particularly crafty young man almost got away. He was hiding in a small home that the bounty hunters searched several times.

This search was a real head-scratcher. They knew he was in there and simply could not find him. After a little frustration and self-condemnation, they realized that the only thing they hadn't physically moved in that house was the sofa in the living room. The sofa was the type that had no legs and sat flush on the floor. They removed the cushions and everything looked normal. Then they tipped the sofa

over and to their surprise, there was the fugitive! He'd removed por-
tions of the sofa frame that allowed him to lie comfortably beneath it
as it sat flat on the floor. He'd also done it in a way that preserved its
structural integrity. If someone sat on it, he or she couldn't tell it had
been altered. It turned out that this guy was a paranoid sicko who
was always hiding from somebody or something. This, according to
him, was the first time his secret spot had failed him.

Mike appreciates when a fugitive challenges him on a search. The
sofa was a good one, but his favorite case happened several months later.

It was a cold, dark winter night when Chris, Mark and Mike
approached a house with the intent of arresting a young guy who was living with his mother. The house was three stories high and large. Chris was
knocking at the front door with one hand and playing with his handcuffs
with the other. Just as somebody from inside the house grabbed the door-
knob and started to open it, Chris closed his cuffs and they made that
familiar ratcheting sound. Anybody who has a habit of going to jail will
instantly recognize that sound. The next thing they heard inside was the
patter of footsteps running away from the door. Chris looked at Mike,
Mike looked at Chris. His shoulders drooped and he rolled his eyes, dis-
playing an disconcerted look. Mike moved quickly to the back of the house
and secured the perimeter while Chris and Mark banged loudly on the
door. After a few threats to kick in the door, the guy's mother finally
opened it. Chris and Mark entered and began their search. Mike
remained out back blocking any escape attempt. After standing in the
yard for over thirty minutes freezing, Mike saw Chris exit the back door.

"We can't find him and Mom's not talking."

"Okay," Mike nodded. "Let me take a shot at it."

Mike walked into the living room and approached the mother. It
was evident that she knew where her son had hidden, but remained
defiant that she wasn't about to give him up.

Mike decided to start the search on the top floor and work his way
down. He looked at everything. He started in one corner of the room

and worked down each wall, pushing on paneling, looking for loose sections, hollow spots or false walls, clearing all closets and checking any access openings or trapdoors. Then he moved on to the objects in the room and turned over all the sofas and chairs, looked in all the cabinets, appliances and anything else that was remotely large enough to hold a body. Slowly working room by room, floor by floor, Mike ended up in the daylight basement.

The basement was one large room, sparsely furnished and took only minutes to search.

The three agents were standing in the middle of the basement trying to figure out what they could have possibly missed. Suddenly Mike spied in the middle of one of the basement walls a large, brick fireplace with a firewood storage section bricked in beside it and pointed to it. Approaching the fireplace, Mark said, "I already looked inside." One thing you know if you search houses looking for fugitives is that you and your partners always double-check one another. It's easy to miss something. Mike cautiously looked inside the fireplace, including up around the flue, but found nothing. Then Mike started looking at the wood storage area. "I've looked in there as well," Mark said.

"Okay," Mike told him, "but if I don't look, it will haunt me forever."

Getting on his back, Mike slid headfirst into the space. Looking upwards, he was surprised to find that he could see the entire fireplace chimney as it traveled its way to the roof, two floors above. He could also see all the framing lumber that made up that portion of the structure. *It might be possible to climb up onto these timbers*, he thought, but he had a clear view of the area and didn't see anything unusual. Shining his flashlight around checking things out, he noticed a spot about six feet above the floor at the front of the chimney. At that spot, the chimney bricks were stepped back about a foot from the wall and formed a kind of shelf. It was the only place that wasn't covered in cobwebs. Putting his flashlight away, Mike climbed up on the bricks, looking between the sheetrock and chimney. He could see what looked like a tunnel running horizontally through the cobwebs leading to the other side of the chimney. It was pitch black and a very tight fit. Mike started to crawl and squeezed between the chimney and wall, stretching out horizontally with the floor about six feet off the ground. Literally he was inside the wall. Finally he worked his way to the far side of the chimney. Peeking around the corner, he could see that the tunnel continued toward the back of the chimney. After more squeezing and crawling, he finally forced his body around that corner and worked his way toward the next corner. At that point his mind started playing tricks on him.

Won't I be surprised if this is a rodent tunnel I'm crawling through and I run into a large nest of rats? If that happens, I'm shooting my way out through the sheetrock and getting the hell out of here! Oh yeah, you dumbass, you're screwed! You've pushed yourself in here like a residential suppository. You can't even reach your gun, let alone shoot anything. Now whatcha gonna do? He took a deep breath and pressed on.

Finally he reached the back of the chimney and started to nervously peek around the corner, this time spotting the bottoms of a pair of tennis shoes.

Triumphantly Mike barked out, "Get your ass out here right now!"

"Yes, sir," squeaked a small voice. "Don't hurt me! I'm coming."

"We're not going to hurt you. Just crawl out of there so we don't have to destroy your mom's wall to get to you."

Then Mike was stuck with the daunting task of getting himself out of the wall. As he backed out, the gear on his gun belt was like barbs on a fishing hook. It was fairly easy going in, but everything was getting hung up on the way out. After considerable grunting and groaning, he finally wiggled free followed by a disheveled fugitive.

"How did you find me in there?" The guy looked perplexed. "I've hidden from the cops for years in that spot and nobody's ever found me."

Mike didn't enlighten him. "Let's go to jail."

Chapter 23

A Lousy Day

Sharkey, a small, sinewy guy with an extensive criminal record, was running around town. He was about thirty years old, so he wasn't a kid, although his lifestyle proved he had not yet learned how to be a man. He sported a lot of tattoos and was considered by many to be a very dangerous fellow.

Pam gave Mike the file one afternoon. "He has missed court on a felony charge and is on the run," she stated.

Soon after, Mark, Chris and Mike started their hunt for him. Some informants stepped forward and they finally tracked him down to a local residence. Mike, Mark and Chris formed a plan, deciding to hit the house at night and waited until dark to depart.

The team members took turns covering the back of the houses. It was Mike's turn, so as soon as they got there he quietly worked his way to the backyard. Once in position, Chris and Mark knocked at the front door, announcing their intentions. A few moments passed and they could hear the sounds of scurrying around inside the house before the front door opened.

"Can we search your house?" Mark asked the residents, who promptly ushered them in.

Mark and Chris were a little uneasy making entry. It appeared that the family living there was not involved in any criminal activity. Looking around, this was definitely not a crack house or some tweeker den. It looked like just Mom, Dad and a couple of kids. However, Mark and Chris's experience kicked in and overcame their initial perceptions. They remembered the unusual sounds coming from within the house and the fact that it took several minutes to open the door. It alerted them that something was not right. Another red flag came up when the guys had asked to make entry to search the house and they were met with no resistance. Any family sitting there watching television together is going to ask a few basic questions before letting a couple of strange guys enter their home looking for a dude with felony warrants who calls himself Sharkey.

Again, Mike was in the backyard freezing, waiting for word from his partners.

As he stood outside of Sharkey's hideout, he shined his flashlight rapidly at all of the windows in the back of the house. From inside the house this would look like several guys might be outside, which forces the bad guy to hide inside. On this particular night, the ploy seemed to be working as designed. Suddenly, the basement door flew open. But it wasn't the fugitive; it was Mark. "We can't find him! The people in the house are acting strange and we're sure he's in here."

"Okay, let's have a look," Mike said as he entered through the basement door that led to the backyard.

"We've searched everything. The family won't talk, but they are acting very guilty. We know he's in here somewhere. Chris is upstairs keeping an eye on everyone."

"Well, Mark, since we're already in the basement, let's start our search down here and work our way up."

"Sounds good to me."

They had just started to search when a small pile of rolled up wall insulation drew Mike's attention. There wasn't really anything unusual about it. It was a roll of R-11 insulation about two feet in diameter with a couple of rags and some loose insulation on top. It was sitting in a bare corner of the basement all by its lonesome. With his gun in one hand, Mike casually picked away at the stuff lying on top of the roll. However, he was concentrating more on the rest of the room than paying attention to the task at hand. Suddenly he felt something odd and glanced down at the pile, seeing several fingertips poking out of the insulation. "Freeze!" he yelled and continued digging in the pile. There sat Sharkey. His hands were resting on his face, fingers extended and eyes fixed on the barrel of Mike's gun with a look of terror. As Mike cuffed Sharkey, Mark started complaining in disgust, "Damn it! I just looked in that pile and didn't dig deep enough!"

About a year later, Sharkey came to the firm's attention again. This time Mark was busy, so Chris and Mike would be running alone. Having three guys is always safer, but not always a reality with this job. Chris and Mike had been in the trenches together, they knew each other inside and out. Mike knew if the trouble got deep and one of them was still standing, the other would never be left alone.

Again, it was a long hunt without much to show for it. Then they got word that Sharkey was hiding out in a house near Lake Steilacoom, just southwest of Tacoma. They were given an exact address, so Chris and Mike drove out there.

It was a nice, sunny day and as their car approached the house, they could see several people outside in front of the place. Some were milling around and a couple of them appeared to be working on a car parked out front. As they drove by slowly trying to get a good look at everybody, they noticed that one of the people in the yard was wearing a hooded sweatshirt. Getting closer they saw the guy pull the hood farther down over his face. It wasn't as though he knew who they were; it seemed like something he was doing as a precaution.

As they drove past, both Chris and Mike said simultaneously, "That's him!" Watching in the rearview mirror, they could see the people checking them out. These guys were tweekers and tweeker groups like this always reminded Mike of meerkats. They are constantly on alert, standing up erect and staring at you at the same time. Their little necks are stretched out, their bodies twitching and their eyeballs bulging, ready to scatter at the slightest hint of danger.

Mike and Chris continued driving, trying not to startle the group. "It looks good," Mike observed. "The guy with the hoodie is the right height and weight and his actions were very suspicious."

Once they were out of the group's sight, they talked over a plan. They were outnumbered and knew they would have to catch the fugitive by surprise. Simply driving up and arresting this guy would never work. The human meerkats would see them coming from a block away and would be running away or shooting at them before they could get out of the car. After kicking ideas back and forth for a few minutes, Mike and Chris decided to go to the end of the block that was the farthest away from the house. They could work their way over the fences and through the yards, allowing them to approach the house from the group's blind side.

Parking the car at the far end of the block, they started their trek. There were a half dozen fenced yards to negotiate. Around fifteen minutes later, Mike and Chris dropped over the last fence and reached the opposite corner of the house, arriving at the scene quietly. There had been one barking dog, but nobody seemed to pay attention. None of the neighbors had come out to challenge them. As far as they could tell, they'd made it this far without being noticed.

Chris went around the left side of the house and Mike to the right. Mike was heading for the front of the house when he heard a female voice yell out, "Sharkey, watch out!" A woman had been vacuuming one of the rooms and spotted Chris through the window as he was sneaking along. As soon as she started screaming, Chris was on the run. He had gotten within a few feet of Sharkey and was closing in on him fast. Mike was also at a full run when he came around his side of the house and saw Chris grab Sharkey by the sweatshirt. The fight was on! Chris hung on fiercely as Sharkey twisted and fought just as vehemently. Mike took four more steps and was within inches of grabbing Sharkey when he spun and took off running with Mike grasping at him, trying to get hold of anything possible. Chris stood there with Sharkey's sweatshirt in his hands. Sharkey had gotten lucky. He had spun around and managed to slip out of the shirt. He was running down the street with Chris and Mike in hot pursuit.

With a great initial burst of speed, Chris got out in front of Mike and took the lead. Chris is a big guy and he was running out of breath. Mike was behind Chris, cheering him on. Chris was running his hardest and was starting to make snorting noises like a bull elk. Mike was behind him, yelling, "You can do it, Chris! Keep it up, keep going!" All the time Mike was thinking, *Chris, for God's sake, catch him 'cause I'm dying back here!* Mike and Chris rounded the block and Sharkey was running uphill in the middle of the street and pulling away from them. Now Mike took the lead from Chris, but Sharkey was getting away.

Suddenly, Mike saw a woman backing out of her driveway right beside him. She was getting ready to drive up the hill toward Sharkey who was moving into the distance. Mike quickly grabbed the passenger door handle of this poor woman's car and to his surprise, it opened. He jumped into the front passenger seat of her car and yelled, "Follow that guy!" Mike turned and looked at her, showing her his badge. Looking back at him, eyes as wide as dinner plates, was an elderly woman. Mike pointed at Sharkey and said, "Go! Go! Go!" She looked like she was scared to death, but without hesitation she hit the gas and away they went.

She covered the half block or so in seconds. As they got within yards of Sharkey, he cut right, running between the houses. "Stop!" Mike yelled. The woman slammed on the brakes and Mike bailed out, closing her door behind him. Still exhausted, he started running after Sharkey. Mike could hear the car behind him speeding away. He only hopes that when she told her family about her adventure, they didn't think she was losing it and have her committed.

At that point, Mike was just a couple of feet behind Sharkey. Sharkey ran to the right behind a house and jumped over a fence into the backyard. Mike saw a wheelbarrow leaning up against the fence and used that as a launch pad. He didn't have the energy to clear the fence so he kind of high centered on it with his body, legs kicking away on one side and arms flailing away on the other. Exhausted, Mike pulled out his pepper spray and just as Sharkey looked up at him, Mike let loose with a stream. Only problem was the wind caught it and blew it straight back into Mike's face. Sharkey let out a grunt and was off again, running through the yards in the direction they had come from. Mike managed to pull himself the rest of the way over the fence and continued sprinting his way after the fugitive. The yards they were running across emptied into Steilacoom Lake. Sharkey was running ahead of him when Mike saw him stumble and fall. Mike could clearly see that Sharkey was faltering. The problem was Mike had very little wind left and it looked like he could still lose him.

Sharkey dragged himself up and started jogging again. He cut to the right behind the houses. Mike got to the spot where Sharkey had fallen and boom, went down like a rock. Tripping on a small wire fence, Mike fell into some type of drainage area that ran between two yards and was draining into the lake. Now he knew why Sharkey had fallen. When he pulled himself up, Mike could see goose shit all over the ground. Mike looked down and saw that his pants were smeared with the toxic fecal matter. Dragging his hind leg, Mike somehow started to go again. Then, to his great delight, he saw Sharkey on the ground about twenty-five yards ahead of him with his hero, Chris Dausch, standing over him. Chris had seen Sharkey run to the back of the houses so he did the same. Meanwhile Sharkey had run right back to Chris.

Mike caught up to Chris as he was cuffing Sharkey. Sharkey was lying on the ground, barely able to breathe. None of them could talk as they tried to catch their breaths.

Chris and Mike stood over their prey, bent at the waist with their hands on their knees sucking in air. Sharkey was lying on the ground sweaty, pale and gasping for breath. At that moment Chris and Mike heard a weak voice behind them, "Do you need help?"

Looking in that direction they saw a family of three sitting on the back deck of their house. A man, his wife and their young daughter were looking at Chris and Mike with eyes wide and mouths hanging open. The wife asked, "Should we call for help?"

Mike responded, panting, "No, we're the good guys. Everything's okay."

She replied, "No, I mean, do I need to call for help for you guys? Are you okay?"

It was then Mike realized they must have all looked like they were near death. "Thanks, but no thanks," Mike told her. "We will need a few minutes before we can get this guy out of here. Will that be okay?"

"Sure, take your time. You sure you don't need help?"

"No, thank you."

They stayed there for about ten minutes until they could breathe normally. Gasping and choking, Sharkey was actually in worse shape than Mike and Chris were. They kept a close eye on him on the way to jail. They thought they might have to take him to the hospital, but he started coming out of it and Chris and Mike were able to book him.

Now he's serving time in prison for murder.

Chapter 24

Creating Tragedy

Business was brisk. Things were so busy the firm hired another bounty hunter. His name was Tony. He made an effort to be pleasant, greeting people when they ran across each other and inquiring as to how everybody was doing. Chris and Mike exchanged pleasantries with him. There was something about this guy that Mike, Chris and Pam liked. He smiled a lot, but had a mischievous air about him. It always looked like Tony was up to something. He had a spark in his eyes that showed a kind of intelligence that was just waiting to come out.

Tony approached Pam, Mike and Chris at the office one day and asked if he could talk to them about a case he was working on.

Tony looked upset. "I need some real advice on this one."

Chris nodded. "Okay," Mike and Pam said at the same time.

Tony told them about the case. The fugitive was staying at a motel somewhere in the area and Tony had developed an informant who gave him a phone number. The target always called from that number. The problem was the caller I.D. showed that the number belonged to a pay phone.

"No problem. Just locate the phone booth. He should be close by," Chris offered.

"Thanks," Tony said and off he went.

The next day Tony approached the three of them again. That guy had spent the entire night driving to every phone booth in the valley that he could find, checking the numbers. Finally, he'd found the location of the phone. He had also checked with the motel manager across the street showing him a picture of the suspect and learned the guy had a room there. Tony now had the room number and a vehicle description. He wanted to know if Chris and Mike would back him up with the arrest.

"Who's going?" Mike asked him.

"Is it okay if just the three of us do it?" Tony asked.

"Sure, no problem. Let's hit the room as soon as we see the car there."

That night, as Chris, Mike and Tony waited, they spotted the car the motel manager had described. The three of them went to the door of the suspect's motel room and knocked. No answer.

They checked with the manager and he told them the subject just got home and was in the room. While Chris and Tony talked with the manager, Mike kept an eye on the room window. The blinds slightly parted and he could see the target peeking out to see if they had left.

"Tony," Mike said. "It's your case. Knock as loud as you can and announce who we are."

Tony started pounding on the door yelling, "Bail enforcement! Open the door! We have a warrant!"

There was no response.

"One more time, Tony, but this time announce that if he doesn't open up, we're going to kick it in."

Bang, bang, bang! He pounded on the door and gave the order.

Again, there was no response.

"What now?" Tony asked, looking at Mike.

"What do you want to do, Tony?"

"I want to kick it in!" he said, the adrenaline now flowing.

"Go for it, kid," Mike ordered. "See if you can cave it in on the first kick."

Tony leaned against the handrail in front of the door using it for leverage and rammed his right foot into the door, ripping half the doorjamb off and slamming the door into the wall behind it. Mike, Chris and Tony entered the room and Tony arrested his first fugitive.

Tony was grinning ear to ear and could barely contain his excitement. They stopped for a beer that night and shared the story about a hundred times.

"That's what you do with a job like this," Mike said proudly. "You share a beer with your comrades and you tell war stories. When it's your first, it's the sweetest—the one you never forget."

For Mike, seeing a new guy this excited was a rush. The new guy doesn't realize it at the time, but his life has just changed.

A couple of days later, Tony asked Mike if he could work with him and Chris. "I've been paying attention to how you and Chris do things and I want you to train me."

"I'll run it by the others, Tony, and we'll let you know."

Chris, Mike and Pam tossed the idea back and forth for a couple of days. They knew the guy had been in some kind of trouble in the past, but they didn't know the details. They also knew he wasn't supposed to have a gun. That might be fixable in the future, but why think about it now. They didn't even know if this guy would be worth the effort until they tried him for awhile. One thing they did know about him was that he had checked every phone booth in town to solve a case and that was impressive. The decision was made to give him a chance.

"You do realize, don't you, that we are the good guys? We play by the rules and no messing around; everything's legal," Mike told Tony.

"I know; that's what I like. I've been stupid in the past, but now I've got a wife and two babies. I want to be a good guy and I see that chance with you."

"Right on, Tony, welcome aboard. Eyes and ears open, mouth shut, okay?"

"You got it, boss!"

Tony was a Native American/Hispanic mix, built like an ox. While he was in great physical shape, he was inexperienced. Later Pam learned he had been a client of Arnie's. He had been bailed on a weapons charge for which he later did time and was recently released from jail.

Tony saw bad guys everywhere. Whenever Mike, Chris and he were driving along, Tony often yelled, "That's him!"

"Tony, are you sure?"

"I'm positive! That was him!"

They turned around and checked the guy out.

"Not even close, Tony. You're wasting our time chasing shadows."

"Sorry guys. I was sure this time."

That's how it went, day in and day out. Mike had high hopes that this initial burst of eagerness would diminish with time. But he would rather have a trainee with a little extra interest in the job than one who didn't care.

Another problem cropped up. Although Tony didn't treat Chris rudely or speak to him with disdain, he just didn't want to learn from Chris. Tony was a lot like an attack dog. He only answered to one master and that master was Mike. Tony knew Mike's background and had a deep respect for the things he had done during his career. Luckily, Chris was a mature guy who wasn't touchy and he let it roll off. Tony, on the other hand, could not see the big picture and thought Chris had nothing to offer him. That could turn out to be a big mistake on Tony's part. He would have to learn to listen to both Chris and Mike if he was smart. Mike hoped he would figure this out with time.

Though Tony's enthusiasm could be worrisome, it was still a pleasure, Mike felt, to watch him try to grow into the job.

One day the three men were hunting a young man down on the east side of Tacoma. They located the apartment he was living in and set up surveillance. After a short period of time, they saw the fugitive walking along the road with his girlfriend. They sat and watched as they entered the ground floor apartment. Luckily for the team, or so they thought, the manager's apartment was the next door over.

They knocked at the manager's door and as a courtesy explained to her who they were and what they would be doing. Right away, they could tell that this wasn't going to be good. She was obviously not impressed with them. Then they knocked at the target door and announced their purpose for being there. Immediately they heard the sound of furniture being pushed up against the door. That jerk was barricading the apartment. Now they had to deal with the manager again. Chris went around back to make sure that the fugitive didn't scoot out the back and with Tony at Mike's side, Mike knocked at the manager's door again.

"Ma'am," he said, "we have a warrant for the guy inside that apartment. He has barricaded the door and we would like a key so we don't have to damage your property."

"You're not getting a key!" she snapped at them. "And if you damage that apartment you're going to pay for it!"

Very calmly Mike explained, "Ma'am, your tenant is the one who is causing this problem. He will have to pay for it."

"What if he doesn't? What then?"

"Then I suggest that you take it out of his damage deposit. Either way, I want you to understand that we are going to enter that apartment with or without your help; whether we damage it or not is your decision."

"I'm not letting you in."

"Okay, we'll do it our way." Mike turned to Tony. "Tony, go back and check on Chris; see if there is a way in through the back."

Tony came back a few minutes later to report that there was a bedroom window and a patio door in the back.

"Mike," Tony said, excited as a little kid again, "let me break the bedroom window out. I can crawl in through the window and get the guy."

"Damn it, Tony. My guys don't crawl. Besides, you'd be in there alone and crawling through a broken window is dangerous. Tell you what: why don't you break the sliding glass door, walk inside like a man and get your guy?"

"You're kidding me," Tony practically squealed, his eyes lit up like a Christmas tree. "You'd really let me break out the glass door?"

"Of course I will. It's the safest way for us to make entry. Then we can all go in together. By the time that door comes down, it will be too late for the guy to move all the crap he's piled up against the front door. You know, Tony, when you think about it, it was quite nice of the guy to block his only escape route."

They all got settled at the back door and Mike handed Tony a heavy metal flashlight.

"Here ya go, Tony. Hit the door at the bottom of the glass. This is safety glass and it will make a nice little shower."

Crash! Tony hit the bottom of the glass and a million small particles of glass rained down. The three of them walked inside and relieved the fugitive of his freedom.

As they drove off, they could hear the squawking of the manager fade into the distance.

"I can't control him," Pam complained about Tony to Mike over a pitcher of beer at their favorite pub a few weeks later. "He doesn't listen to me. I tell him not to go alone; he should *make* someone go with him. I tell him where the guy is, whether he has weapons, whether he's on dope. I outline the scenario and tell him how to approach it. He nods like he's listening then he takes the case and does it his way. He has almost gotten himself killed a few times. The fact that I can't control him bothers me."

By then, Mike had the same problem with the inexperienced bounty hunter. Tony's enthusiasm to get the job done was great, but the way he went about it had become troublesome. Mike was not happy about Tony's tendency to not listen to Pam's and Chris's directions. In actuality, Mike was becoming unhappy about a lot of things. As a former police officer, he was offended by bounty hunters who were unregulated and unskilled. He didn't like it that some had no formal training, not even firearms certification.

Mike and Pam both had a real problem with all the Joeys in the world: convicted felons who ran around bashing in cars and waving guns in the faces of innocent people. Mike couldn't believe the lack of regulation.

"That's one of the reasons why most police officers look at bounty hunters with suspicion," Mike commented. "Most are illiterate imbeciles, braggarts with very little skill. The scary part is they're walking disasters just waiting to happen. I wonder how many innocent people have been injured or even killed directly or indirectly due to bounty hunters' actions.

"At the very least," Mike told Pam, "we need SOPs—standard operating procedures—for bounty hunters. Like police officers, they should learn the escalation of force. When it is—and isn't—appropriate to pull their weapons. Bounty hunters should have clean police records, should go through vigorous training before being allowed on the street, should be licensed by the state and held accountable for their actions."

Pam couldn't agree more.

"Tony's okay," Mike continued. "He's a young guy who hasn't had any training. To have untrained bounty hunters out on the street who don't have a clue of what they're doing just doubles our chances of someone getting seriously injured or even killed on the job. And I'm not going to be around when that happens."

"Mike, you wouldn't quit!" Pam looked at him in horror.

"I would. The way this is going, it isn't fun. For your sake, I'll hang out as long as I can, but I'm not making any promises."

A few weeks later, Mike was gone. When Pam arrived at the office one morning, she learned he'd quit the night before.

Mike called Chris and told him that he'd quit. Chris wasn't happy but he understood. "I'm going to stick it out with Tony as long as I can. I have bills to pay and I can't imagine doing anything else."

"Good luck, Chris. I'm going to spend some time on my bike and drink some beer. Don't let the bad guys get you. If something looks bad, call me. I'll always help if you need it, but I can't handle the lack of rules."

"See ya, Beak," Chris said sadly.

Chapter 25

Fatal Prediction

Not long after Mike quit, Pam was handed the case of an eighteen-year-old male who failed to appear in court. His name was Sean Brown. He'd been arrested for felony drug possession with intent to deliver and his bail was $5000.

Pam tried to find him. She called all the numbers on the application. She researched all the databases trying to get an address, some idea of where he might be. After working the case for a few days, she was stymied. She handed the case to Chris and Tony, instructing them to start nosing around on the street to see if an informant would snitch.

Tony and Chris headed to the house where they knew Brown's cousin and possibly his girlfriend were living. The cousin was Brown's cosigner, which gave them the right to search the house if they needed. Driving to the house, they turned a corner and saw Brown standing out in the street selling rock. They got about thirty feet from him before he spotted them. He took off running through the front door of his cousin's house, out the back door then downhill between the houses. He kept running through the nearby vacant lots.

Chris chased Brown for about two blocks before he lost him. About ten minutes later, Tony spotted him running down the alley. Tony swore he saw a gun in Brown's hand, but lost him when Brown cut between some other houses. They decided to leave the area for awhile and let Brown calm down.

A few hours later Chris and Tony returned to the house and decided to search it. Brown's cousin was there and she was one very tough woman. They began searching a bedroom with the woman yelling at them the entire time. "He's not here! He's not here!" she screamed. Then she reached down and grabbed hold of a metal-framed twin bed that was in the room. She snatched the bed off the ground and literally held it above her head screaming, "See he's not under here!" Then she slammed the bed to the floor. Chris tried to reason with the woman. He tried to convince her that it would be better for her cousin and everybody involved if Brown just turned himself in. Brown's cousin calmed down a bit and told Chris she would try to talk her cousin.

For about a week, Tony and Chris came in and out of the office. They related the latest news on Sean to Pam. "He was seen here; we chased him without success; we were close to getting him; it is only a matter of time."

There was something about their exuberance that gave Pam an uneasy feeling. One afternoon Pam received a telephone call from a reliable informant. The informant told her Sean was a high-ranking gang member—a CRIP—recruited from California to reorganize the gang in the Tacoma area. According to the source, Sean was a bad one and knew the bounty hunters were looking for him.

"Better watch your back," she was told. "He's packing and he'll shoot you without blinking."

When Tony and Chris came into the office, Pam related what she had learned. Both shrugged.

"We've chased dangerous criminals before. Sean isn't anything to be concerned about," they reassured her. "We have it under control."

The next day, while Chris and Tony related their progress on chasing Sean, Pam felt nervous. Tony's most recent lead on the case had involved an unnecessary and reckless high-speed chase. It not only jeopardized innocent bystanders, but also could have easily gotten Tony and Chris killed. The car chase coupled with Tony seeing Brown with a gun was the end for Pam.

"That's it!" Pam shouted. "You're off the case. This is too dangerous. You're going to get yourselves or somebody else killed. It isn't worth it. Don't chase Sean anymore. Leave him alone for now. That's an order!" Pam pointed her finger in Tony's face.

Tony argued with her. "I'm this close," he held his thumb and forefinger an inch apart. "It'd be unfair to take me off the case now."

"I don't care," Pam responded sternly, shaking her head. "This has gotten way too dangerous. Let things cool off for a minute. We'll give Brown's defense attorney a chance to try and get him into court. Go home. I'll give you another case tomorrow."

Tony had driven that day and Chris asked him for a ride home.

They were driving up a street near the area they had chased Brown when Tony suddenly turned left toward the cousin's house.

"Tony, don't do it!" Chris said. "I know what you're up to. We are done for the day!"

But Tony didn't like listening to Chris—only to Mike. When Tony got a scheme into his head, it was about impossible to reason with him. "I just want to look one more time," Tony kept saying.

"Knock it off and take me home," Chris said repeatedly. Tony was too stubborn. As Mike had predicted, it was only a matter of time before that stubbornness got him into trouble.

Tony kept driving in the direction of the house despite Chris's protests. When they pulled up, Brown was outside selling rock again. Just like the first time, he spotted Chris and Tony and took off running. Tony bailed out of the car and started chasing him. Tony went around the house on one side and Chris followed Brown. He took the exact same route he ran the first time Chris had chased him. This time when Chris lost him, he hid behind some hedges that were at the top of an old set of concrete stairs in one of the vacant lots. Chris thought, *I'll stay here for awhile and see if he surfaces.*

After a few minutes, Chris saw Brown running up from the lower vacant lot. He had been hiding in an old building on the lower lot. Chris was still hiding behind the hedge when Brown started up the stairs. Chris waited for Brown to get to the top of the stairs then he stepped out and sprayed pepper spray at Brown. The next thing Chris saw was Brown turn and, with one leap, jump and clear six to eight steps, landing at the bottom, running. It was pretty incredible to see. The guy was either very athletic or very scared.

Chris started chasing him again. This time, Chris saw him run into the back door of his cousin's house. Tony was already in front of the house so they had him pinned. A window on the side of the house flew open. Brown looked out, spotted Chris and ducked back inside, closing the window. Chris and Tony had Brown fairly well-contained. Chris wanted to call the police for help, but Tony had Chris's phone and Tony didn't want to wait for the police. Tony wanted to kick the door in right away. Chris couldn't let him kick it in alone, because Tony wasn't armed, so he went around front and joined him. Again, Tony refused to listen to reason from Chris.

Tony kicked the door and they found four screaming women in the living room. Tony stayed with the women and tried to calm them down while Chris started searching the house. He entered one of the bedrooms and found a man sleeping in a bed. Chris knew it wasn't Brown so he continued clearing the room. He grabbed the closet door-knob and started to open it. Just as he was getting ready to search the closet, Tony and the women began yelling at one another at the top of their lungs. It sounded like things were getting out of hand. Chris went back to the living room and told Tony to finish clearing the bedroom while he tried to calm everything down. Tony was pretty angry by now, but agreed and he disappeared into the bedroom. Chris had just started talking to the women when he suddenly heard five rapid-fire gunshots come from Tony's direction. The women screamed and took off running.

Chris drew his weapon just as Brown came around the bedroom door. He was crouched down low and pointing a gun at Chris. Chris fired off one fast round, hitting Brown in the chest, pushing him backwards. Brown then took cover behind the wall next to the door. Chris fired six or seven rounds into the wall where he was hiding, hoping to end this thing. He didn't hear Brown moving, so he started clearing the doorway. Chris entered the bedroom, hoping Brown was down. Turned out he wasn't, as Brown immediately attacked Chris, trying to wrestle the gun away from him. Fighting for his life, Chris was able to shove his gun into the hollow part of Brown's throat just above the area where the collarbones meet. Chris pulled the trigger and the round blasted through Brown's throat, exiting out the back and hitting the wall behind him. Brown jerked backwards, turned and jumped out the window. Chris was right behind him and saw him land headfirst on the concrete about ten feet below. Brown then jumped up and started running. By this time, his cousin had pulled her car around back and was waiting for him. As he reached her car, Chris yelled at him to stop. Brown spun around as though he was going to shoot at Chris again. Chris fired one more round at him before he turned, jumped into the car and sped away.

Now Chris's attention turned to Tony. Chris went to check on him and saw that he had crawled out of the bedroom and into the living room. At the same time, Chris noticed that Brown had dropped his gun just inside the doorway to the bedroom. Chris picked it up and put it in his belt in case somebody else was in the house. It looked like he had dropped it the first time Chris shot him. The man sleeping in the bed was still lying there not moving or making a sound when Chris returned. In fact, he never moved or said a word the entire time of the fight.

Approaching Tony to check on him, Chris could see that Tony had crawled over to use the phone. Chris thought he had called 911 so he grabbed the phone from him thinking he could give police dispatch clearer information. When Chris began yelling in to the phone what had happened he realized that Tony's wife was on the other end of the line. All Tony could think of was calling his wife. He had called to let her know that he had been shot, he might be dying and that he loved her. It was more important for him to call and say goodbye to his wife, letting her know that he loved her, than calling for help for himself. Now Chris had to get Tony's wife off the phone so he could call the police. Things were bad enough, but having to hang up on Tony's wife made Chris feel like his guts were being ripped out.

After calling 911, who told him help was coming, Chris tried to do first aid on Tony. He assessed his wounds and saw a lot of holes. He was bleeding everywhere. Chris spotted a sucking chest wound and tried to stop the bleeding with his hands but couldn't; there were just too many holes and too much bleeding. Chris found a piece of plastic wrap on the floor and used it in an attempt to slow the bleeding.

Suddenly Chris heard someone call, "Help! Help me!" There was nothing more Chris could do for Tony at that point, so he went into the bedroom to check on the guy who had been sleeping. The bed was directly across the room from the closet and in a direct line of fire from Brown when he was shooting from inside the closet. Chris searched the guy's body and found a bullet hole in his left shoulder blade. He also had a divot along the back of his head where one of the bullets had creased it. The guy looked up at Chris scared and asked, "Am I going to die?" Chris assured him that he would be fine and then went back to Tony. All Chris could do was try to comfort him until police and an ambulance arrived.

Within minutes the police arrived. They started coming down the sidewalk and Chris yelled out to them, "In here!" As soon as they got into the house, Chris started telling them what had happened and that he had the bad guy's gun in the back of his belt. The police quickly cleared the rest of the house then let the medical people in. They took Chris's and Brown's guns from Chris then rushed him to a police car. At first Chris thought he was under arrest, but then he realized that a crowd had been forming. A lot of gang members were showing up and the police wanted to get Chris out of there as quickly as possible for his own safety.

Pam had just gotten home from work when she received a frantic phone call from one of the staff at the office. "Tony has just been shot! Turn on the news."

Flipping on the television news, Pam saw Chris sitting in the back of a police car, head down with his lips moving. The camera panned out to show the street, a dozen police cars with their lights flashing, officers talking to one another, others walking down the street, obviously searching for something. According to the television reporter broadcasting live from the scene, "A local bounty hunter has just been shot and is in critical condition. He's been taken to the hospital. We'll continue following this developing story. Stay tuned for further news."

Frantically Pam called Mike. "Chris just called me and I'm on my way to the police station to meet up with him. I'll call you back once I know the details," Mike told her.

At the police department, Mike saw one of the detectives he'd known for years. She escorted him back to an interview room where Chris was sitting alone. He looked angry and concerned at the same time.

"Chris, is Tony okay?" Mike asked urgently.

"We don't know yet. He got hit four or five times in the stomach. He looked pretty bad when they hauled him away."

"How are you holding up? You seem angry."

"I'm doing okay. I shot the guy, but he still got away. I think the cops might have picked him up by now. They're not telling me a lot until they get all this stuff sorted out."

"How bad did you wound the guy?"

"He should be dead. I think I hit him twice, once in the chest and once in the throat."

"Holy shit, what happened?" Mike asked, sitting in a chair across from Chris. Chris began relating the details of the case to Mike.

"Chris, it sounds like you were doing a damn good job to me and had things under control. What happened to make everything go so sideways?"

"Tony's stubbornness," Chris replied and described their final confrontation with Brown and the gunfight to Mike.

"Has a detective interviewed you yet?"

"Not in any depth so far. A female detective spoke to me for a couple of minutes. She said that they are going to handle it the same way they would if a police officer was involved in a shooting. That makes me feel a lot better. At first, I just assumed that I was going to be under arrest no matter what had happened. I told the detective that I had been working with you. She let me call you. She's been very cool with me and is treating me well."

"How about you, Chris? How are you holding up?"

"To tell you the truth, Mike, I'm not sure. I'm really worried about Tony. He looked bad. I don't think he is going to make it."

"I'll stay here with you until the detective comes back then I should head up to the hospital and see what's going on."

A short time later, the detectives arrived and started their interview with Chris.

Mike went to the hospital and found Tony's family already there. After several hours passed, they were told Tony's condition was uncertain. He had survived surgery but the next hours would be critical. There was no guarantee that he would make it through the night.

Once Mike learned of Tony's condition he called Pam. "Tony has been shot five times in the belly by Sean Brown, the defendant he was chasing. He's undergone emergency surgery and the doctors have successfully removed all the bullets. Tony is conscious and talking, but it will be touch and go for awhile. I'll keep you updated on his progress."

The next morning Chris called and wanted to take some time off. Under the circumstances, Pam felt he should and obliged his request.

As the days passed, Mike called Pam regularly. He reported that Tony was able to hold down food and water. "That's a good sign," Mike reassured Pam. "He just might be okay."

Sean had been wounded in the battle, but not seriously. After he was released from the hospital, he was booked into jail. It was Pam's duty to appear in court and request that since Sean had been apprehended, the bail bond be exonerated.

When Pam appeared in court, the jailer brought Sean before the judge. Pam and Sean were standing less than five feet from each other. When Pam explained to the judge that this defendant had shot the firm's bounty hunter, she looked over at Sean. He looked at Pam. His eyes were cold. Ice cold. Pam could tell he'd shot Tony just as easily as he would swat a fly. There was no expression, no emotion in his eyes. He didn't even blink.

The judge exonerated the bond and placed a no-bail hold on him. Later Sean was charged with attempted murder.

Tony's family kept vigil over him. A few times over the next two weeks, Mike got frantic phone calls from members of Tony's family.

"Mike!" the callers said. "We need you down here right now. Tony's losing it. He keeps saying he is going to die. He's panicking. He won't listen to anyone. He keeps asking for you. Please hurry!"

Each time Mike got to the hospital as fast as he could. Tony's eyes were wide with fear. Mike bent over his bed and Tony grabbed him in a bear hug.

"Mike, I'm going to die! I know I'm going to die and I don't want to!"

"Easy, Tony," Mike said into his ear. "You're going to be alright. You're not going to die. Tony, listen to me. You're not going to die; you've got to believe me. You know I've seen a lot of bad stuff in my life. I've seen a lot worse than this and guys have pulled through. You're going to be fine."

"Promise me, Mike! Promise me I'm going to live."

"Tony, I promise you. You will live, I promise."

"Okay, Mike, you're sure?"

"Yes, I'm sure, Tony; I wouldn't lie to you about something like this. I promise you, you'll make it."

A nurse gave Tony an injection and he finally started to calm down. The medication the nurse gave him started to kick in and Tony went back to sleep.

However, Mike's reassurances proved to be wrong. During the next three weeks an infection started raging in Tony's body and could not be controlled. Tony passed away in his sleep.

Everyone was devastated by Tony's death. Tony's family was beyond grief. Chris and Mike felt the irony of what had happened. They had taken Tony under their wing, because the guy had potential as a bounty hunter and, best of all, he wanted to become one of the good guys. They had felt he would have a better chance of surviving the job if they trained and mentored him the proper way. And now he was gone.

Not long after Tony's death, Mike's phone rang.

"Mike," Chris said, his voice weak. It was obvious that something was terribly wrong.

"What's wrong, Chris? You don't sound so good."

"I'm not good," he said, his voice cracking. "I just got off the phone with the police detective. He told me that the killing shot hit Tony high on the torso and angled down through his chest taking out both lungs. Mike, he told me that the bullet came from my gun. *I* killed Tony. Now what do I do?"

Chapter 26

Picking Up the Pieces

The press was having a field day. Tony had been the first bounty hunter to die in the line of duty in the state and that made him newsworthy. Television and newspapers covered the story nonstop for weeks.

Cameras were stationed outside Arnie's office. Reporters tried to stop employees as they walked in and out of the building. Pam had plenty to say, but she wasn't able to. No one was supposed to comment; if they did they'd be fired. She thought the silence made the company look even worse and that at least the firm needed to do damage control. She felt they should have held a press conference.

Tony's widow was understandably devastated. Only eighteen years old, she had two small children under age five. In her grief, she openly blasted the company in the press for hiring her husband to begin with. "He shouldn't have been allowed to chase dangerous criminals when he was unarmed," she sobbed. "All he had was pepper spray."

After Tony's death, everybody felt numb. The tension in the office was thick. Phones were still ringing; people were still lining up at the front counter waiting to be helped. They all did their jobs, but the mood was different. The employees usually laughed and joked among themselves and clients, but not anymore. No one said anything to another unrelated to the work at hand.

Chris was doing his best to cope with the knowledge that his bullet was the one that killed Tony. Mike spent a lot of time with Chris trying to reassure him that Tony's death was not his fault. It was, in fact, the bad guy's fault. Chris understood, but at that point it didn't help. He had lost his fire. His normally gregarious self was replaced by a somber, quiet person with a deeply troubled and unhappy exterior. Mike knew from experience that only time could dull the pain.

Pam was devastated over Tony's death. Pam and Tony had spent hours and hours talking about the bail bond industry and he'd spent a considerable amount of time over at Pam's apartment. She truly loved and missed him.

"I blame Chris for Tony's death," Pam told Mike one night when they met for drinks.

"Why?" Mike cocked his head to the side.

"Because Chris knew better. He knew Sean was armed. Tony wasn't. Chris shouldn't have left Tony alone when all he had was pepper spray."

"It's not Chris's fault," Mike said thoughtfully. "The police ruled it a clean shoot, so he didn't do anything wrong. Chris is a good bounty hunter. He was put in a tough spot. Tony could be reckless and was inexperienced. There wasn't time to train him properly. I warned everybody somebody was going to get killed."

Tony's funeral passed and a fund-raising event for his wife and children was planned. Tony had died without any insurance or benefits.

The memorial was held at the same lounge at which Mike had been shot as a police officer. Mike had maintained a friendship with the owners and they said they were honored to host the event. Tony's widow was grateful for the benefit, but her loss was enormous.

Mark, Chris, Pam and Mike were all there. It was good to have the old crew back together for the day. This was an occasion that required ignoring personal differences. This was for Tony's family.

It was a sunny evening and the turnout was incredible. The parking lot had been fenced off and the owners supplied a band, a dunk tank and several other activities for the guests. Beer was flowing and everybody was having a good time. Mike, Chris and Pam stood together watching the festivities and the feeling of shared camaraderie between them strengthened again.

"Mike," Chris leaned toward his friend. "You know I need a partner. I cannot work with those other knot heads. Would you consider coming back?"

"Please, Mike," Pam chimed in. "Chris and I both need you."

"Will Arnie let me come back? After all, I did quit," Mike said tentatively.

Pam smiled, "I'm sure Arnie will be happy about it."

And he was. So, that was it. Chris and Mike hit the streets together again.

A couple of weeks went by and Chris was getting back to his old self. Mike soon got a call from Mark. He was picking up some cases for a couple of different bail bond companies and wanted some help.

At about the same time, Pam gave Chris and Mike a case involving a heroin-addicted hooker with felony warrants. They talked to every contact they could think of. Finally they got a break and learned of an apartment complex where she was hanging around. Mike and Chris located her van parked outside the activity center at the apartments. They walked into the swimming pool area and there she sat. She was in the community swimming pool rinsing out a huge open lesion on her left forearm. The wound, about four inches long and about an inch and a half wide, was disgusting. It was on the top of her forearm and had been caused by shooting way too much heroin in the same area. It was so bad they could actually see the muscle tissue and what looked like tendons in her flesh. Mike and Chris yarded her out of the pool, got her dressed, wrapped her arm in a clean towel and had her put a coat on. Then they hauled her to jail and booked her.

The jailer called the bond company about a half hour after Mike and Chris had booked the hooker. He was highly agitated. Sometimes jailers like to pick and chose whom they accept. Jailers do not like to book people with existing medical issues and understandably so. It takes more time, expense and effort to deal with these people and a lot of jails are severely understaffed to begin with. But the judge had ordered Mike and Chris to bring the fugitive back into the system or pay the outstanding bond. Mike and Chris had no choice and the courts do not accept any excuses from the bail bond company. They must produce the defendant or pay the amount of the bond.

The next day Pam dropped another felony case on Mike's desk.

He got hold of Chris. "Let's hit it, Chris. This guy should be a piece of cake. He's got felony warrants, but we already have tracked him to his grandmother's house. The guy can't hold down a job, so I think he will be at home. You and I can handle this one."

Mike and Chris approached the grandmother's house with the usual caution, parking down the block and walking the rest of the way. As they started up the sidewalk to the front door, a large brown dog started yapping. As the pooch was sounding off, a man peered out the window and saw Mike and Chris. The drapes closed and the deadbolt clicked on the front door. Mike pounded on the door announcing himself and Chris, telling the guy inside to give it up. The suspect started yelling excuses.

"I was going to turn myself in today," he first proclaimed.

Next, he pleaded, "I can't go to jail now; my grandma is sick and I need to watch her."

"Nobody told me I had a court date," he concluded.

Mike was thinking: *What's his next excuse going to be, his hemorrhoids are flaring and his ulcers are kicking up?*

"Whatever, dude, but make no mistake: We're coming through the door whether you open it or not."

The next thing they heard was sounds of the guy running toward the back of the house. They ran around back through the yard just in time to see the fugitive enter a garage and slam the door.

Chris immediately tried kicking the door in but it was a solid-core door on a heavy frame. The door wouldn't budge. As Mike was running around to the back of the building, the suspect jumped out a side window. Chris heard him escape and yelled to Mike, "He's heading for the front!" and the chase was on.

Mike ran through the yard and saw Chris chasing the guy down the street. Mike joined in, following behind Chris. Suddenly Mike saw Chris go down. He fell to the shoulder of the road. Just as Mike was catching up to him, he saw the suspect duck into a house a couple of doors down.

Reaching Chris, Mike asked, "What's wrong? Quit being a pussy and let's get this guy."

Then Mike realized that Chris was hurt.

"Chris, are you okay? What happened?"

"Did you hear that loud pop?" Chris asked.

"I didn't hear anything."

"It was my ankle!" Chris responded. "I thought I got shot in the back. Then I heard a loud pop and hit the ground hard. I think I broke it; I can't get up."

"Okay, I'll get medical on the way."

Mike stayed with Chris until help arrived. Soon they heard the sirens coming. The fire department arrived as did an ambulance and rescue rig. When Chris was in good hands, Mike ran toward the house the suspect had disappeared into. He wasn't sure whether the fugitive had gone inside or was hiding somewhere on the outside of the house. Mike milled around the gathering crowd of neighbors. It wasn't long before the suspect emerged. He must have been thinking that he might slip away during all the commotion. He didn't see Mike coming until Mike threw the cuffs on him.

After booking the guy into jail, Mike went to the emergency room to check on Chris.

"How ya doing, buddy?"

"Not so good, Mike. They're telling me I trashed my ankle. They think I tore all the ligaments, tendons and that kind of stuff. The doctor says I'm a pretty big guy and I may never be able to run again. He says my bounty hunting days are probably over. This really sucks."

And sucked it did. Chris had to pull the plug. Now it would be just Mike and Mark when he could join in.

The only reason Mike had come back to Arnie's was to help Chris and still be able to work with Pam. So Mike talked to Mark. He was working for a couple of different bail bond outfits and was getting pretty busy.

"Do you have enough to keep both of us busy?" Mike asked Mark.

"I sure do. Why do you ask?"

"I don't want to work at Arnie's with Chris gone. I think I'm going to call it quits with the bounty hunting business. That is, unless you need the help."

Mark nodded. "Let's work together whenever we can. We know we can trust each other."

Mike nodded. "I'm going to quit Arnie's today."

Returning to the office, Mike pulled Pam aside and told her his decision.

"I've told you before that I don't *have* to work. I work because I want to. I don't want to work where I always have to watch my back and without Chris here I'll have to. If you ever want to leave Arnie's, call me or Mark. I think we could find another bond company that would love to scoop you up."

With both Mike and Chris gone, Pam disliked work. Now when she had to get up in the morning to go to the office, her stomach twisted in knots. For the first time ever, she thought seriously about leaving her job at Arnie's.

Mike knew Pam was unhappy and suggested she apply for a position at one of the companies where he was working. He was partnering with Mark and picking up skips for several different companies. He was sure Pam wouldn't have any trouble finding another job.

Pam was tempted, but she wasn't sure she wanted to leave. She told herself: *Arnie needs me.*

Chapter 27

Liar, Liar

Pam was having a drink at the bar several nights later when a defense attorney she knew walked over, drink in hand, and sat down at her table. He told Pam he'd heard about Tony and offered his condolences. Pam looked down and nodded her head. After some small talk, he told Pam he had it on good authority that Sean Brown had pled not guilty and was planning on claiming self-defense. Before she could ask him any questions, he said he had to go, finished his drink and left.

"How can he claim self-defense?" Pam asked Mike. "Tony wasn't armed; Sean was."

"You know how those guys are—they'll say anything." Mike sipped his drink. "That doesn't mean he can prove it. Juries aren't dumb. They can usually figure it out."

"He can't get away with it," Pam whispered.

"No, he can't," Mike's eyes narrowed. "If Brown walks, that'll give license to every criminal on the street to take potshots at bounty hunters and get away with it. We'll all be fair game. That *can't* happen."

"I know."

Not long after, Brown's attorney contacted Pam. He spent hours asking her questions. Pam told the truth: She'd ordered Tony off the case. He chased Brown anyway. Then he was shot.

"What did you do after you found out Tony was shot?" the attorney asked.

"I called Mike," Pam answered truthfully.

"Was he with Mark?"

"I think he was with Mark. I'm not sure."

"That's all I wanted to know." He thanked Pam for her time and left.

Chris had been out of state going to commercial diver's school. His ankle had healed up and he was feeling good. He was back in town, because Sean Brown's trial for shooting Tony was about to begin.

This was hitting Chris hard. All those memories were dragged back. Mike hated to see that sadness back on his friend's face.

Chris was going through the motions trying to get through it all when he called Mike.

"Mike!" Chris shouted excitedly. "You're never going to believe this!"

Immediately Mike thought that Brown had pleaded guilty to some lesser charge for a ridiculously small sentence.

"I didn't do it, Mike! I didn't do it!"

"Do what, Chris?"

"I didn't shoot Tony! I just left the prosecutor's office. I was asking him how to handle the testimony about my round being the one that killed Tony. I didn't want that jerk to get away with it because some defense attorney would say that I killed Tony, not Brown. That's when the prosecutor said, 'Oh, nobody told you? We matched that round to Brown's gun a long time ago.' Unbelievable, Mike, that the police nor district attorney's office never told me of this development in the case. They let me carry this burden around for almost two years. I'm so pissed off, but I'm so happy at the same time. I'm running around the room hooting and hollering."

Mike jumped up from his chair. "Outstanding, Chris. I'm so happy for you. Now let's make sure Brown is found guilty."

Finally came the day of the trial. Pam was called as a witness to testify, she assumed it was due to the fact that she had been Tony's boss.

While waiting to testify, she saw Joey being escorted by a guard through the waiting room into the courtroom.

Why is he here? Pam thought to herself, confused. *Joey didn't have anything to do with this.*

When she was called into the courtroom, she testified to all she knew. Just when she thought she was about finished, the defense attorney asked Pam a final question: "Who did you call after you learned Tony had been shot?"

"Mike."

"Was he with Mark?"

"I think so. I don't really know."

"Thank you."

Since there were no further questions, Pam was dismissed.

They all waited anxiously for the verdict. They felt Sean Brown was guilty of murder and, for Tony's sake, *had* to be convicted.

Hours later, Mike called Pam. He had been at the closing arguments. "Sean Brown walked," he said somberly. "It just came over the news."

Mike told Pam he and Mark were standing outside the jail when Sean walked out—a free man.

Pam couldn't understand it. *How could Sean claim self-defense when Tony was unarmed? How could the jury believe his story? How could they be so gullible that he literally got away with murder?*

Chris and Mike talked after the trial. They were understandably upset.

"Justice might be blind, but it shouldn't be lazy. Damn it. What are your plans now, Chris?"

"I'm going to head back to dive school and see where that takes me."

"Good, sounds like a good opportunity. How's your ankle doing?"

"It's doing real well. I've worked hard rehabilitating it and it's pretty much back to normal as far as I'm concerned."

"I'm glad to hear that things are going well for you, but I would like you to do me a favor."

"What's that?"

"See if you can keep your options open for some time. Mark has gotten tied into a nationwide bail bond company. These guys are offering big bucks to their bounty hunters. Mark is already in with them and he's bringing me along. It sounds like this company is going to get very busy and we will probably need some help."

"I don't know, Mike. After all of this with Tony and all, I just don't know."

"Chris, you might be able to bullshit yourself, but not your old partner. Just talking about it, I can see the look in your eyes. Trust me buddy, you are what you are and you're not ready to give it up yet. We'll be in touch."

It took quite awhile to fit all the pieces together.

According to the court docket, Sean testified that he knew the bounty hunters were chasing him. They searched a house in which he'd been hiding and though they didn't discover him that day, he said he heard the bounty hunters say when they found him they were going to kill him.

Afraid for his life, he kept moving from place to place. He called his girlfriend and asked her to bring him his gun. She testified she brought it to him.

When Tony opened the closet door where Sean was hiding, Sean claimed Tony had a gun. When Sean saw the weapon, he opened fire.

"Tony was unarmed," Chris testified. "Tony had been convicted of a weapons charge and, as a convicted felon, couldn't carry a gun. All he had was a small black can of pepper spray."

According to the police, when they arrived at the scene and searched the house, there was no weapon. They hadn't found one on the floor or on the grounds.

"Wouldn't it make sense to you that if Tony had a gun, after he'd been shot it would be lying on the floor next to him?" Chris asked. "I know, because I was there. Tony *did not* have a gun!"

Joey got on the witness stand and testified that after Tony was shot, Chris called him on his cell phone. Chris asked him to come to the scene and remove Tony's weapon. When he refused, Joey testified that Chris then called Mike and Mark—who did.

That didn't make sense to Pam. Joey hadn't been anywhere around during the shooting. He'd been fired years before. She felt even if he was around, Chris wouldn't have called him; he didn't like Joey and certainly wouldn't have had his cell phone number. Chris wouldn't have done that anyway. He was a moral man who did everything by the book. In her opinion, even if they had been called, Mike and Mark wouldn't have disposed of the weapon either. That would have gone against their natures. Even if asked, they *wouldn't* have disposed of evidence used in a crime.

Another element that wasn't discussed at the trial was the all-important time frame. According to Chris's testimony, the police arrived at the scene within fifteen to twenty minutes of the 911 call. That wouldn't have given Mike and Mark enough time to drive across town (assuming they were in town), remove Tony's weapon and dispose of it before the police arrived.

Mike complained to Pam bitterly a few days later. "When we were interviewed, we both told the prosecutor we were nowhere near the scene. I was at a bar with some friends and Mark had been truck driving that day. I had plenty of witnesses who could have testified to my whereabouts and Mark's hours were clearly stated on a company time card. Had that been brought into evidence—as it should have— Brown's plea of self-defense wouldn't have held up in court."

In their opinions, Joey's story was outrageous and didn't square with the real truth about what happened to Tony. In addition, the prosecution hadn't followed up on Mike's evidence, the end result was the jury believed that Tony had a gun on him, that it had been removed from the scene by Mike and Mark and that Brown had killed Tony in self-defense.

The "not guilty" verdict shook Pam's faith in the justice system. She always believed that the truth would come out—the innocent would be found innocent, the guilty would be punished. Now Pam knew that wasn't always true.

The real truth was that sometimes Lady Justice *is* blind.

Chapter 28

Opening and Shutting Doors

Mark was picking up a lot of cases for a lot of different companies and Mike was joining him on some. Not all cases were hair-raising dances with the devil. Bounty hunting is a lot like police work: You have a lot of routine days and you can go months without anything exciting happening. In fact, sometimes the more interesting cases have no excitement at all; they are just different in circumstance.

Mark got a case from one bail company that was only a $500 bond. It was some twenty-year-old guy with a warrant for a suspended driver's license. The owner of the company found out that the kid moved back home with his parents in San Francisco. So far, so good. The owner called the kid's father, who also happened to be the one on the bail bond contract for his son. Once the owner got the father on the line and explained the situation to him, things went downhill. The father told the owner that he was not going to pay for the bail bond and he was not going to send his son back to Washington to take care of a traffic charge. Further, he told the owner that he had checked with his attorney and found out that the warrant was not extraditable from out of state.

The owner of the bail company was so beside himself, Mark and Mike thought he was going to stroke out. The bondsman yelled, "I'm renting a car and you guys are going to go to Frisco to pick this little bastard up! Don't come back without him. I don't care what it costs or how long it takes!"

"Boss," Mark said, "it's only $500."

"I don't care! I want him! When can you leave?"

Mark and Mike looked at each other and shrugged. "Is tomorrow morning okay?"

"Do it!" he yelled.

They grabbed a rental car the next morning and headed for San Francisco. They drove straight through the day, stopping only for burgers, coffee and pit stops. As soon as they got into town they located the parents' house. Nobody was home at the time so they sat across the street and waited. After three hours the family came home and they had their son with them. Mike and Mark knocked at the door, the fugitive answered and Mike grabbed him. The father tried to come to his son's rescue. They were causing quite a ruckus, so Mark had to give them a little taste of pepper spray to help him make an exit.

Mark and Mike stuffed the kid into the car and headed back up north. Just on the California side of the Oregon border, they informed the guy that this would be his last bathroom break for a few hours. The problem was Oregon does not recognize bail bond agents or bounty hunters. Oregon is one of a few states that will actually arrest the good guys if bounty hunters try to arrest a criminal. As stupid as that sounds, it's a fact of life. Mike and Mark weren't sure what Oregon would do to them for simply transporting a fugitive through the state, but they didn't want to find out. Any state that is comfortable with arresting someone who is following court orders from another jurisdiction and willing to charge them with felony kidnapping is a state that is not to be trusted—at least that's Mike's opinion.

They got the fugitive back to Tacoma, booked him into jail and took the next day off. They had spent twenty-nine hours in the car, but got the job done. The owner was happy. Mark and Mike were happy. However, the father was quite angry.

Mark had established contacts with a large bail bond outfit that was spreading out all over the country. The company was going to open up in Washington and Mark was its go-to guy in the state. It sounded like the big time for a couple of bounty hunters: salaried positions with substantial pay and other benefits.

Meanwhile, Pam was becoming increasingly unhappy working at Arnie's. Even though she still adored Arnie, she questioned some of the decisions being made and felt the new supervisor Arnie had hired didn't have the knowledge or people skills to run the office efficiently.

For several days there had been a lot of whispering in the forfeiture room. Whenever Pam walked in, suddenly the talking stopped. She knew something was up, but she didn't know what. And that bothered her.

Pam soon found out.

His name was Guy. He had been a regular of Pam's for the past several years. His dad always came in and bailed him. He was often arrested for some pretty heavy stuff—drug possession, unlawful possession with the intent to deliver, gun possession. But for some reason, he was never convicted. He always managed to walk.

One morning Pam received a telephone call from Guy. He was in jail.

"Why am I here?" Guy shouted. "Why did you pick me up?"

"What are you talking about? I didn't pick you up."

"Yes, you did," he insisted. "Last night I was in bed sleeping when your supervisor barged in with some guy and handcuffed me. He took me to jail."

"What?"

"So what the hell?" Guy yelled. "What the hell do you think you're doing? I haven't missed court."

"I don't know anything about it," Pam said honestly. "I'm the one who dispatches the bounty hunters. I didn't order your arrest."

"Then get me out. I shouldn't be here."

Pam immediately confronted her supervisor.

"Yeah, I went and got him. So what?"

Pam paced around the room. "Did he miss court?"

"No."

"Then why did you arrest him?"

"Because I wanted to! Pam, you're not the boss. *I* am! I can do any goddamned thing I want to. I don't have to answer to you. Why don't you mind your own business?"

"Whom you arrest and whom you don't *is* my business," Pam shouted back. "You can't arrest somebody just because you feel like it. It's unethical to pick someone up because the person owes us money or you felt like it. The only ethical reason to pick people up is because they threaten not to go to court or they've already missed. Linda taught me that."

"Linda's dead. She's not in charge anymore. *I* am. Seems to me you have a real problem with that."

"I do! You're not the one who has to go into court and explain to the judge why we arrested someone when he doesn't have a warrant and didn't miss court. How am I going to explain it to the judge?"

"I don't give a damn what you say. Just tell him we wanted off the bond. Period. That's all you have to say."

"I'm not doing it. You go into court and explain it to the judge. I'm *not* doing it." Pam stormed out of the room.

When the phone rang again, Pam knew it was Guy. She didn't know what to tell him. She couldn't justify her supervisor's actions. Guy shouldn't have been picked up and returned to custody. He hadn't done anything wrong.

The phone kept ringing and ringing. Pam reached out to answer it, but she couldn't force herself to pick up the receiver.

"That's it!" Pam shouted.

Impulsively, she reached out her arm and pushed all the files she had on her desk to the floor. Loose papers flew everywhere.

"You can take this job and shove it!" Pam said to no one in particular. "I quit!"

Pam slammed the front door so hard, the front window rattled when she walked out.

Chapter 29

Nirvana

B ounty Hunters in the area had never seen anything like it. Mark's contacts with a large nationwide outfit called Donovan's Bail Bonds paid off big time. Mark had negotiated a nice monthly salary for himself with bonuses for every case closed and mileage expenses for his vehicle. He had also insisted that Mike be brought on as his partner and receive the same pay and benefits that he did. The company agreed to everything.

Periodically, the company picked certain employees from offices all over the country and flew them to Las Vegas to shoot in competitive three gun tactical matches. The company supplied all the ammo and some top notch weapons. It was Donovan's way of encouraging agents throughout his company to get to know one another.

Often when Mark and Mike were out working, they got a call, "We're partying in Frisco this weekend; we expect to see you here" or "Get down to Vegas tomorrow; we're meeting the guys from Jersey."

In the bail bond world, they had hit the big time. As bounty hunters, they couldn't ask for more.

Donovan's was just getting into Washington.The company's plan was to enter a new market, bail everyone out cheaper than the next guy and run the competition out of town. With this business philosophy, the cases started to pile up fast and they needed more help.

Chris had graduated from dive school and was enjoying a new career in commercial diving. One phone call and Chris was sitting at a desk at Donovan's, a pile of files in front of him.

"Chris!" Mike chuckled.

"Yeah, Mike."

"I thought you were done with this crap."

Chris slowly looked up from the case he was working on. "Asshole!" he said then calmly went back to work, smiling as he continued reading his case.

Mark, Chris and Mike were back together and working hard. They were clearing at least fifty cases or more a month. The work was becoming routine again. The three of them had worked together for so long that they made it look easy. For every one hundred arrests they made, Mike bet they didn't have to wrestle with more than one person, if that.

The only close call came from a guy they were going to pick up in an apartment. This pinhead had locked himself inside and wasn't coming out. Mark and Chris went around to the sliding glass door in the back while Mike pounded on the front door. The boys were prying at the slider when suddenly the entire piece of glass popped out and fell inside on the floor in one piece. They made entry and let Mike in through the front. They started searching the apartment. Mike checked the front hallway and Chris, the living room. Mark started clearing one of the bedrooms and found the guy. He dragged the suspect into the hallway and was bent over cuffing him when another guy in a different bedroom came out with a baseball bat. Mark, being preoccupied, never noticed the second guy. Chris spotted the attacker just as he was about to swing the bat down on Mark's head. Chris pulled his gun out and shoved it into the attacker's face yelling, "Freeze!" Mike heard the commotion and swung around the corner of the hallway, aiming his gun at the guy's head. As soon as the guy with the baseball bat saw what was about to happen to him, he made the right decision and gave up. Chris had almost capped the guy. He had pulled his trigger halfway down and if the idiot hadn't dropped the bat, he would be a dead man today.

The guy with the bat didn't have any warrants. They arrested their defendant, scared the shit out of the roommate and left.

These cases were rare, but technology was speeding along and they were developing some databases that were making life easier. Mike was especially enjoying some of the new resources.

One fugitive skipped out of Seattle and fled to Texas. Mike heard he might be somewhere in the Dallas/Fort Worth area. He also knew that the fugitive was calling his girlfriend on a regular basis and he was more than likely staying at a motel. At one point, the fugitive had mentioned that he thought bounty hunters and bail bond companies were jokes and they would never find him. This guy didn't heed a major lesson: Never piss off your bail bond agent. Searching some of the new records that were available to him, Mike was able to get the physical location of a phone booth the fugitive always called from.

Not wanting to take the time or expense to go to Texas, Mike got in touch with a fugitive task force working the area. They looked for about two weeks, but didn't have any luck finding him. Mike's company wanted the case solved and Mike had a gut feeling about finding the fugitive. Mark backed Mike's idea and the company agreed to the trip. Mike and Mark caught the redeye to Dallas and arrived around 3 A.M. They rented a car at the airport, bought a map and found their way to the booth. Once there, they noted that there were several motels along that street. They also noticed that the phone booth was right next to a freeway overpass. The overpass was like a natural barrier with one lone motel on the other side of it.

"Let's try it," Mike said. They woke up the motel manager and showed him a picture of the fugitive.

"Oh sure," the manager said, "That guy is in room eight. He drives the white car that's parked there."

How sweet was this? They hadn't been in town for an hour and they'd located their guy. One problem though. They were from out of state, it was the middle of the night and nobody there knew them. Mike thought they'd better wait and make contact with the task force to avoid problems.

They got a motel room and a couple hours of sleep then made their calls.

The task force met them close to the motel. They contacted motel management and made entry into the room. The bad guy wasn't home and his car was not there. The task force guys had other things to do than hang around with a couple of bounty hunters all day. So with a "Good luck, call us if you need us," they left.

Mark and Mike watched the motel until 5 o'clock that evening, waiting for the guy to come home. Finally the fugitive drove his car into the parking lot. They watched as he parked the car and went into his room. Mike made a call to the task force and they replied they were on the way. They geared up with vests and weapons about a block away and came up with an entry plan.

Mark and Mike stayed in the parking lot while the task force agents did their thing. They hit the room and the defendant put up a short fight. When the task force had the fugitive lying on his stomach on the sidewalk in front of his room, Mike and Mark walked up and introduced themselves, letting the fugitive know that it was the dumb bounty hunters he had criticized who found him.

The cops took custody of the fugitive and he was later extradited back to Seattle. Mike and Mark drove to the airport and caught the next flight back. They felt pretty good. Their trip took less than twenty-four hours and their case was solved.

After Pam left Arnie's, she called Mike. She needed a friend to talk to, someone who knew her, someone who would understand. Mike was sympathetic. He knew what the problems were. That's why he'd left.

"Mark and I are just going to lunch," he said calmly. "Why don't you meet us? We'll talk. It'll be okay."

"I don't know...," Pam said.

"Come on. I'll even spring for lunch."

"Okay. I'll be there in fifteen minutes."

When Pam walked in, Mark and Mike were already seated at a table in the small delicatessen.

"So what happened?" Mark asked, interested.

Pam told him about Guy—the illegal arrest and how she walked out in frustration.

"Don't worry about it." Mike put his hand on Pam's shoulder. "You did what you had to do."

"I guess," Pam said slowly. "Actually, I don't know what I'm doing. I must be crazy! I have rent and bills and here I walk out on my job. How am I going to pay my rent now? I can't get unemployment, because I quit."

"You'll come work with us," Mark smiled. "I just got hooked up with Donovan's, a nationwide bail bond company. Because every state has different rules and regulations with regard to bail bonds, they're looking for an office manager who doesn't need any training. They want someone local who knows the business inside and out. You'd be perfect for the job. I don't know anyone more experienced or better than you."

"I don't know if I want to be a bail bond agent or not—especially after Tony." Pam looked at Mark. "But after all these years, I don't know how to do anything else."

"Come with us to the office right after lunch and we'll introduce you. You're just what they need," Mike said soothingly.

Donovan's was much larger than any bonding office Pam had ever seen. It was airy and clean with large picture windows that let in all the light, unlike the small offices at Arnie's. Pam was impressed.

Mark brought Pam over to Frank, a man in his mid-thirties dressed immaculately in a dark blue three-piece suit. He outlined the position.

They had just opened this office and the office manager, whom Frank said was doing a good job, was leaving. Unfortunately the office was losing money on a regular basis. What they were looking for was an experienced office manager—someone who would come in, evaluate and change whatever needed to be changed to turn the office into a profitable one.

When he mentioned the salary, Pam's eyes opened wide. Never in her wildest dreams did she think she'd ever make that kind of money. When Frank also mentioned she'd have medical, dental, two weeks paid vacation *and* a 401K, Pam was totally amazed.

No bail bond company to her knowledge offered any kind of paid vacation and/or sick leave. Bail bond companies don't have unions. Most experienced bond agents like Pam work incredibly long hours for years and often for minimum wage.

Pam thanked Frank and told him she needed to think about it. He thanked her for coming and told her to make up her mind soon. They were in desperate need of an office manager. He'd have to fill the position right away.

"Go for it!" Mike encouraged Pam. "If you turn that down, you're crazy!"

"I know you're right. I'm just worried."

"About what?"

"I don't know who these other guys are. Maybe they're dirty, too."

"Do you think Mark and I would work for somebody like that? No! With us there already, you can't lose."

"Okay. I'll do it. I'll call Frank and let him know right away."

Mike could tell Pam was ecstatic; she would finally get the pay and respect she deserved. Mike wished Pam had her own business and they both worked together there, but this was the next best thing. At least, that's what he thought then.

When Pam walked into Donovan's to begin working her first day, Mark brought her into his office. Frank quickly joined them, closing the door after himself.

"There's been a slight change in plans," Frank said. "Don't worry. You still have a job. It's just that we have a situation. See, the other manager was supposed to be gone by now. But his new job doesn't start for another week or so. He asked if he could stay a while longer.

He's been with us a long time and the owner, Donovan, agreed. So, I don't want you to introduce yourself as the new office manager. Not yet, at any rate. Go ahead and start working as a bond agent. While we're waiting for him to leave, check out the crew. See if they're doing their jobs. If not, you might not want to keep them. Just let me know what you find and we'll go from there."

After Pam met the crew, she liked them all right away. She inherited three male bond agents. All of them were young and wearing suits. All were cordial to Pam and welcomed her aboard.

Two weeks came and went. Pam was alarmed to find the previous manager still there. He was still doing all the scheduling and the appearances in court that were necessary. She wondered if she had been promised an office manager position only to work as just another bond agent.

One day, Pam walked into the office to hear the other manager protesting—loudly. He had just been fired. He walked around the office telling everyone who'd listen that it was bullshit. He'd grown up with Donovan and Frank—the three of them had been friends for years. He'd worked for Donovan before when he owned a different company. He couldn't believe Donovan or Frank would do this to him.

As he gathered up his things, he told Pam and the other bond agents, "You all need to watch your backs. Donovan and Frank can't be trusted." He slammed the front door hard when he walked out.

"Don't mind him," Frank reassured Pam. "His new job fell through and he just assumed he could still work for us. That wasn't possible, as we'd already hired you. So we had no choice. We had to let him go."

Frank informed Pam that Donovan's main office was located in the East. Donovan would be flying out within the next few days to check out their office and to meet her, the new office manager.

Soon Pam was working around the clock. The filing system was a nightmare. She created new forms to comply with state law, organized files, redistributed job duties, created office policy and revamped the scheduling. By the time Donovan was due to arrive, the office had been newly reorganized.

Donovan, an attractive man in his early forties, wore a custom-made three-piece suit. He stood up very straight, giving the impression that he was a very important man, too busy to deal with any sort of trivialities. He had a certain presence—an air of importance about him.

Frank introduced Pam to Donovan's entourage—the corporate attorney, the corporate accountant and Donovan's personal secretary, who walked directly behind him with a notebook in hand, listening to his every word and frantically taking notes. Donovan talked so fast and walked so briskly, they all had a hard time keeping up.

After he toured the office, they sat at the conference table and Pam briefly outlined her plan to increase production. "Sounds good," Donovan nodded. "How much money do you need?"

"Not much," Pam said. "Five hundred ought to do it."

"Write her a check," he instructed his accountant. "Make it for a thousand just in case she needs a little extra. Okay." Donovan stood up. "Everything looks good here. Let's go."

Frank told Pam that Donovan had sent him to Washington only long enough to secure a replacement for the office manager. Since Frank lived back East and worked in Donovan's main office, he'd be flying back with Donovan in the morning.

"I'll call you," Frank whispered. "By the way, the office looks great. Good job."

After Pam got to know him better, she had to admit Donovan was brilliant. He'd thought of a way to double production in half the time. Due to his innovation, which he practiced in all his offices, he was making a great deal of money. Mark told Pam that Donovan was a millionaire several times over. Rather than be content with that, his goal was to dominate the industry. He planned on owning and operating the largest chain of bail bond companies in the nation. And with offices in forty-two states when Pam was hired, he was well on his way.

The only problem was Donovan was hyperactive and impatient. He didn't sleep more than three to four hours a day and he didn't like to wait for results. He wanted them immediately. He called Pam at all hours of the day and night. He thought of something he wanted to tell her, picked up the phone and dialed. It didn't matter if it was 9 A.M. or 3 A.M. Pam quickly learned to have pen and paper handy, because the first words out of his mouth were always, "Write this down."

Frank and Pam planned their strategy—how Donovan's was going to be the largest bail bond company in the state.

She knew that wasn't going to be easy. Arnie's was still the king-pin. Toppling him off his throne wouldn't be easy. However, Frank assured Pam that if she listened to his advice and they planned care-fully, it could be done.

Pam's regular clients were calling around looking for her. Soon they found her at Donovan's. The phones were ringing. Bonds were being written. Production was going up.

Frank wanted Pam to hire more people. He said Pam needed "bod-ies" to answer the phones. If the phones weren't being answered, bonds wouldn't be written and they wouldn't grow like Donovan wanted them to.

Pam didn't know any bond agents she wanted to hire; they were either already working or corrupt. She suggested that she put an advertisement in the paper.

"No," Frank said firmly. "Don't you have any friends or relatives you can hire? Someone you can train?"

"What?" Pam asked surprised. "You want me to hire friends and family? The other companies don't do that. They don't want family working together."

"I don't care about what other companies do," Frank said. "Donovan and I have relatives here. He wants a family-oriented busi-ness. As long as they can do the job, that is. So why don't you check around and see if there's somebody you know. You might be sur-prised."

After Pam talked it over with some family and friends, a few agreed to begin training as bond agents. With a full staff, the phones began ringing around the clock. Production doubled—then tripled.

Within a year of Pam's hire, Donovan's had become the largest bail bond company in the state with sales of over two million dollars a month.

Pam was promoted from office manager to state manager with an impressive increase in salary. She opened two branch offices that she directly supervised with forty-one employees scattered across the state. She flew across the country several times to visit Donovan's out-of-state offices and confer with other state managers. She attended nationwide bail bond conventions and attended meetings at the state bail bond association. She was totally, thoroughly exhausted from working around the clock. But when Donovan's skyrocketed, all the effort was worth it.

For the first time ever, she was making great money. Since she'd always been poor, she spent it wildly. She bought new furniture, rented one of the houses Mike owned instead of an apartment, spent hundreds promoting the company by buying all the bar patrons a round or two on her tab and gave away a lot to family and friends.

When Donovan sent her a plane ticket and invitation to attend an annual award ceremony held for all his employees at his main office in the East, she was thrilled. She bought an expensive cocktail dress just for the occasion.

At the ceremony, Pam's name was unexpectedly called to receive an award from the company. When she stood up in front of hundreds of people—all employees of Donovan's and all from different states across the United States—to receive the award, thanking her for her "outstanding contribution and dedication to the company," she was so overwhelmed that she cried.

After years and years of long hours, low salary, the constant struggle to stay clean instead of the much easier dirty road, constantly fighting the corruption both inside and outside the industry and the male chauvinism that was so prevalent in the business, she thought this was her reward.

This was it.

She'd found nirvana.

Chapter 30

Buried in the Woods

Most bonding companies have a policy that once a defendant is arrested, if he or she has a good reason for missing court, the bounty hunters can bring the defendant into the office before taking the fugitive to jail. After hearing the reason, if management thinks it is good enough, the agents ask the hunters to release the defendant with the understanding a new court date will immediately be set and payments will begin on the bounty hunter fees.

It never ceased to amaze Pam and Mike how tough macho guys, talking tough on the street, cried like babies when the guys brought them in. They cried, they whined, they begged, they pleaded. Mike, Mark and Pam have been offered sexual favors, drugs, cash and cars—if only they'd let the fugitives go—all of which they turned down. In all these years, Pam heard only one or two excuses that were good enough to let the fugitives go. Pam felt there was no excuse to justify running. Scared or not, innocent or guilty, if she bailed them, they *had* to go to court. That was the deal.

So Pam was surprised when Mike and Mark brought Betsy into her office. Donovan's had the policy that once bounty hunters were dispatched, defendants were to be taken directly to jail. Most of their excuses were feeble: The court never sent a date; they never received a notice in the mail; they forgot; they were sick; the car broke down; they were evicted and had to move. Pam thought she'd heard every excuse in the book—until she met Betsy.

When Mike and Mark brought her in, Pam raised her eyebrows. Looking directly at them, Pam silently questioned why Betsy was there. Mike sat the young woman down in the chair next to Pam then asked if he could speak to Pam privately for a moment. Mark stayed with Betsy as Mike and Pam walked into another room.

"You've got to hear this!" Mike said, animated. "Wait until you hear why she missed court."

"Mike, you know I don't want to hear that stuff. Why don't you just take her in? Man, I don't want to hear all her excuses. It's always the same anyway."

"Not this time. Trust me. You'll want to hear *this* from her directly."

"Okay, okay," Pam sighed.

When they re-entered the room, Betsy was calm and composed.

"So why did you miss court?" Pam asked.

"It's a long story...," she paused.

"I have time," Pam said in an attempt to sound patient.

"Okay," Betsy took a deep breath. "My boyfriend and I were methamphetamine addicts. When I first met him, I didn't do the stuff. But after a while, he talked me into it. Then we did it regularly. When I became involved with him, I didn't know he was part of a very large crew that cooked meth out in the woods. My boyfriend wasn't the cook; he just dealt the stuff to make a little money and have enough meth for the two of us."

Betsy said when she first started visiting the woods, it was all fun and games. They did a little meth, had roaring campfires and drank a few beers. "It was great." She smiled wistfully.

About a year after visiting the woods for the first time, Betsy and her boyfriend were there on a Friday night, as usual. Everything seemed okay. They were cooking meth and bagging it for distribution.

"Suddenly the leader of the crew appeared. I recognized him. I knew he was a bad one and I was instantly afraid."

Shouting some words she didn't understand, the guys grabbed her boyfriend, dragged him over to the campfire and quickly tied him up. The leader accused him of being a snitch.

"I was terrified." Betsy's eyes widened. "I'd heard about what happened to those accused of being snitches or stealing the dope. My boyfriend had told me they were tortured and murdered, their bodies buried deep within the woods; so far, they'd never been discovered. He was innocent!" She started to cry. "We'd never snitch. We'd never do that. We knew better."

Betsy told Pam how her boyfriend kept saying he didn't snitch. The leader and his crew hit, punched and kicked him. Betsy said she tried to defend him, but one of the guys told her to shut up or she'd be next. Frightened, she watched in silence.

"They kept kicking him over and over again." Betsy became hysterical. Her voice rose and she spoke faster. "They wouldn't stop! They dragged him into a chicken coop where I could hear him screaming. Then they brought him out, close to the campfire. The leader poured gasoline all over him and lit a match! Oh my God!" she screamed. "They killed him right in front of me! They *killed* him!"

Pam put her arm around Betsy's shoulder. For several minutes, the young woman sobbed so hard that she struggled to breathe.

After Betsy calmed down a bit, Pam asked how she escaped.

"I ran. While they were watching him burn, I ran into the woods and kept running. I could hear them searching for me and I was scared to death they were going to find me. But they didn't. I stayed in the woods all night and in the morning found my way out."

Pam interrupted her. "And you missed court because?"

"I couldn't go. The gang knew when I had court and I was afraid they'd be in the courthouse waiting for me. I couldn't go home. They know where I live, too. I've been moving from one place to another, staying with friends here and there. I know they're looking for me. I witnessed them murdering my boyfriend! They're not going to let me get away with that. They won't rest until they kill me, too!"

"Well, you're safe now. Nobody's going to get you here. Not with Mike and Mark around."

"That's good." Betsy wiped her eyes with the tissue Pam handed her. "It's not safe anywhere. I can't sleep; I can't eat. I keep seeing my boyfriend over and over again in my mind, hearing his screams . . . going up in flames."

"So, guys, what are we going to do now?" Pam looked at Mark.

"We're going to take her to a safe place," Mark said firmly.

"Where?"

"Never mind," Mike said. "We'll help her reschedule her court date then we'll take her to this place we know where they'll never find her. She'll be safe there."

"Okay."

Pam told Betsy she was so sorry Betsy had to go through that ordeal. Pam encouraged her to tell the police everything she had told Pam when she was ready. Those guys had gotten away with murder. She owed it to her boyfriend—and all the other victims—to tell the police everything she knew. They *had* to be stopped.

As Betsy stood up to go with the guys, Pam had one final question. "By the way, do you know the leader who did this?"

"Yes," she said softly.

"What's his name?"

"Eric is the older guy. But it's really not him who runs it. His son's in charge of the whole thing. He's the one who accused my boyfriend of being a snitch. He's the one who poured gasoline all over him and lit the match."

"And his name?" Pam prompted her.

She spoke over her shoulder as she walked out the front door: "Guy."

Guy was the one responsible for Betsy's boyfriend's death. The same man one of Pam's former co-workers had illegally arrested while he was sleeping; the one who called and demanded to know why he was in jail; the one whose case prompted Pam to quit Arnie's.

Guy had stood in front of Pam, almost shoulder to shoulder, for years. She knew his dad, Eric, too. Eric was soft-spoken and very quiet, a man of few words. He always signed for Guy and brought him over to the office immediately upon his release. When Betsy told Pam they were the ones running this huge meth operation, that they were the ones responsible for all the deaths out in the woods, she was astonished.

Pam wondered if her former supervisor knew what Guy had been doing, if that's why he'd arrested him even though Guy hadn't missed court.

Mike and Mark took Betsy to a safe house. They helped her arrange a new court date. They accompanied her to court then helped her get out of town. Mike assured Pam that she was safe. They'd covered their tracks so well, she'd never be found.

"Do you think she'll ever go to the cops and tell them what she knows?" Pam asked Mike.

"I don't think so. She's too terrified. She's too afraid that if she does, Guy and Eric will kill her too."

"Damn, these guys have to be stopped. They're killing people out in the woods. Somebody's got to know."

"Don't worry. I talked to a few people. They know all about Eric and Guy. It's only a matter of time before they're arrested."

"You really think so?"

"Yeah. Cops aren't stupid. I've heard they've been watching Eric and Guy for some time. They're just waiting for the right moment to catch them with the goods. Once the cops do, they'll be going away for a long time."

A few months later, Pam received a phone call. She didn't recognize the voice at first. It took her a minute to realize it was Guy.

Pam didn't want to talk to him. He was a cold-blooded murderer. While he was talking, a picture of the terrified Betsy came to Pam's mind.

Guy insisted Pam bail him out. Pam checked his bail and charges. He was in jail for UMCS—unlawful manufacture of a controlled substance—and UDCS—unlawful distribution of a controlled substance with intent to deliver—both felonies. His bail was $100,000.

"Have your dad come over and put up the house for collateral," Pam said. "Then I'll see what I can do."

"He's in jail with me," Guy replied.

"For what?"

"I don't know. The cops came to the house and arrested a bunch of us. I don't know what for."

Eric had the same charges with the same bail Pam learned after looking into it.

"I don't have anybody to sign for me," Guy whimpered. "Not with my dad in jail with me. Get me out. Just throw in a bond and I'll pay you the moment I'm out. I have some cash at home. I'll even pay you extra—I'll pay you double. As soon as I'm out, I'll bring it right over."

"Guy, you know I can't do that. I have to have a house for a bail that large to secure the hundred grand. Our fee is $10,000. I have to have that, too—up front."

"Get me out!" Guy demanded.

Pam hung up the phone.

A few moments later, the phone rang again. Even before Pam picked it up, she knew it was Guy. When the recording asked if she'd accept a collect call from Guy at the jail, Pam hung up the phone.

As a bail bond agent, it's Pam's duty to bail people out of jail. It's their constitutional right to be free on bail pending the outcomes of their court cases. However, it is also Pam's responsibility to protect the general public. If, in her opinion, someone could be injured by an inmate's release, then she wouldn't bail that person. Pam never said "no" exactly. She just made the defendants jump through so many hoops eventually they didn't want to use her. Ultimately, they'd call somebody else.

Guy called repeatedly for several days, but Pam didn't accept his calls. Finally the calls stopped.

When Pam checked a few weeks later, she learned Eric and Guy pled guilty to the charges and were sentenced to prison. Pam was just sorry they weren't charged with murder. The police must not have found the bodies buried in the woods.

Even though they weren't sentenced to life in prison, at least they were off the street for a long while. They couldn't hurt anybody else.

Pam was usually saddened when her clients went to prison, but not this time. As far as Pam was concerned, Guy and Eric were right where they *deserved* to be.

Chapter 31

Extra Hard to Find

One of the problems with some huge national companies is that there are a lot of people who, instead of pursuing excellence in their jobs, are dishonest, drug-addicted or corrupt. It can make for a hostile work environment. Pam was bound and determined to run a clean operation. She didn't tolerate any dirt—none.

When she caught a bond agent pocketing money and forging receipts, she fired him immediately.

One employee went out one night and broke into several cars, removing stereo equipment. His conscience got the better of him and he confessed before Pam discovered the stolen goods. Despite his confession, Pam fired him as well.

Another employee decided to take his lunch break outside in his car. It was parked right near the office's large picture window. An office worker reported the employee went outside, got in his car, placed a large mirror on the dashboard, pushed some powder around with a razor blade, picked up a straw and snorted the powder up his nose. Pam fired him the moment he walked back in the front door.

Connie, another employee, was young, enthusiastic and smart. Pam felt she was a real joy to work with. Whenever Pam walked by her, she always had some smart-ass comment that made Pam roar with laughter.

The firm had been looking for a large forfeiture that had, so far, escaped them. It was critical they find him and soon. The court was demanding a huge payment.

Mike and Mark looked for him everywhere without success.

One day, Pam was quietly working at her desk when Mike approached her. Clearing his throat, he said softly, "We got him."

"Terrific!" Pam yelled, jumping up from her desk and giving him a hug. "Where?"

"You'll never guess where." He didn't look happy.

"Tell me."

"Okay. At Connie's house."

"You found him at Connie's?"

"Yes," Mike confirmed somberly. "Someone gave us an address and when we checked it out, it was Connie's house. He was living there."

"You've got to be kidding me."

"I wish I were."

Now Pam had a decision to make. Certainly, since Connie entered all the forfeitures on the computer, she knew they were looking for him. She *had* to have known. So the real question remained: Why did she hide him?

When Pam asked Connie about it, she hung her head. She said she knew they were looking for him, but she was trying to come up with the money to get him a lawyer. "He can't go to jail now," Connie shook her head, tears running down her face.

It was one of the hardest things Pam ever had to do. No matter what the reason, the firm couldn't have employees hiding known fugitives. Pam quietly told Connie she was fired and to clean out her desk. She ignored Connie's tears as she walked away.

Then there was Danny.

During his job interview, Danny made a good impression on Pam. He was serious, smart and badly wanted to get into the bond business. He said one day he hoped to own an agency. After Pam hired him, he made several suggestions Pam immediately implemented. He was hard-working, ambitious and he volunteered for extra hours. Pam was impressed.

Then one afternoon, Mike asked to speak to Pam privately. That was unusual. Knowing it must be important, Pam stopped what she was doing and immediately walked into the back office. Mark followed them inside.

"What's up?" Pam asked.

Apparently, Mark and Mike had gone to arrest Shelly, a prostitute who'd missed court. They went to her house, found Shelly there, arrested her and were on the way to jail when she started talking. What she said surprised them both.

"She said she was checking in with one of our bond agents regularly. When she was bailed, the agent told her she had to call him every day just to check in. She said she was calling him daily and she didn't know she'd missed court. She talked to him this morning and he never said anything."

"That's weird." Pam frowned. "Sometimes when we're insecure on a bond, we have them call once a week just so we know they're still around. But every day? That's unusual."

"Yeah," Mark piped up. "And lately he's been calling her telling her she *has* to sleep with him or he'll personally take her back to jail."

"What? Who the hell did that?"

"You'll never guess," Mike shook his head.

"Tell me."

"Danny," both said in unison.

"Are you sure she's telling the truth?"

"She's in the van. We'll bring her inside so you can talk to her."

Shelly was trembling when she walked into Pam's office. Pam assured her she could tell the truth—the whole truth—without repercussions. Pam needed to know what was going on.

She related everything Mike and Mark had told Pam.

"How do I know he's harassing you? Do you have any proof?"

"I think so." Shelly opened her purse and pulled out an address book. Under the listing of the firm, she'd written Danny's home telephone number along with a comment that read "Call once a day. Important!!!"

Pam apologized to her. "We don't work that way. I'm sorry you had to go through this. The employee will be immediately fired."

Pam told Mike and Mark to return the woman to where they picked her up and let her go. Under the circumstances, she could contact Pam later and make another court date. Shelly was visibly relieved.

After Shelly left, Pam called Danny into her office and confronted him with the evidence. He didn't deny it.

"Why did you think you could get away with sexually harassing a client?"

He shrugged his shoulders.

"Do you have any defense to the allegations?"

He shook his head no.

When Pam told him he was fired, he merely nodded and walked out the door.

A few months later, Danny called the firm from jail and spoke to one of the other bond agents. He'd been arrested for drug possession and his bail was $5000. He said he hoped there were no hard feelings. They'd still bail him, wouldn't they, if he had a good cosigner? They did. The cosigner appeared, signed the paperwork and Danny was bailed.

A few days later, Pam opened up the mail and read the letter from the court: Danny had failed to appear. Pam turned the matter over to Mike. She was sure he and Mark would do whatever they thought was best.

A short while later, Mike walked into Pam's office and said, "You'll never believe what happened. Danny isn't living at the address he listed on the application; all the phone numbers are disconnected. And the cosigner took off. He's gone."

"You can't find the cosigner?"

"No, but we finally learned Danny might be staying with a friend, so we went over to that apartment. According to our source, it was an apartment complex and he lived upstairs in one of the units. Mark went around back while I went to the front. When I knocked on the front door, Mark saw Danny open the sliding glass door on the back porch. We thought we had him trapped. Mark was coming around the front to help me arrest him when he jumped off the second floor balcony and got away."

"What?"

"Don't worry. We'll get him. We won't let up until we do. Our informant said he broke his leg in the fall, but he hobbled away before we could reach him. We didn't expect him to jump. That was a long fall. He's lucky all he broke was a leg; he could have been killed. Do me a favor. Don't bail out any more bond agents. They know the game. They know all our tricks, the various ways we find them. They're extra hard to find but not impossible. We will find Danny and put him back in jail. But they're harder. And frankly, I'm getting older and I'm tired of working that hard."

Laughing, Pam agreed.

A few days later, Mike and Mark found Danny, arrested him and put him in jail—cast and all.

Chapter 32

Best Place to Hide

O n the traditional weekly get-together Friday nights, Pam, Mike and Mark went to a nearby bar with some of Pam's crew.

To promote his business, the owner had purchased black polo shirts with "Donovan's" written across the front and back that only the employees wore. Similar white cotton T-shirts were given out by the hundreds to clients.

Typically, looking around the room, Pam would see at least a dozen black polo shirts along with a similar amount of white T-shirts. Because so many employees frequented the place, Pam laughingly called it "our (Donovan's) bar."

On their night out a few weeks later, a group was meeting at the bar after work. Pam was running a little late, so some of her crew was already there when she arrived. Pam sat down at her usual table. One of the agents and a longtime personal friend, Brian, poured a glass of beer from his pitcher, handed it to Pam and asked if she wanted to shoot some darts.

Pam shook her head no. "I just want to sit down and relax. It's been a really long day."

A few minutes later, Brian brought Pam over to the couple who were seated at the table next to them.

"I'm Michelle." The tall, attractive brunette extended her hand and as Pam gave her a second, more lingering look at her, Pam noticed a scar on her chin.

"I'm Grant." The man extended his hand.

Introducing herself, Pam shook both hands and engaged in some small talk before Brian, Grant and Michelle went off to shoot darts.

Soon, Mike entered the room and sat down with Pam. Pam ordered him a beer.

"Who's that girl shooting darts with Brian?" Mike asked after a minute or two.

"Oh, you mean Michelle?" Pam answered nonchalantly.

"Is that what she said her name was?"

"Yeah, why?"

"I think I'm looking for her," Mike whispered. "Tell me, does she have a scar right here?" He traced his index finger across his chin.

"Yeah."

Just then, Michelle looked over at Mike before bolting past them and running out the back door. Mike ran after her, Brian ran after him, the bar's security guard ran after Brian and the guard's partner ran after the guard. Pam quickly followed.

By the time Pam got to the parking lot, Mike already had the woman handcuffed. The others were standing around watching in silence as he placed her in his car. "I'll be back," he grinned.

An hour or so later, Mike rejoined Brian and Pam at the table. "We *were* looking for her," Mike sipped his drink. "Her name isn't Michelle, it is really Erin. And she is worth ten grand."

"Ten thousand dollars?"

Mike nodded.

Pam hung her head. "I'm so busy I don't even know who we're looking for anymore. I don't look at the pictures. I just give you the file."

"Well, maybe you should look from now on. I knew it was her when you told me about her scar. I had noticed that when I saw her picture."

"I can't believe I was sitting next to an FTA!" Pam said incredulously. "I even shook her hand!"

"And Brian was shooting darts with her!" Mike looked at Brian.

"I did that on purpose." Brian laughed. "I was trying to keep her here long enough for you to come in, arrest her and take her to jail."

"Thanks." Mike laughed out loud.

"Well, you got her," Pam said gratefully.

"I almost didn't. I wasn't sure if it was Erin or not. I didn't have time to go out to the van and check her photo. After she ran out the back door and I ran after her, I stopped running and yelled, 'Erin!' She turned around and looked at me. That's how I knew it was her.

"I wish all my cases were this easy," Mike sighed. "I wish all I had to do was walk into my favorite bar, sit down, put my feet up, order a beer and all our FTAs walked in the door asking to play darts with the state manager. Wouldn't that be great? That'd make my job so much easier."

"You wish."

"Well," Mike leaned back in his chair, "serves her right."

"What do you mean?" Brian asked.

"Well, she should have known," Mike said slowly.

"Known what?"

"Look around you. Donovan's shirts are everywhere. If I'd jumped bail on this bonding company, I wouldn't have walked in the door. Or if I did walk in and saw the shirts, I would have immediately left. The fact is she didn't. She came in and started shooting darts with Brian...drinking...how long was she here? A couple of hours? That takes nerve. Actually, it's pretty clever of her if you think about it. She probably figured that of all the places to hide in this town, this was probably the best place to hide. She could come in, drink beer, shoot some darts—mingle with us and no one would ever suspect her of being one of our bail jumpers. And it almost worked. She probably would have pulled it off, too, if I hadn't walked through the door. She had that deer-in-the-headlights look as soon as she saw me. That's probably why she ran.

"The ironic part is," Mike paused to sip his drink and then went on, "I'd been looking for her for weeks. I couldn't find her anywhere. I went to the address listed on the application; she wasn't there. The cosigner's gone; he'd moved. I thought she was long gone. Who knew that out of the hundreds of thousands of places to hide in this town, I'd walk in and find her playing darts and partying in 'our bar'?"

Chapter 33

In the End

After working at Donovan's for nearly two years, Pam's office was doing very well financially. Then suddenly employees' paychecks started bouncing. First it happened only once or twice; then everyone's check bounced every single payday—including Pam's. She got on the phone to complain to Frank and Donovan. Both were suddenly unavailable to take her calls according to the person who answered the phone and promised to give them the message. But no one ever called Pam back.

Pam learned that if she waited a day or two after payday, the money would be in the account and people were able to cash their checks. Out of frustration, some employees quit. Pam couldn't blame them. Donovan's was a twenty-four-hour, seven-day-a-week operation. They never closed. To work that hard and not be paid on time was a real disappointment. Pam couldn't understand it, because her office alone was bringing in more than a quarter million dollars a month in premiums.

Soon Frank was replaced as Pam's supervisor. She never knew why. She was told by Mark—who always knew the latest scoop—a guy named Fred would be taking his place.

When Fred flew up with another employee, Lyle, to check out Pam's operation, they both struck Pam as very cold and abrupt.

The very first thing Lyle did was demote Pam's assistant. Pam wasn't consulted or even warned in advance. Pam protested, but Lyle just shrugged. He said Fred made the decision; he was only following orders.

Fred walked through the office, barking orders at Pam. He changed some office procedures Pam had carefully put into place, fired some employees outright that he considered "excess baggage," changed the pay scale from an hourly wage to commission and ordered Pam to start writing every bond that walked in the door no matter how shaky.

Pam protested. She wanted to write good solid bail. As far as she was concerned, if they wrote every bond that walked in the door, their FTA rate would triple. Once the bounty hunters were dispatched, they'd already lost. Since the bounty hunters were paid the premium they'd taken in on the bond, after attorney fees and other expenses were added, doing it Fred's way would lose more money than the company would be taking in.

Fred brushed off Pam's concerns with a wave of his arm.

As the fired employees were cleaning out their desks, they looked at Pam questioningly. She shrugged her shoulders. She couldn't do anything. She was powerless to stop it.

Just before he left, Fred ordered Pam to catch a plane in the next few days to travel to his office. "I want to show you how it's really done," he said curtly. "I'll expect you on that plane by the end of the week."

After creating total chaos in what used to be a calm, organized office, Fred and Lyle left as abruptly as they came.

A few days later, Fred met Pam at the airport. He didn't believe in small talk. As Pam and he drove to his office from the airport, Pam felt extremely uncomfortable. She just wanted to get this over with, have him teach her what he thought she should know and go home.

His office was much smaller than hers and, Pam thought, not as well run. He was the boss and made sure everybody knew it.

The employees answered the phones in monotone voices and didn't laugh and joke among each other as Pam's did. They were strictly business.

During the week Pam spent at his office, Fred spent absolutely no time with her. She busied herself checking their office procedures and talking with some of the employees when they had time. Fred always went into his office by mid-morning and slammed the door. Pam wouldn't see him for the rest of the day.

The night before she was to fly back home, she was in her hotel room planning to go to dinner in the hotel's dining room then maybe take a swim in the pool. She was grateful the week was over. As far as she was concerned, it had been a colossal waste of time, money and energy.

Unexpectedly Lyle called Pam. He told Pam he was downstairs waiting for her in the dining room. He wanted to talk to her before she left and told her to meet him there in five minutes. The macho culture of the business was evident.

Pam bristled. She didn't like being given orders as if he was the sergeant and she was the private. However, she had no choice. She went.

Lyle ordered and devoured his meal in short order. While he was eating, she felt he treated her like a hired date. They didn't talk of anything important about the business and, though he seemed to her to be flirting, she made sure she let him know she wasn't open to anything else. Pam tried to be cordial, which was really a stretch, and she couldn't wait for the meal to be over.

About a week or so later, Pam was back at her office when she felt a nudge on her shoulder. Looking up, she saw Mark. "Follow me," he said curtly.

When Pam approached the back office, the company attorney was standing in the doorway. Wordlessly, she was handed a sealed letter.

She opened it. The letter said due to the recent reorganization of the company's infrastructure, she'd been downsized. She was to immediately leave the premises.

She'd been *fired*!

While she was standing off to the side of the doorway trying to absorb what she'd just read, she noticed a whole line of people being given similar envelopes with the same instructions.

These were all the people who had helped Pam. The people who volunteered for extra hours, worked round the clock with her, hoping, praying, making it work above all else. The people who stood by Pam and sacrificed their personal lives to make Donovan's so successful. These were her friends and family.

She had never cried in any office before, but she couldn't hold back the tears. As Pam walked to her desk and started gathering her things, she tried to calm herself. She had so many personal things at the office—she didn't have a box to put them in. Her car was parked far away from the front door. Mark was standing next to her.

"Mark, can't I come back over the weekend and get my things? I mean, then I could do it privately without the employees staring at me."

"No." He shook his head. "If you want them, you have to get them now or not at all. I'm sorry, Pam, I really am. But those are my instructions."

"Okay."

Leaving most of her personal things behind, Pam gathered up what she could carry in her arms and Mark escorted her out the door.

Chapter 34

Riches to Rags

"You wanna know why you were fired?" Mike leaned back in his chair as he and Pam were sipping drinks at their favorite bar.

"Yeah."

"I overhead two of the bosses saying they were going to fire you, because you're a woman. They don't believe a woman should have such an important position in the corporation. Too much emotional bullshit."

"What? I was fired because I'm a woman?"

"That's my opinion," Mike nodded.

"Well, I was the only female state manager in the entire corporation," Pam said angrily. "But last I checked, women were given the right to vote."

"I know. It isn't right," Mike agreed. "You never should have been fired. You were doing a great job. Both Mark and I thought so."

"I'm going to see a lawyer," Pam suddenly decided.

"If you need me to testify, I'll be happy to."

"You bet I will. They are not going to get away with what they did to me."

A few weeks later, Pam was seated in a lawyer's office—along with everyone who'd been fired with her. All of them were women with the exception of two men—both longtime family friends.

"This doesn't smell right," the lawyer said. "Let me check into this and get back to you. You might have a class action suit for sexual discrimination."

"I hope so."

"In the meantime," the lawyer addressed all of them, "this is going to take a long time to get into court. All of you need to go on with your lives. This is going to take years before it is finally resolved. Don't wait for the outcome. You can't afford to wait. All of you have to go out and find other jobs and somehow go on with your lives until this is all over."

Pam knew she was right. She applied for unemployment and tried to put her life back together. She was certain that with her credentials she could find another job as a bail bond agent. That's what she loved to do and had been doing so well for over fifteen years.

Pam went to several different bail bond companies with her resume.

All the doors that she had thought were wide open, to her great amazement, *slammed* shut one by one. No one would hire her. Pam was told later by a reliable source that she'd been blacklisted.

When Pam's unemployment compensation was about to run out, Pam knew she had to take whatever job she could get. No matter how lowly. No matter how unimportant or trivial.

After making all the rounds, she was forced to accept the only job she'd been offered: cleaning houses for a small cleaning firm for minimum wage.

After all those hours, all that hard work, fighting her way to the top and now it was over—just like that. In a blink of an eye, she was no longer a bail bond agent.

She had become a maid, on her hands and knees, scrubbing strangers' toilets for minimum wage, but she kept on fighting.

Pam's lawyer informed her that her employment had been "at will," that state law gave her employer all the rights.

She explained, "*At will* means they can fire you for any reason whatsoever. They don't even have to give you a reason. It could be for something as simple as they don't like the color of your hair."

"So what you're saying is I don't have a legal leg to stand on."

"Pretty much. We can file suit of course."

Pam stopped her. "Well, I'm going to fight it. This kind of discrimination isn't right and we can't just sit back and take it."

Her lawyer nodded. "Okay, just as long as you understand this is an uphill battle."

"I understand," Pam said grimly.

Mark had worked long and hard at getting the cooperation of a Federal Fugitive Task Force in the area. These guys were the best and when the firm had occasion to call on them, it was always a pleasure. On one particular case, Mark suggested to one of his bosses that they should touch base with the task force regarding a fugitive, but his response was, "Fuck the feds. All they do is run around with their fanny packs on while we do all the work!"

Soon after, someone in the company decided Mark's job as supervisor should be handed over to a new company guy. Mike is very particular about whom he works with while chasing criminals. When a guy showed up to work the first day wearing a custom made T-shirt with big block letters silk-screened on it that read, "Large and in Charge," it set the tone of things to come. Mike could feel they wouldn't get along.

Meanwhile, there were other problems with the company. Things weren't adding up. The company was offering plans that didn't seem quite right. Mike had seen a lot of scammers in his day and his instincts were talking to him. Nothing specific, just a nervous gut. But other people were noticing things, too, and the rumors were growing every day.

For Mike, the writing was on the wall. He emptied his desk, put his feet up and waited to be fired.

Soon Mike was terminated. He shook their hands and politely said, "Goodbye."

Remodeling houses had always been a hobby of Mike's. Maybe it was time to switch careers. He wouldn't go back to bounty hunting unless some day Pam had her own business and Mike felt there wasn't much chance of that.

During this time, Mike brought his cause to the state legislature. Mike felt the major problem with bounty hunting was the policies of Washington State or rather, lack of policies. The State had no requirements for licensing, training or background checks. All that was required to be a bounty hunter was permission from the bail bond company to arrest their clients. The potential for corruption was unbelievable. All the bail bond companies cared about was the bottom line. If they could hire some knuckle-dragger to go out and arrest their skips for next to nothing, they did it. Criminals arresting criminals seemed to be the industry standard. Somehow these people had gotten it into their heads that it took a criminal to catch a criminal. Mike had also been around long enough to learn about some of the dirty little secrets of the business. You always hear of the rumors, but if you keep your eyes and ears open, you can learn quite a bit firsthand.

One of the more serious problems that Mike saw emerging was the violation of personal freedoms. Personal freedom is the most valuable thing people own. The bail bond companies had in effect turned a bunch of criminals loose with other people's freedoms as bargaining chips. Of course, a prostitute might trade her freedom for sexual favors or a drug dealer might give up some dope or cash in exchange for not going to jail at that moment. Now, imagine a bounty hunter with a criminal mindset soliciting favors or contraband for a person's freedom. This system was a nightmare.

Mike had always believed that bounty hunters should have training similar to police officers, standard operating procedures, training in the escalation of force and certification in firearms. He believed they should have clean police records, no felonies, should be licensed by the state and held criminally and civilly accountable for their actions. All he could do was conduct himself ethically and professionally and find a partner who believed in doing it the same way.

Mike decided it was time to speak up. He knew nothing about writing laws or changing legislation but he knew something had to change. Fortunately, others agreed.

One of the best things to come out of working at Donovan's was that Mike had been introduced to a Washington State senator named Mike Carrell. He, too, wanted to see some serious changes in the bounty hunting business. He felt that training and licensing were needed and was trying to change all the things about bounty hunting that Mike had been objecting to for years. Mike Carrell became the driving force behind the new laws being implemented in Washington.

The two Mikes had a meeting in Olympia with other legislators, attorneys and bail bond owners. They presented their case to the Police Chief Association. Mike's part was letting the decision makers know what worked and what didn't work in real life situations with real bad guys. If you haven't been in the mix, you may have your own feelings about how things should work, but reality has a way of screwing up a lot of good theories.

Everyone agreed that things had to change. In 2004, a new law was passed in the state, the first of its kind in the nation, incorporating all of Mike's guidelines and, at the beginning of 2006, the new law took effect. No more felons arresting felons. No more goofs running around with guns and zero training. Background checks were required along with firearms training and Taser, baton and pepper spray certification. The State also agreed to provide some training in building searches and to teach the laws pertaining to bail enforcement. Mike personally made sure no more men like Tony would be killed due to their inexperience and no more guys like Joey would be running the street. Although things still weren't perfect, with Mike Carrell's help they were better.

Nevertheless, Pam felt deeply depressed, reflecting:

I didn't take my firing lightly or, for that matter, graciously. I was often angry and hurt and depressed all at the same time. In order to cope, I spent many, many hours all by myself in my bedroom—alternating between crying and being depressed. Losing Donovan's had hurt. Not only was I dependent upon it for my livelihood, but also I'd put my heart and soul into that company. I lived, breathed and slept bail bonds. I talked of little else. To have my "baby" (as I called Donovan's) taken away from me like that, hurt almost as much as losing custody of a precious child to an unfit parent. I hurt. And I bled. I told everyone who'd listen how totally, utterly miserable I felt. And I did. Nothing eased the pain. . .

However, Pam was a survivor and, somehow, she got through it.

For several years she struggled to survive. She held a succession of minimum wage jobs—housecleaner, receptionist for a non-profit organization and caregiver for elderly clients in their homes. She went to college, graduated and passed state boards to become a licensed certified nursing assistant—a license she still holds.

But she wanted to be a bail bond agent again. That was always Pam's secret dream.

Chapter 35

A New Beginning

Five years after Pam was fired, her case against Donovan's was close to trial. Mike had testified on her behalf. Near the date the court ordered arbitration to see if the case could be settled out of court.

During arbitration, Pam contended she hadn't done anything wrong. She was fired simply because one of the bosses was a male chauvinist who was prejudiced against women having authority in Donovan's corporation. In her opinion, the others were fired because the bosses had assumed they'd be loyal to Pam and retaliate against the company for letting Pam go—none of which would have ever happened. As a victim of sexual discrimination, she was entitled to a substantial cash settlement—as were all the others. They agreed to take the money.

When they were waiting to get their settlements from Donovan's, Pam discussed with her former employees her dream of opening her own business. They all agreed to pool their money and open a bail bond company. However, Donovan's firm crashed and burned shortly after the agreement to settle. The corporation declared bankruptcy and Pam and the others never received the settlement. The entire conglomerate was gone.

When they didn't receive that settlement, they couldn't open their own business.

Pam continued to talk about her dream for so long and so often even her closest friends and family rolled their eyes. They all told her they loved her, but they were tired of hearing about it. They pleaded with Pam to accept the reality that it was never going to happen, so it was time to quit dreaming. But though Pam wisely kept her thoughts to herself, she still dreamed.

One day, Pam's mom asked her to come over to the house as she and Pam's father wanted to discuss something important with her. After Pam arrived, Pam's mother talked with her daughter seriously about opening her own bail bond company.

"I'm not making any promises," Pam's mom said slowly, "but I've been talking to your father about it. We both feel so bad you lost your job. Especially when you didn't do anything wrong. Obviously, you're not happy doing anything else. Let me talk to your father a little bit more. If I can arrange it, I will get you the funds you need. Just give me a little more time."

Pam knew her parents loved her and wanted to help. However, though both were retired and living on comfortable pensions, they weren't rich. Pam felt opening her own company was a pipe dream and probably would never realistically happen.

A few months later, Pam's mom called and asked her to drop by. After Pam arrived, her mother handed her a sizable check made out to Pam and told her, smiling, "This is for you to open that bail bond company you've always dreamed about. Your dad and I talked it over. We believe in you and what you are trying to do. Do you think this will be enough?"

Though she knew nothing about the business, she had talked her husband into taking a second mortgage on a house they owned to obtain the funds Pam needed.

With tears streaming down her face, Pam assured her mother it was enough. Pam gratefully accepted the check, made arrangements to repay the loan then danced to the bank.

A few days later, after the initial excitement wore down, the doubts began.

Pam knew if she was to open her own place, it would be a very risky venture. She didn't know of any other woman who owned her own business. Most female owners Pam knew worked alongside their owner husbands. Pam didn't have that luxury. She'd have to go it alone.

If she was to open her own place, there was one key player she'd desperately need—Mike.

In Pam's opinion, Mike was the best bounty hunter on the planet. There wasn't anyone qualified enough to take his place—or anyone Pam trusted as much. She knew from experience that on average, three out of ten people jump bail. She'd need Mike to chase, find and arrest those skips if she ever hoped to stay in business.

They were still in touch, still friends, but would he have the necessary faith in her to commit? She wasn't sure.

Would he even want to? Pam asked herself. They both knew what working in the bond industry meant—long hours with little pay. And what if he said no?

Finally Pam decided all she could do was ask him. If he said no, that would be that. She'd never risk opening without him. She'd give the funds back to her parents and her longtime dream would officially be dead.

That weekend, Pam asked Mike to come by.

They were sitting on the back porch in the warm spring sunshine, shooting the breeze when Pam blurted out, "Mike, if I were to open my own bail bond company, would you work for me?"

He shook his head and scowled. "Pam! Haven't you gotten over that yet? You've been dreaming about your own place for years. Isn't it about time you gave it up? When are you going to accept the fact that your bonding days are over? Give it a rest, will ya?"

Pam didn't blame him. For twenty years, she'd been talking about opening her own place. "Mike," Pam said slowly, "this time there's a difference. This time I *have* the money."

He didn't say anything for a minute. "You have the money?"

"Yes," Pam nodded.

He looked down, sipped his beer and didn't say anything. Pam anxiously held her breath. A slow grin spread across his face. Finally, he said, "I can't believe it, Pam! I never thought this would happen! When I got out of the business I said I'd never go back and work for anyone *but* you."

He paused for a moment. "If you open a company," he sighed, "I'll come back."

Pam let out a small scream and hugged him.

"You'll need a partner," Pam speculated. "What about Mark? Do you think he might be interested in working for me?"

Mike looked surprised. "Don't you have bad feelings about Mark? Since he fired you, I mean. Didn't you tell me you had some bad feelings about that?"

"I did in the beginning," Pam admitted. "It hurt that Mark escorted me out the door at Donovan's. After I thought about it, I realized Mark had to do what he'd been ordered to do. If he refused, he probably would have been fired right along with me. It wasn't his fault. He did what he had to do—what he was forced to do. It wasn't personal. I know that now."

Mike paused. "After Donovan's closed, Mark got out of the business like I did. For the past few years, he's been driving trucks for a large firm and making good money. He has a good pension. He won't want to give that up."

"Just thought I'd ask. What about Chris?"

"Chris is a police officer now working in Tacoma. He can't bounty hunt. That's a conflict of interest."

"Good for Chris! He's always wanted to be a cop. Well, you'll have to find another partner then."

"Oh great!" Mike rolled his eyes. "Just what I wanted to do! Just when I thought I'd take it easy, being retired and all, here you go making me interview another progression of goobers wanting to be bounty hunters. Maybe I'd better rethink this." He feigned a frown. "It sounds too much like work to me."

They both laughed.

When Pam started working in the business twenty-three years ago, there was only a handful of female bail bond agents. Over the years, more and more women have entered the field. The powers that be finally decided that "bail bondsman" is a sexist term and officially changed the name to the more appropriate "bail bond agent."

As the weeks moved on, Pam kept Mike updated.

"Mike, I've worked up a budget. I know what it's going to cost to open up."

"Pam, do yourself a favor. I'm not trying to discourage you, but whatever your presumed budget is double it. Then you just might have enough without getting caught by surprise."

"Really?"

"Yes, Pam, really and that's experience talking, so please believe me."

"Okay."

Mike continued to be skeptical of Pam's ability to see her plan through. A few weeks passed and she called again.

"Mike, I've formed a corporation and filed it with the State."

"That's nice, Pam," Mike said while thinking, *Doesn't she know this will never work?*

"Mike, I'm so excited, I've found a surety company that will back my bonds."

"That's nice, Pam."

"Mike, I got my bail bond agency license and my bail bond agent license. The State made me take some tests, because I've been out of the business for so long, but I passed them."

"That's nice, Pam," Mike repeated, while thinking to himself, *I wish she would stop. This is really going to hurt when it all comes crashing down.*

However, Pam was determined and made him a believer. She found a suitable office in an old building that needed extensive remodeling. Since her budget was limited, friends and family pitched in to lay carpet, paint walls and buy office furniture to help her settle in.

"Mike! I've rented an office space and we've started remodeling! We should have our doors open in a month. Aren't you excited about coming back to work? I'm so happy. I've done it, Mike, I've done it!"

Mike had to jump through his own hoops to become licensed as a fugitive recovery agent. In the years since he'd been in the business, state law (helped passed by him) required Mike to become recertified in firearms, pass a test on the escalation of force and become properly licensed with the state. All of which he did, easily.

Pam hired back all the people who had been fired along with her for her business.

A month later, Pam was sitting at her new desk.

Finally, after months of hard labor, she proudly opened *PHREE* Bail Bonds for business in Tacoma, Washington. Pam didn't want to be the biggest bail bond company in Washington State—she just wanted to be the *best*.

Pam quickly learned that dreaming and reality are two different things. After considerable expenses and challenges to open her own business, it wasn't smooth sailing. Within three months of opening the doors, Pam's office was burglarized. When Pam drove up outside the office one morning, the back door was wide open. The alarm system hadn't been installed yet and the night agent had forgotten to lock the back door. It didn't take long to discover all the computers were missing as well as the 400-pound safe. It cost Pam thousands of dollars to replace the stolen equipment; that nearly closed her doors before she'd even begun.

Then, due to a series of freak weather systems, Pam's office had to close when a nearby river overflowed. Snow and ice came down so heavily, no one ventured outside until the streets were cleared. Since the storms came almost back-to-back, that meant absolutely no business for nearly a month. Pam was already on a shoestring budget. Her meager savings was running out the door in leaps and bounds. With no money coming in, it was all she could do to pay expenses.

Soon, a lot of other people decided to open bonding companies in the area. Bail bond companies sprang up so fast that the field was inundated. Due to stiff competition with big money, Pam's little company struggled to survive. She was forced to lay off most of her agents and worked twelve-hour days, seven days a week—a schedule she still maintains—but thankfully her doors stayed open and business began to pick up. Later, she celebrated *PHREE*'s second anniversary.

Chapter 36

Nothing's for *PHREE*

The numbers are impressive: 95 percent of Pam's customers fulfilled their responsibilities of appearing in court. To catch the other 5 percent, Mike had to hire a partner. As Pam sat at her desk at 9 o'clock one morning trying to decide where to look, the front door of the office opened.

"Hi, Byron," Pam greeted a young man. "I heard you stopped by the other day, but I missed you. I haven't seen you in a long time. How are you doing?"

"Great," the guy replied. "How have you been, Pam?"

"Real good. As you can see, I finally got my own business. Are you back bounty hunting again?"

"Yeah, I'm working for a couple of other bond companies. I meant to get in sooner to see you, but I've been swamped."

"I'm glad you stopped by. My friend, bounty hunter Mike Beakley, is working with me—you guys should meet. Maybe you could help each other out sometime."

Coming into Mike's office, Pam introduced Byron Gross. Mike noticed the man she brought with her looked like a cross between the actor Vin Diesel and the singer Chris Daughtry from the television show *American Idol*. He was about twenty years Mike's junior. Mike thought a little youth and vigor was a plus doing a job like bounty hunting.

After the usual small talk and pleasantries, it became apparent that Gross had quite a bit of experience. He was also very busy. He was working a lot of cases for an outfit called Liberty Bail Bonds.

Pam had run into Byron several years before when he was bounty hunting a defendant whom Pam had bailed out on a separate matter. Byron had heard about the other bond and checked with Pam to see if she had any information she could share with him. She told him what he needed to know to make the arrest. From then on they had a mutual respect for each other. Both believed the other to be ethical and honest.

Mike could tell right away that Byron had an inherent distrust of other bounty hunters. It was obvious that he had seen some foul stuff and did not like it. After the initial sniff test Byron and Mike agreed to call on each other as needed.

It didn't take long to figure out that Byron was a workaholic. He could work twenty-four hours a day and it wouldn't be enough. He took on any case thrown at him and still asked for more. Byron was so busy that it wasn't long before he and Mike were working together constantly. Because of his penchant for not only distrusting but also genuinely disliking most bounty hunters, Byron had developed a habit of working alone most of the time. He wasn't really sure how to handle a partner and Mike had to appreciate the fact that he was as wary of a new partner as Mike was.

Byron explained to Mike that working alone had its benefits. First of all, you did not have to share the commission for the arrests. Second, you didn't have to worry about some inexperienced or dishonest bounty hunter stealing something or screwing something up and getting you into trouble.

Mike argued that money doesn't come in very useful in intensive care when you're on a ventilator and you can't spend a dime from the cemetery. Besides the obvious physical danger of working alone, you also need a witness. The savages on the streets will accuse you of anything you can imagine and then you find yourself in deep trouble trying to prove you didn't do something you were wrongly accused of in the first place.

To make extra money Pam let Mike work for other companies. A couple of weeks went by and Mike and Byron were working well together. They were closing a lot of cases.

Liberty gave Byron a thirty thousand dollar skip that wasn't looking good. One thing about the big bonds, the bail bond company will usually work the larger cases before handing them over to the bounty hunters. If they can solve the cases with a few phone calls, it saves the company a lot of money. If they can't solve them, the cases have now been trampled on and the defendants are alerted, making bounty hunters' jobs that much tougher.

This was one of those cases. All the information on the bail applications was turning out to be false. It was obvious that this guy had planned on running even before he'd been bailed out. Every indication showed he had gang ties and, to make things worse, his charge was a felony possession of a firearm.

Byron had worked the phones and was coming up empty-handed. He asked for Mike's help with the investigation. Mike had access to some sources and soon they got a tentative location for the guy in Arizona. They now had to decide if they were going to take the time and money to go all the way to Arizona to knock on one door.

They decided to work it from Washington for a couple more weeks and see what they could come up with.

Byron, the workaholic, was out of town tied up on another job when Mike got an urgent call from him.

"Mike! Jake, our thirty grander, is back in town! He is living in Arizona, but he came back to cut a rap album. He's supposed to be in a studio in Tacoma right now. The company got a call from the cosigner. The guy left him hanging, so he's willing to help."

"Good deal; let's go get him."

"I can't. I'm out of town on another job. You've got to do this one alone. The cosigner says it will be no problem. He says the guy won't resist. He knows you are coming and he'll just turn himself over to you if the cosigner asks him to. Can you do it?"

"You know how I feel about doing this stuff alone. Especially a gangbanger with a gun charge. If the guy's up here cutting an album, why don't we just pick him up when you get back into town?"

"We can't. The cosigner says Jake's flying out tonight. He'll be gone if we don't get him now."

"Okay, I'll try. Call the cosigner and ask him where I can meet him. I'll know more when I talk to him in person."

As soon as Mike met with the cosigner, he could tell things were going to be dicey. The cosigner was no stranger to thug life himself. It turned out that the bail company had him out on a large bond as well and the bond agent was threatening to put him back in jail if he didn't help clean up this mess. He wasn't doing Mike and Byron a favor; he was working for his own freedom.

"How many people are we looking at in this studio?" Mike asked the cosigner.

"Oh, about six guys and a few girlfriends."

"You've got to be kidding me. How are we going to put this guy in jail without his friends helping him?"

"They might help him; they're all part of the same crew. I can go home and get my gun if you want. Then when they all come out to the parking lot, we can run up on them and arrest them."

"No!" Mike blurted out. "I don't want you getting your gun! Is there a way you can get this guy outside alone? Tell him you need to talk in private; you've got something to show him or whatever other bullshit you can come up with."

"Yeah, that should work. I'm sure I can get him outside alone. I can tell him I got something for him."

"Okay, I'll follow you over and check out the location first."

On the way to the studio, Mike called Byron.

"Byron, it sounds like you're sending me into a hornets' nest. This guy isn't going to just give himself up. He has no idea I'm coming for him."

"Really? I was told that by someone in the office. This cosigner is close with one of the bond agents and I'm getting the info from him."

"Well, someone is making this seem a lot easier than it is because they don't want to pay the thirty thousand."

"Mike, man, if it looks too dangerous, don't do it."

"I'm here now and the cosigner thinks he can get the guy outside without the rest of the crew. I'll check it out and see how it feels."

"Just be careful and call me right away. Now I'm not going to be able to do anything else here until I know you're alright."

At the studio, Mike found a back door that led to a smoking area. It was concealed from the rest of the building and nobody from the inside could see what was going on. He could also park the van within a couple of feet of the area.

The cosigner went inside and Mike stood at the backside of the door. Within a few minutes the door opened and out came the cosigner with the skip. As they walked toward the van, neither one of them could see Mike. Suddenly, Mike came up behind them and grabbed the fugitive by the shoulder telling him, "Jake, I'm from the bail bond company and you're under arrest." Instantly the guy started squirming, trying to get out of Mike's grip. He pushed Jake up against the van trying to control him and repeated his identification. The cosigner grabbed Jake's arm and tried to calm him down. As if he didn't hear Mike, Jake kept yelling, "Who are you? Who are you?"

He knew exactly who Mike was. Mike's badge was out and Mike kept telling him he was from the bail bond company and that he was under arrest.

He refused to give up so Mike pulled his Taser out. "I'm going to light you up if you don't quit fighting." Jake agreed to stop resisting. But as soon as Mike put his Taser away Jake started fighting again. They played this game about three times. Mike kept pulling out the Taser and he would give up until Mike put it away and tried to cuff him. They'd been wrestling for a couple of minutes now. The cosigner was holding one of the fugitive's arms, but wouldn't commit any further than that and Jake was fighting back and resisting arrest. Mike was getting worried that some of the friends might come out to see what was going on. This had to stop. Mike took the Taser out again and tased the guy from about two feet away. This time Mike hit him in the chest with it and the fugitive immediately dropped to the ground. It was the first time Mike had tased anyone so he wasn't sure what to expect. The guy lay on the ground, but as Mike started to cuff him he began struggling again. Mike yelled, "Stop!" but to no avail. Mike shot him again with the Taser and that was all it took. The fight was gone, but time was getting short. With all the commotion, Mike's fears grew that the guy's friends would be bursting out the door at any second. Mike opened the side door of the van and pushed the defendant toward it as fast as he could. The entire time Mike was asking, "Do you have any weapons on you?"

"No!" he yelled. "I don't have anything."

As Mike shoved him in the backseat of the van, Mike grabbed at Jake's clothes, feeling for anything he could find. Jake was wearing a very long thick jacket and Mike didn't have time to do a proper search. The only thing Mike could think of was to get the hell out of there.

Slamming the door shut, Mike jumped in the driver's seat, jammed the key into the ignition, started the motor and took off. They were in the middle of the Hilltop area of Tacoma, which was this guy's turf. Mike wasn't about to stop and search him, because he probably had a lot of friends in the area. Watching him in the mirror whenever he could, Mike saw the guy moving all over the place.

Mike yelled, "Quit moving around. Do you have anything on you?"
He yelled back, "I don't have anything."

As he was moving around, Mike pushed the guy back into the seat with his left hand grabbing at his clothes trying to do a search while they were moving. He was wearing baggy cargo pants and Mike felt several hard objects in his pockets. First Mike pulled out a portable scale, then a bag of pot and finally, a large water bong.

"Jake, I thought you didn't have anything on you."

"That's all I had. I don't have anything else."

"Are you sure? Do you have anything else? Any weapons? Now's the time to tell me. Once you get to the jail, it's too late."

"No, man, that's all I have."

"Okay, but you'd better be sure."

"I'm sure, man," Jake sat back in the seat. "I don't have anything else."

Mike had been around long enough to know better than to let his guard down. He tried to keep an eye on Jake as he drove towards the jail. The guy was young and skinny and Mike knew from experience that the skinny ones are very flexible. Even though their hands are cuffed behind their backs, they can still move around quite a bit.

As they got closer to the jail, Mike sensed that the guy's stress levels were going up again. He was starting to wiggle a bit. Meanwhile, Mike was weaving the car through traffic and trying to keep an eye on Jake without getting into an accident. Mike took a second to turn and get a good look at his prisoner and noticed that he had worked his arms around to his right side and had his thumb and forefinger digging into the cargo pocket of his pants.

"What are you doing?" Mike yelled, grabbing the guy's hand and pants. Instantly Mike felt the revolver, his finger just touching it.

"Damn you!" Mike yelled even louder as he squeezed the gun, pinning Jake's finger against the butt. "What the hell are you doing?"

"Don't squeeze it!" Jake yelled back. "It's loaded!"

Mike ripped the gun out of the guy's pocket, throwing it on the floor of the front seat.

After that there was no more conversation. The guy knew what he had just tried to do as well as Mike did. If Mike hadn't been alert and wary, Jake would have shot him and run. Mike had only been seconds away from being wounded or dead.

Mike wanted to pull over and beat the guy up, but Mike knew that would only create sympathy for Jake and turn Mike into the bad guy.

Mike drove to the bail bond company. He needed to do a proper search on the fugitive and get some help in booking him. Once Mike got to the jail, he had to walk the paperwork up to a window and Mike didn't want to leave Jake in the van alone. A bail bond agent in the office agreed to ride to the jail and help Mike out.

Mike had been booking people in this new jail for about a year. The procedure was simple enough: You bring the paperwork up to an outside window, then you drive the defendant into a secured parking lot and walk him into the jail. On this particular occasion, Mike told the agent to go ahead and go back to the office. With the paperwork already handed in, Mike felt he wouldn't have any more trouble since he was in the secured parking area and Jake had nothing else on his person.

Mike entered the covered parking area and started pulling the prisoner out of the van when he was challenged by a corrections officer just coming to work. Mike didn't blame him. Neither the van nor Mike looked like they belonged there. Mike explained that he was a bail recovery agent and was booking a guy.

"I don't care who you are!" he bellowed. "You can't park here!"

"But, sir, this is where I've always parked in the past. Can I book this guy first?"

"No, you can't! Get that car out of here right now!" The corrections officer raised his arm.

Great, this guy just tried to shoot me dead and now I have the pleasure of running into a real jerk. Mike was thinking. *Be polite, you can't win this one.*

"Okay, whatever you say," Mike held onto his temper, keeping his voice even.

Mike had to go out and find street parking then walk Jake back to the jail while hoping nobody who would have an interest in helping Jake escape would see them.

As soon as Mike booked Jake, he called Byron and filled him in.

"If anything had happened to you, I would never have forgiven myself for getting you hurt," Byron said.

"Byron, if I did get hurt, it would have nothing to do with you. If I'm out there alone and get messed up, it's no one's fault but mine."

"Okay, Mike. I'm just happy you're alright. I do know one thing: I've never wanted a partner before, but I have one now."

Chapter 37

Backup

Chantel, an attractive brunette with a slim, athletic build, was also a bounty hunter. New at the game, she was working cases for Liberty Bail Bonds. She had contacted Byron, whom she had heard about from other employees, and Mike wanting to work a few cases with them. She was looking for experienced partners to work with and was hungry to get some additional training. Chantel was not yet qualified to carry a firearm, but was still working cases alone. Byron and Mike both chastised her for this practice, but she was already addicted to the hunt and wouldn't listen. Mike had to admire her guts and hoped it didn't get her into something she couldn't handle. Finding fugitives can be easy; getting them in handcuffs and safely tucked into jail can get a little tricky.

One day Chantel called Byron for help on a case she was trying to solve. She explained to Mike and Byron that she was looking for Mia, a young woman with a lot of mental issues and had tracked the skip to a house belonging to a relative of her boyfriend, Warren.

Chantel had gone to the house alone and tried to arrest Mia. However, once Chantel entered the house the boyfriend started giving her a hard time.

"He's a big guy and very threatening," she told Mike and Byron. "I think he was blocking my way while his girlfriend hid in the house. I tried to look around, but he was very intimidating and I had to get out of there. Would you guys be willing to help me with this one?"

"Of course we'll help," Byron told her.

They had information that the relatives would be out of town for a few days and felt that the time to strike would be while Mia and her boyfriend were home alone.

They scouted the location and could not find the suspect's vehicle parked outside. It was decided that Byron and Chantel would enter and search the house while Mike waited outside. If the couple were not home at this time, they would wait. Byron and Chantel would wait inside and Mike would let them know when the car pulled up.

The couple was home when Byron and Chantel entered the house, but managed to hide before either bounty hunter saw them. Suddenly, Byron heard a noise in the bedroom. Quickly heading for the room, both Byron and Chantel searched it and discovered Mia and her boyfriend hiding under the bed.

Mike had been sitting outside about ten minutes when Byron called, "Get in here, Mike! They're home and the boyfriend's being a jerk."

Mike entered the front door to find Byron arguing with Warren, the boyfriend, in the living room. He could also hear what sounded like some wild animal wailing from deeper inside the house.

Warren was very tall, around six feet six inches. He was advancing on Byron, trying to push by him and intimidate him. Byron gave the guy a double-handed push to the chest, sending him back about five feet. That stopped the guy's physical advances, but not his mouth. In these situations, the bad guy usually likes to pick out one person he doesn't like and will focus on them. In this case it was Byron. Warren was trying to do everything he could, short of actual physical violence, to cause a confrontation. Quickly they assessed Warren and let him know that they would give him little pain if he resisted.

Meanwhile, the screeching continued. Knowing Byron could handle this guy, Mike went deeper into the house to make sure Chantel was okay and to check on the source of all the noise.

Chantel was in the bedroom with the suspect Mia. The young woman was lying on the floor acting as though she was having some sort of seizure and screaming her lungs out. Warren was now running around the house yelling at everybody and calling Byron every foul name he could think of. It was quite a chaotic scene.

Mike felt that Mia just didn't want to go to jail. She wasn't having this mental and physical apocalypse prior to being told she was under arrest and during his career he'd met a lot of people with convenient conditions.

Mia continued flopping around on the ground refusing to calm down while Warren continued pushing Byron's buttons. Mike knew it was a matter of time before Byron granted this jerk his wish and gave him a little something to remember him by. Realizing he was about one word away from being turned into a human pretzel, Warren headed for the kitchen, grabbed the phone and called 911. Mike told Byron, "You help Chantel and I'll keep an eye on this guy."

As Mike stood in the kitchen, Warren yelled at the 911 dispatcher, accusing the bounty hunters of everything in the book. Most of his complaints were about Byron. He referred to Mike as the older one who might be in charge. Mike kept telling him that he would talk to the dispatcher. After several minutes Warren handed Mike the phone, partially at the insistence of the dispatcher.

Once on the phone, Mike was able to let the operator know who he was and what was going on. She asked if they needed police assistance. Mike assured her they were fine. She then asked if they needed medical assistance for the girlfriend.

"That's probably a good idea," Mike agreed. "Let's play it safe and have rescue check her out. She's been going through these contortions for about ten minutes now and has worked herself into quite a tizzy."

Mike gave the dispatcher the address.

"We already have an aid unit coming to that address. We have somebody named Byron on the other line asking for rescue."

"That's my partner. I guess he wants to play it safe also."

Byron had called dispatch on his cell phone and had asked for a medical unit.

Waiting for rescue to arrive, Warren never let up. He must have felt safe, because the medics were coming. Byron and Mike just ignored the guy. As he stood there screaming insults at them, they continued to pay him no mind, but it was getting more difficult.

Soon men from the fire department arrived and started evaluating Mia. The boyfriend would not stay out of their way and started giving them a bad time as well. He was being so disruptive and threatening towards them that they called dispatch for police backup.

Mike and Byron were standing in the hallway by the front door leaning against the wall talking about the next case to avoid getting in the firefighters' way when the police showed up.

A fireman greeted the police at the front door. As soon as they heard that bounty hunters were on the scene, the police officers informed the firefighter that they could not and would not assist them, because bounty hunters were involved. The cops wouldn't even enter the house.

By now the rescue workers decided that they were going to transport Mia to the hospital. They felt that they couldn't take a chance and not do anything. Chantel was going to go to the hospital with Mia and book her into jail if they released her. Chantel seemed very concerned that Warren would also go to the hospital and cause more problems.

Mike decided to tell the police, who were still standing on the front porch, what was going on, including Chantel's concerns about Warren.

As Mike approached them, they both looked down and away from him. One of them put his hand up as if to block Mike saying, "No, no, no; we can't talk to you."

"Come on, guys. I simply want to let you know what's going on."

"Nope, policy says we can't have anything to do with you. We don't want to hear it."

"You're kidding, right? I just want to let you know that this guy might be going to the hospital causing trouble."

"Nope, don't want to hear it."

"Unbelievable!" Mike said after returning to Byron and relaying what the cops said. "You'd think we were the devil himself the way these guys are acting. It was like they were afraid to even look at me. What the hell? I've got to keep this in perspective and keep telling myself it's not the guys on the street, it's the bureaucratic policy makers."

A lot of the smaller agencies in the area were more than happy to assist bounty hunters if it looked like a dangerous situation. They were also happy to put the bad guys in jail. It's the larger agencies that absolutely refused. One time, a father was inside a house waving a gun around protecting his adult son from being arrested by Mike and Byron. Mike called the nearest sheriff's office and told the dispatcher they could see the gun in the father's hand through the window. All the dispatcher said was, "You're on your own. We don't assist bounty hunters."

The thing that really bothered Mike about this was that when he was a cop and another law enforcement agency came into their jurisdiction needing assistance, his office would drop everything to help them. Granted, bail bond agents and their bounty hunters are not an official enforcement agency, but they are trained and licensed by the State. They are also under court orders to return the bad guy to the system. Any citizen can call for police assistance and they will respond. Any citizen can call Crime Stoppers and report the location of a wanted person and they will respond. But when bounty hunters call with a situation that could get out of control, becoming a danger to not only themselves but the general public as well, they are basically told that their "lives are not our concern."

Over the years, Mike had asked several officers what the deal was. Nobody seemed to know. It was like a bad habit that can't be fixed. One officer told Mike that it was the decision of the city or county attorney's office not to assist because of the fear of liability. But in Mike's opinion, the situation didn't make sense—how is it that if bail bond agents called an agency for assistance on active felony warrants on a situation that appeared to be too dangerous for two agents to handle, that agency refused to even drive by and keep an eye on things? Because the liability was still there and the agents' families can sue and collect.

One night, Mike and Byron had a skip to pick up for Pam. It was very dark when they approached the house. They decided to let local law enforcement know who they were, where they were and what they were up to in case a commotion broke out. They called in the address and the dispatcher told them that they were very familiar with that particular location. Right away, that raised some serious red flags. The only reason dispatch would be that familiar with a location was because of problems in the past. Mike and Byron thought it was best to ask for police assistance.

A few minutes later, four marked units showed up.

One of the officers approached Mike and Byron. "Why are we here? Why should the taxpayers be paying for us to do your job?"

"That's not why we called," Byron tried to explain. "Your dispatcher told us that you guys were very familiar with the people here. We thought it would be best to call you."

The officer wouldn't let up. "So what do you want us to do? You want us to do your job at the taxpayer's expense?"

"No, we don't want you to do our job. If you could just stand by for safety's sake, we will go try to arrest him."

"That's not going to happen! Since we're here, we'll arrest him and you guys will stay out of our way."

"Fine with us; it doesn't matter who arrests him. If you grab him and sign our paperwork showing he was arrested, we still can get off the bond."

"We're going to arrest him and we're not signing any paperwork."

This guy absolutely refused to do it. Luckily, the lieutenant on the scene was ultimately in charge. She asked Byron and Mike a few questions about how bail bonds worked and decided that there was no reason not to sign the paperwork if they arrested the guy.

The four officers approached the house to make the arrest, one of them going to the back of the house to block any escape. At the lieutenant's request, Mike and Byron waited at the corner. Several minutes later, the lieutenant informed them that they were unable to locate the subject. Byron and Mike thanked her and the police left.

After the police cleared the area, Byron and Mike knocked at the door of the house and made entry. Byron kept the family members in the living room while Mike searched the house. While Mike was searching, he noticed that the patio door was unlocked. The backyard was huge with a lot of large shrubbery. Mike began at one corner of the yard and started working his way around. As soon as he started shaking bushes near the far corner of the yard, Mike heard a voice quietly say, "I don't have any weapon."

For a second, Mike wasn't sure if he'd heard right.

"What was that?" Mike asked, peering into the darkness.

"I don't have any weapons."

"Okay, come on out here."

The fugitive emerged from behind a bush. Mike cuffed him and away they went.

Meanwhile, the ambulance took Mia to the hospital and the doctors decided it would be best to keep her for observation.

Chapter 38

Shocking

The industry standard for bounty hunters is usually 10 percent of the bond value, so when Byron called and said, "We just got a fifty thousand dollar skip," Mike was excited. Byron continued, "We're going to have to be careful on this one. Looks like he's a big dude and built like a gorilla with some heavy duty charges on him. I think he ran from the cops then gave them a good fight when they caught up to him."

"I'm getting my gear on right now," Mike told him. "I'll meet you in the office as soon as I can."

"Okay, I'm already dressed. I'll be waiting."

When they both were ready and met up, they looked at each other and smiled. Getting dressed up in all this gear might sound like Mike and Byron were a couple of cartoon characters but that's not the way they did business. They worked together, because they had the same philosophy on a lot of issues.

Mike and Byron kept low profiles. When they were dressed for work, nobody could ever tell who they were.

Weapons, badges, Tasers and other equipment were covered. Clothes were everyday, casual attire. The vehicle they drove had to fit into the area of town they were searching in. In fact what they chose had been so effective, they often had targets approach the vehicle trying to sell Byron and Mike drugs. When dealers walked up to the vehicle and asked, "What you lookin' for?" and Mike and Byron said, "You!" Many times the fugitives were so shocked and confused that their brains didn't have time to tell their feet to run before Mike and Byron had them.

Everyone in this industry has seen the "posers"—the guys who like to drive around in old surplus cop cars and wear stuff that would make Rambo blush. Mike has seen guys dressed up in full SWAT gear. These guys are wearing short sleeve t-shirts with the sleeves rolled up, load bearing mesh vests with all the pouches stuffed full of who knows what, guns strapped to their thighs, camouflaged battle dress pants complete with combat boots and a shitload of shiny stuff hanging off of them.

While waiting for Byron to arrive to pick up the skip, Mike posted a blog about these kind of guys from the office: "You guys are an embarrassment to the rest of us. I know for a fact that you are also a big part of the reason that the cops think we're all a bunch of idiots. Knock it off! If you want to be a cop, join the department. I'm guessing some of you've already tried and didn't get very far.

"My advice to bail bond company owners is this: The local SWAT team is not going to show up on your doorstep and offer to solve your cases. If you see someone like that coming, lock your doors.

"To my fellow police officers: please do not judge all of us on account of a few jerks. Every time an officer screws up and is plastered all over the news, people love to assume that all cops are corrupt. Even I catch some heat because of those guys. Everybody who knows me knows I'm a former Tacoma cop. There are always a few who like to point out how bad we all are.

"Same thing goes with bounty hunters. In my travels, I have met a lot of people who go about this job in a quiet, professional manner. The only ones you hear about are the same kind of cops you hear about: either wrongfully accused or a blight to us all."

Upon his arrival, Byron broke in on Mike's heated blogging. "Let's head for Seattle, Mike. I think I've got a good address on this fifty grander. I would love to get this guy in one day."

"Yeah, that would be outstanding," Mike replied enthusiastically.

Byron and Mike got to the address the skip gave to the bonding company only to discover that the apartments were all vacated and the building was in the middle of being renovated and turned into condos.

"Shit, now what?"

"Let's find the girlfriend. If we find her, we'll find him."

Byron was all over this one. He and Mike started doing the usual investigative things, looking for forwarding address and so forth when Byron came up with a brilliant idea. Within a half hour, they had their skip's new address. He was staying in a little place in the Alki neighborhood of Seattle. The neighborhood is picturesque, flanked by a street that runs along the waterway and a beautiful view of downtown Seattle. A lot of high-priced condos and other choice real estate line the west side of the street with beaches and a running path on the east side.

They located the address in an older building and watched the building for a while, but quickly grew anxious.

"Let's just knock," Byron said. "What have we got to lose?"

"Only a multi-thousand dollar payday. Let's hit it."

Byron knocked and nothing. Not one to give up, he knocked again, this time louder and harder, announcing who they were. This time the door slowly swung open.

Still not knowing if anyone was home, they entered cautiously into a nicely decorated studio apartment. There were pictures of the guy on the wall and his mail was on the table. It was the right place.

Inside the bedroom closet there was a short ladder set up directly under the attic access, which was partially open.

Mike climbed up the ladder and stuck his head into the attic, which was a very tight space, maybe two feet high with short rafters. It also went the full length of the apartment building with a lot of shadows and hiding places.

Mike dropped back into the room and told Byron what he didn't see.

"Screw it," Byron said. "I'll crawl up there and look around. Can I borrow your Taser in case he's up there?"

"No problem. Just don't get into a battle with this guy, if you can avoid it. If he is up there, we can fill the space with pepper spray. He'll come out then."

Byron squeezed himself into the attic and began working his way towards the back.

Mike stood in the living room listening to Byron clunking around in the attic when his guts started talking to him. At first he was anxious about Byron being in the attic alone. Then he began to feel nervous about being in the guy's living room alone. If the fugitive came home at that point, Mike would have his hands full. This guy was a lot bigger and younger than he was with a history of violence. Mike's partner and Taser were in the attic and would be of no help for several possibly painful moments. Listening to his instincts, Mike locked the deadbolt on the door and kept his pepper spray in his hands. Suddenly, somebody tried to open the front door.

"Hey, I didn't bring my key with me. Let me in."

Mike's thoughts quickly evolved: *Damn, he thinks somebody is home and locked him out. That's why the door was unlatched. I can't yell for my partner, the gorilla would hear me and take off.*

"Goddammit, let me in!" the fugitive yelled as he continued pounding at the door.

Mike could tell that Byron didn't hear the guy knocking. If he did, he would have been crawling out of the attic as fast as he could.

Again Mike's gut kicked in: *I don't want to lose this guy. If he leaves now, we might not see him again. Go on, open the door and see what happens.*

He turned the deadbolt, grabbed the knob and opened the door, standing behind it as it opened and the defendant stormed in angrily after being locked out.

"Why didn't you let me in?" He started growling before noticing that nobody was there.

Mike slammed the door shut, locking the deadbolt at the same time. The fugitive spun around and yelled, "Who the hell are you?"

"Bail enforcement! You're under arrest!" Mike yelled with the best macho voice he could come up with.

Instantly the guy charged towards Mike. His eyes were opened with surprise when Mike filled them with pepper spray.

He continued toward Mike, grabbing him and throwing him to the other side of the room like a rag doll. He threw Mike into the couch and Mike's hands hit the wall behind it. As he recovered his balance, the fugitive was able to open the door and run outside. At the same time Mike could hear Byron crashing through the attic trying to come to Mike's aid.

Mike ran after the guy, who was now jumping into a car that he had parked next to the building. It was a hot day out and the car windows were down. Mike covered him with the remaining pepper spray and was trying to wrestle him out of the vehicle. Mike grabbed at the fugitive's head and arms, anything to slow him down and prevent him from starting the car. Suddenly, the fugitive lurched in the seat and threw his arms out. His left arm sent Mike sprawling to the gravel parking lot about six feet away. Just as the fugitive launched Mike into the air, Mike saw Byron on the passenger side of the vehicle. Almost at the same moment Mike also saw the suspect wielding a large screwdriver, swinging it in the air like a knife. As Mike was going through the air, he yelled back at Byron, "Watch the screwdriver!"

Mike landed hard on the gravel, tearing up his jeans and his knees, but quickly got back to his feet to rejoin the fight. Then he noticed that Byron had fired Mike's Taser at the guy and had him dancing in his seat. It appeared as though the guy was still fighting, but what he was really doing was jerking wildly from the massive electric jolt that Byron was sending through his body.

Byron had never used Mike's Taser before and didn't know how to turn it off. He kept pulling the trigger and this poor bastard kept jumping around.

In the excitement, Byron grabbed the Taser wires to pull them out and started doing a little dance of his own. The wires were still charged and he was shocking himself.

Mike had the driver's door open now and was able to get a cuff slapped onto the fugitive's left wrist. Mike grabbed the other end of the cuffs and jerked as hard as he could, pulling the guy out of the vehicle and onto the ground.

A little more wrestling and the cuffs were securely on both wrists.

Byron was very happy that they had solved a fifty grander in one day. After a couple of high fives, he and Mike rinsed the pepper spray off the guy and took him to jail.

Chapter 39

Two for One

Byron called into the office one morning with some exciting news: "We've got a two-for-one deal just dropped on us."

"What are you talking about, Byron?" Mike queried.

"Liberty just gave me a case in which two cousins are on the run. One of them has some misdemeanor warrants but the other one has some pretty heavy-duty felony charges. We've got a lot of addresses, but I think these guys are going to be hard to find. The cousin with the felony warrants never checked in with the bond company after he got bailed out. They weren't able to get a picture of him."

Mike and Byron worked this case for several weeks. They raided addresses given to them by informants where family members still lived. They checked the local motels and known local drug dens. The cousins had been seen from time to time but never stayed in one place.

Then Mike and Byron got word that Tina, a local call girl, was tight with these guys, so the two bounty agents started tracking her down. They finally tracked her to an apartment.

Knocking at the door, Mike and Byron identified themselves and called her name. They heard a male voice from inside.

The guy called out that Tina wasn't there and he'd have her call them.

A few days later, to their surprise, Tina indeed called Byron. She was very familiar with the cousins and knew where they were staying; turned out she bought dope from them.

After some negotiating, she realized that it was going to be a lot better getting a little reward money from Mike and Byron and staying out of jail, at least until the cops caught up with her. She told Mike and Byron what motel the cousins were staying in. She also warned them that they were probably armed, had at least three adult females with them and several of their children.

Byron and Mike felt a little uneasy about this one. First of all, there were two fugitives, both of whom had the potential of making the situation a whole lot more dangerous. Second, women and children might be present and these guys were armed.

They decided to set up surveillance on the motel.

The motel was an old but popular one with paper-thin walls and if gunfire erupted, it could penetrate several rooms and also cause problems for anyone in the parking lot.

They had another major problem, as the motel was at full capacity. People were running around everywhere. They were walking around the parking lot, sitting in front of their rooms and visiting back and forth from room to room. It looked like everyone was there together as a group.

This thing was shaping up to be a nightmare.

Mike and Byron talked things over and decided that the best thing to do was attempt to get the police involved. They thought they'd better give it a shot.

They drove to the police department, only to find that the building had closed just five minutes before they got there. No problem. Byron called dispatch and told them what they had going on. Dispatch said they would have someone call them right back.

About forty-five minutes later, Byron's cell phone finally rang. Byron explained everything to the police officer. He gave the names of the suspects, the charges, the situation with the motel, the kids, the women, everything.

The officer replied, "If you think it's that dangerous, I recommend that you don't do it. And no, we're not going to help you."

"We have to get these guys. The one guy has felony warrants from your city and the company can't afford to pay the bonds. Do you have a number we should call if things go bad?"

"You're still going after them?"

"Of course we are."

"Okay, but don't call us."

Now what were they going to do? This could get tricky. At least they now knew what the one cousin looked like. Luckily, earlier in the investigation a sympathetic police officer had given Mike and Byron a mug shot of the felon.

That's another oddity about this business. The bondsmen usually have privy to every piece of personal information about their clients that you can imagine. They can get credit checks, social security numbers and full access to court records and the clients sign release forms allowing the bond agents to get information from every agency you can imagine. However, try to get a mug shot of them and you run into a wall.

Here's how the situation stacks up.

Let's say a bond agent has a white male, twenty-three years old, five feet ten inches tall and 160 pounds with brown hair and he misses court. The court sends the agent an order. The bond agent has between thirty to sixty days to return this subject back to the system or pay the entire amount of the bond to the courts. The clock starts ticking the day the defendant doesn't show. Oh, and one other condition: They're not going to show the agent what the defendant looks like.

In order to locate the defendant, Mike could take one of these courses of action: Go to various official Web sites and check out the mug shots of the county's fifty most wanted; open the Sunday paper and see mug shots of a recent bunch of sex offenders they released into the community; go down to the post office and look at mug shots or turn on *America's Most Wanted* and several other television true crime shows and see mug shots plastered all over the place. What he couldn't do was get a picture of the defendant he had been ordered to arrest from the Department of Justice.

After a little strategizing, Mike and Byron decided to get a third guy to help them. They also decided to hit the motel room early in the morning while everyone was asleep.

Luckily for Byron and Mike, the motel management understood the situation and didn't want to put any innocents in jeopardy. The manager decided to give the bounty hunters a key after confirming that their target was indeed in the room.

At 6 A.M. the three men hit the room and surprised the two fugitives, both of whom were sound asleep. Mike and Byron took these dangerous individuals into custody without any resistance.

Chapter 40

Dead or Alive

One morning, Byron came into the office with some startling news to share with Mike: "You're not going to believe what I just heard. The prosecutor's office is totally screwing Liberty on a $150,000 skip."

"How are they doing that?" Mike questioned.

"Do you know Shelby? She sells bail."

"Yeah, I know her."

"Apparently she bailed some drug dealer out on a hundred and fifty grand and then he ripped off the money in the safe at Liberty. From what I hear, she gave him the keys and he grabbed the cash. Then they split it down the middle."

"So the guy went on the run and left them stuck with the bond."

"No, the company busted Shelby. I heard she confessed. Then the owner Gary and his right hand man, Mike Savant, arrested the fugitive when he showed up for his next court date."

"What's the problem? Sounds like this case is finished to me."

"It's not. Gary and Savant picked the dealer up and had a couple of police detectives with them. The detectives were working the burglary case against Shelby and this dealer. After they arrested him they took him over to Liberty's office to interview him. Next thing you know this dude is giving the cops a bunch of info about organized crime and drug dealing and he also claims he has a military missile he can turn over to them."

"Yeah, that's all good, but what's the problem with the bond?"

"After the cops hear about the missile, they call the FBI. Those guys hotfoot it down to the office and talk to this fugitive. Next thing you know the cops and the Feds signed Gary's surrender forms and took custody of the fugitive. He's rolled over and they are using him as a snitch."

"That's great, but I still don't see what the problem is. The Feds took this guy off Gary's hands."

"That's where the problem starts. The attorney goes to the prosecutor's office and talks to some guy who basically says, 'That's tough, pay the bond or produce the fugitive.'"

"Byron, someone's feeding you a line. There's no way a prosecutor would screw up a Federal investigation by making bounty hunters chase their informant around. I don't believe it."

"I'm telling you, Mike, it's true. I guess this guy in the prosecutor's office told the company attorney that the bond company has to turn the defendant over to the jail. He says that giving him to the cops or the FBI isn't good enough."

"I've been around a long time, Byron, and I've never heard of anything like this before."

"Well, according to the guy in the prosecutor's office, the law states that we have to put him in the jail or he's not going to waiver."

"I know the law. What it says is that we can put a fugitive in the facility he was bailed out of or return him to the city or county affiliated with the court issuing the warrant. Turning him over to the police in that jurisdiction for booking is returning him to the issuing court."

"Not according to this guy."

"Too many districts have bounty hunters turn their prisoners over to police officers who sign the paperwork and book the fugitives for them. The bond companies always get off these bonds. In fact, some districts won't let bounty hunters near their jails and they always get off the bonds."

"I know, I guess this guy's being a real jerk about it."

"Byron, it's not up to the prosecutor; it's up to the judge. Who cares what that guy in the prosecutor's office thinks? Have the attorney go before the judge. I guarantee the company will be okay."

"I guess the attorney's working on that right now, but until then Gary doesn't want to take any chances. There's a lot of money on the line."

"Do the Feds know that this prosecutor is forcing us to screw up their case?"

"Nobody knows. I'll be talking with Gary to see if he needs our help."

A couple of days later Mike heard from Byron, who had been helping Gary and Mike Savant with the case. Byron said that Gary and Savant almost had the fugitive one night, but the guy took off in his car. They followed him as long as they could before he spotted them and took off at high speed.

"I went with Gary and Savant to see the fugitive's wife and kids," Byron told Mike. "You should see the place; it was a dump. They had no food in the place and the power was shut off. They had to run an extension cord to the next house so the kids could keep warm. The fugitive's name is Roberto Roque. He's running around town with thousands of dollars on him from his drug deals, but he won't take care of his kids."

"How'd the visit with the wife go? Is she cooperating at all?" Mike asked.

"Not at first. I told her we would get Child Protective Services involved if she didn't help. Finally she got Roque on the phone for me.

I appealed to him to turn himself in, at least for his kids' sake. He told me he was coming over to the house in three minutes and was going to kill me. We waited for several hours, but he never showed."

"Was the wife able to give any useful info?" Mike inquired.

"No, other than the fact that she believes he will try to shoot us if we catch up to him. She even pleaded with us to wear bulletproof vests. She is convinced that he will kill us if given a chance."

"Wonderful. What now?" Mike asked.

"Gary wants you on board with me. Sounds like this could be a bad one."

"No problem partner."

"Great, let's get to work."

Mike and Byron started putting the word out with their informants that they needed this guy and there was going to be a reward for anyone who could come up with any information that pertained to his whereabouts. Roque was in the meth world and they knew a lot of people in that realm.

It didn't take long for the tips to start coming in. They were getting several addresses that he was supposed to frequent and a list of known associates was starting to come together.

They also discovered that Roque had taken the money he stole from Gary and used it to bail out Shelby through a different bail bond company posing as her cousin. Somehow he had gotten a Washington State driver's license with his picture on it identifying him as Juan Alvarez and had a social security card with the same name on it. It was now very probable that if the cops stopped him on a routine traffic violation they would not know who they had.

They got a frantic call from an informant: "Roque bought a new car. He's driving a black sports car and it was just spotted at a duplex near here." He was supposed to be wearing a goofy looking hat and a wig.

Mike and Byron drove westbound. As they drove past the duplex, they immediately spotted Roque, standing on the front porch. There were about five other guys with him and Mike and Byron had to assume that they were all shooters. They drove past the duplex for about two blocks and turned around. They needed a plan, because bailing out of the vehicle and trying to grab Roque was not going to happen. Roque had too much backup with him and Mike and Byron would have to negotiate a chain-link fence, which would give Roque too much time to react.

Just then, they spotted a police car coming toward them. They flagged it down and told the officer what was happening. "These guys are probably all armed and Roque has several outstanding felony warrants, including a felony for possession of a firearm," Byron warned him. Mike also let the officer know that he was a former Tacoma police officer. The officer asked Mike if he knew a specific sergeant and Mike told him that he did. The officer then called the sergeant about the situation. The reply came back: "Good luck, we're not going to help with the arrest of this dangerous felon."

"Can you at least drive up to the house while we hit it?" Mike pleaded with the officer. "Maybe a show of force will make the guy think twice before pulling a gun."

"Nope," the officer told Mike. "I'll hang around the area for awhile in case something happens, but I can't be involved. You're on your own."

Mike turned to Byron after the officer left, "Well, partner, this sucks. What do you want to do?"

"I don't know. There's too many of them for just the two of us."

"I know. Let's drive by again and take another look. The duplex is on the alley. Maybe we can sneak down the alley and catch him by surprise. One of us can deal with Roque and the other can keep his buddies at bay."

They drove past the duplex again. The guys were all standing in the front yard. Mike went another block farther then began to circle the block and head toward the alley. On the next street over, some jersey barriers had been placed in the street. Mike and Byron had to

park a block away from the alley and head out on foot. As they worked
their way down the alley, they were within a couple of houses away
when Roque and his buddies suddenly got into one of the vehicles
parked there and slowly drove away.

A perfect opportunity. If the police had agreed to help, they could
have done a felony traffic stop and this would have been over. Mike
and Byron walked back to their vehicle and the drawing board.

Then a week later Dawn called and told Pam that Mike had been
involved in a shooting...

As the hours slowly ticked by without further word from anyone,
Pam was a nervous wreck.

Mike was so much more than Pam's bounty hunter. Mike was
Pam's closest friend. Over the years, they'd gone through hell together.

As Pam paced the floor, she could still see him in his police uniform
arresting that junkie in the bar. Pam could see him standing in the
hallway of the courthouse, his arm in a sling, surrounded by a small
mob of admirers just days after he was shot. She remembered her
absolute astonishment when he walked in the front door of Arnie's.
Pam had introduced him to his eventual partners, Mark Straub, Chris
Dausch and then Byron Gross. She leaned on him during awful days
and cried on his shoulder after Tony's tragic death. He testified for
Pam, which tipped the scales in her favor after her firing from
Donovan's.

Throughout all the slime, filth and corruption, through all the
betrayal, murder and greed, Mike had always stood by Pam, encouraging her, helping her, defending her when necessary. Without Mike, Pam
never would have had the strength or the courage to open her own
place. If it hadn't been for him, she wouldn't be where she was: the only
single female who owned and operated her own bail bond business.

It occurred to her at that moment that she'd never once told Mike
how grateful she was for him for standing by her all these years. She

had never once thanked him for helping her do it "the right way." Because of him, the industry had changed and for the better. The moment Mike's licensing proposal went into effect, most bounty hunters they knew working on the street at that time went out of business.

Mike not only worked with Pam but, due to his expertise, he also freelanced for other bonding companies. They both felt it was a necessary step in promoting public safety.

All politics aside, despite the fact most companies bicker with their competition and play price wars, the bottom line is dangerous criminals jump bail every day and are running helter-skelter on the streets. In the interest of public safety, bounty hunters have to re-arrest those criminals as soon as possible before they have a chance to re-offend. And Roberto Roque was one dangerous guy. Shooting off guns in drive-bys and having a missile in his living room showed that Roberto was in the big leagues. Pam knew if anyone could find and arrest him, Mike could.

But at what cost? After thirty-four years in law enforcement, this time, did the bad guy win? In one pivotal moment, did the bad guy fire his weapon taking Mike out? All it would take was Mike turning his back on the defendant for one split second; one moment of being distracted...one lucky shot...

"There's a phone call for you," one of Pam's bail agents said quietly, interrupting her thoughts.

This was it. This might be the call. How was Pam going to handle it if it was Mike's wife, Dawn, calling to tell her that Mike had died at the scene?

Pam took a deep breath and picked up the phone. "Hello?"

"Hello, boss."

"Mike!" Pam burst into tears. "You're not dead after all!"

"Not the last time I checked," he chuckled.

"Then who was shot?"

"The bad guy."

"Did you shoot him, Mike?"

"Yes ma'am. I had to. It was either him or me and it wasn't going to be me."

"What happened?"

"It's a long story. I don't have time to go into now."

"When are you coming back to the office?"

"All four of us are together: Gary, Savant, Byron and me. The police just let us go. We decided to go back to Gary's office but it's surrounded by reporters. I guess the shooting's all over the news. Gary doesn't want to deal with that right now. Why don't you meet us at our favorite pub and I'll tell you all about it . . . Your bounty hunter could really use a beer."

"You got it!"

A few minutes later, they were seated at the pub. Though Gary and Savant didn't drink, they graciously ordered sodas and Pam ordered a pitcher.

After it was delivered, Mike poured Pam a glass. Before he could say a word, Pam stopped him.

"I know this is corny, you guys, but please indulge me. When I heard someone was shot today and I didn't know who, I nearly went out of my mind. This was one of the worst days in my entire life. But you all came home. That's always the goal," Pam choked up. "You all came home."

Ceremoniously, Pam and Mike clinked glasses together.

"*Now* can I tell you what happened?" Mike said, smiling.

"Let's hear it," Pam smiled back.

"Okay," he took a deep breath. "Here's how it all went down..."

Chapter 41

The Big One

Soon after losing Roque at the duplex, Mike and Byron heard through the grapevine that Roque had trouble with the trunk lock on his new black sports car. He couldn't open the trunk and screwed up the lock trying to force it open. He had to return it to the car lot for repairs.

Mike and Byron drove by the used car lot and saw Roque's vehicle. They got the plate number and a good look at it. The car lot owner then took the vehicle to a repair shop he owned on the other side of town. Now for the hard part: They had to keep their eyes on the car until it was repaired and returned to Roque. Some of the surveillance would go well into the night. They had gotten word that Roque was friends with some of the employees and partied with them at the shop. Mike and Byron didn't want him to pick the car up after hours and miss him.

Taking turns, Gary and Savant sat watching the car while Byron and Mike pounded the streets with informants looking for him.

A week after the surveillance started, Byron and Mike headed out to a nearby neighborhood. The route took them past the car lot. As they were driving by Byron yelled, "There's the car!"

290 The Big One

The car was sitting in the exact same spot that they had seen it a week earlier. This was it! The car was fixed and Roque should be showing up to get it.

Byron called Gary and told him the car was back at the used car lot. Gary thought he and Mike were crazy. He told them that he and Savant were looking at the car at the repair shop across town.

"No, you're not!" Byron told him. "There were two small black cars at the shop; you're looking at the other one!"

"You're right!" Gary said. "They put the other black car in that stall. We're on our way."

Byron and Mike set up across the street from the lot in Mike's car. They'd been swapping vehicles throughout the investigation to keep the tweekers confused.

Roque's car was parked in a perfect spot. The lot was surrounded by a chain-link fence and jammed full of cars all bumper-to-bumper. There was a narrow opening in the fence and Roque's car was wedged between the fence and a wall of vehicles. If Byron and Mike pulled up behind him, there was no way out.

A few agonizing moments later they saw a large SUV that Roque was associated with drive slowly by the car lot.

"That's him on the corner! They just dropped him off!"

Roque was walking along the sidewalk toward the car lot. This time he had a fuzzy brown wig on that looked more like roadkill than hair and was wearing a backpack. Byron and Mike watched him walk up to the black car then continue to the small office in the center of the lot.

Byron and Mike bantered back and forth, "Should we take him in the office?"

"No, there might be a way out the back."

"Should we walk into the lot like customers and take him out in the open?"

"No, innocent people might get involved. He would also have a chance to run if he spotted us."

"That's it, then. We'll take him in the car. We can block him in and he'll never see us coming."

About two minutes later, Roque exited the office and walked directly to the car. He took the backpack off and put it in vehicle. The driver's door was open and he was just starting to get inside. The time was now! They were on a busy street but luckily there was no traffic to slow them down. Savant and Gary wouldn't be so lucky.

Mike powered his car over and came to a sliding stop directly behind Roque's car. His car's passenger door was now only a few feet from Roque's trunk. Byron tried to bail out of the car before it came to a complete stop, but he couldn't get out. Mike slammed the car into park as Byron manually unlocked the door. He hit the ground running toward the passenger side of Roque's vehicle screaming, "Bail enforcement! Warrant for your arrest!" Mike piled out of the drivers side running around the front of his car and up to Roque's driver's side door also yelling, "Bail enforcement! We have a warrant for your arrest!"

As Mike approached Roque's door, he noticed that the window was heavily tinted. Mike could just make out Roque's silhouette in the driver's seat. As soon as he got close enough to grab the door handle, Mike saw Roque's body stiffen and he sat straight up. A moment later he slammed the car into reverse and almost stood out of his seat pushing on the accelerator. The rear end of the car started bouncing off the pavement as the tires squealed and billowed smoke. The car finally got enough traction to move and it took off in reverse with Roque turning the steering wheel to the right. At that point Mike didn't think Roque knew he was blocked in. At the same time, Mike saw Byron on the other side of the car lurch backward and to the side as though the car had hit him. Then came the sound of metal smashing together as Roque rammed Mike's car. As soon as he hit Mike's car, he threw the vehicle into drive, turned the wheel toward Mike and lit up the tires again.

Mike was trapped with nowhere to go. They were surrounded by cars from the lot and Mike didn't dare take the time to turn and look for an escape route. Roque was heading toward Mike fast. At this point Mike had made up his mind what to do. He took one step backward pulling out his gun and aimed. Just as Mike was pulling his trigger he heard Byron shoot one round at the car. Then Bam! Bam! Mike fired two rounds as fast as he could squeeze them off into Roque's driver's side window from mere inches away. The tinted glass seemed to instantly disappear and the car screeched to a halt. Roque was sitting upright in the driver's seat staring straight ahead. Mike knew he had found his mark.

Byron ran toward the passenger door yelling, "I shot at his tire hoping it would stop him!"

Just as Byron was starting to open the passenger door, Roque suddenly lurched toward the passenger side of the vehicle, throwing his upper body over the console and shoving his left hand under the passenger seat. Byron had the door open by then and grabbed Roque's left arm.

"I think he's grabbing a gun! I think he's grabbing a gun!"

Mike had the driver's door open now and yelled at Byron to hang onto Roque's arm; if he came up with a gun, Mike had him covered.

"Hang on to him, Byron!" Mike yelled as he looked at Byron bent over Roque, hanging on as hard as he could. "Don't let him pull that arm out!"

If Mike had to shoot Roque again, he would have to shoot low to avoid hitting Byron. Roque was bent over the console at the waist and Mike was looking directly at his butt. The only lethal shot he had at this angle was one he didn't want to take. Some refer to it as the old Texas Heart Shot.

Slowly the fight left Roque. He looked up at Byron's face and gasped. Then his head slowly sank to the seat as he vomited a massive amount of blood on Byron.

Mike knew it was over. He moved back and holstered his weapon. Byron stepped back from the car covered in Roque's blood.

Gary and Savant had finally fought their way through traffic to the car lot. Mike signaled thumbs down. Gary knew what Mike meant. "Call 911," Mike hollered.

Byron asked, "Should we pull Roque out of the vehicle and do something?"

"No, don't!" Mike instructed all of them. "It's over; do not move a thing. This is a crime scene now and we've got to leave everything just as it is."

Then a thought struck Mike: *This is going to be all over the news in about a half hour.* Mike needed to call his wife and let her know he was okay. He knew if she heard about the scene without hearing his voice she would be sick with worry. He grabbed his cell phone and called her work number. The answering machine came on and that's when Mike remembered that she had stayed home.

Quickly he started dialing his home number. Before he could finish the commands started in.

"Everybody on the ground! Drop your weapons! Everybody down!"

Mike looked up to see a very impressive army of police officers bearing down on them. There were too many of them walking abreast toward the lot to count. The street was a four lane main arterial and all traffic had been stopped; they were coming hard, AR-15s and handguns pointed. They weren't playing.

Mike hit the ground and pushed his cell phone away. He'd lived through the fight to get Roque and didn't need any mistakes now.

As soon as Mike was on the ground, an officer came from behind him and started to cuff him. Mike looked up at the officer, told him his name and that he was a former cop.

"I'm the shooter and that's the gun that was used," Mike said, motioning to his duty belt and holster.

"Okay," the officer said and he relayed the information to the other officers.

Then he handcuffed Mike, removed Mike's gun from its holster, helped Mike to his feet and led him to a police car.

"I've got to pat you down and take everything from you."

"I know you do. You've got to do your job."

The officer emptied Mike's pockets, removed his duty belt and placed him in the back of a police car shutting the door.

Mike was wearing a heavy jacket and vest. His hands were cuffed behind his back in the back of a cop car. It was hot out and Mike was starting to sweat profusely.

From the back of the squad car Mike could see the medical personnel working on the suspect. Roque was on a gurney and they were performing CPR.

Mike knew all of these officers' adrenaline had to be spiked. They had approached four armed men only knowing that a shooting had occurred. Despite the intensity of the situation, Mike was very impressed with the professionalism of these officers and their treatment of Mike and his partners. Job well done by Lakewood PD.

Several minutes later, the officer returned to the car and he and Mike headed to the Lakewood Police Station.

He told Mike, "I've got to take you to the station and you will be meeting with some detectives. You doing okay back there?"

"Yeah, I'm good."

Mike thought: *Thirty years of putting people in this position, I never dreamt that I would be the one getting cuffed and stuffed.*

They arrived at the station and Mike was put in an interview room. Two detectives joined him. Immediately they asked if Mike was okay and if he needed anything as they took the handcuffs off.

"I could really use some water. It was hot as hell in the prowl car."

"No problem."

"Is there any way," Mike asked worriedly, "you can let me call my wife? This is probably already on the news. I've got to let her know I'm alright."

"Sure thing," the detective said and handed Mike his cell phone.

Mike's wife's voice was shaky and weak when she answered the phone. Immediately Mike could tell she'd already heard the news.

"It's me. How ya doing?" Mike asked as casually as he could.

"Are you okay?"

"I'm fine; everybody's okay."

"You're not hurt? Are you sure you're alright?"

"I'm good, I promise. I'm at the police station now talking with some detectives. They're treating me very well. Everybody's fine, all the guys are okay. None of us was hurt, I promise you."

"Okay, I was scared."

"I know, but now I've got to talk with the detectives for awhile. We will probably be here several hours. I can't talk right now but I'll call again as soon as I can."

"Okay, I love you. Bye."

Mike handed the detective's phone back to him and he nodded to Mike with approval. It was his job to listen carefully to everything Mike said and he seemed to appreciate the way Mike handled that call.

The interview was by the book. Mike told his story to two detectives. After they finished questioning him they went over it again; this time it was recorded.

During the interview, Mike told them this never should have happened. He mentioned seeing Roque on the porch in front of the duplex and the refusal of the police in the area to help.

One of the detectives told Mike that Lakewood didn't operate that way. If bounty hunters called in with felony warrants, the police were happy to assist.

After interviewing Mike, they placed him in a holding cell that was about four feet by six feet with no window. He was in that cell for around an hour, although it seemed like an eternity. Mike tried to sit on the concrete bench, yet couldn't stay put for more than a couple of seconds. He wound up spending the entire time pacing back and forth.

Finally, the detectives finished interviewing the rest of the guys and told them they were going to cut them loose. They would then forward the results of their investigation to the prosecutor's office.

Mike felt compelled to ask the detectives about the suspect. Inside he knew the answer; he had watched Roque die after he was shot, but he still had to know conclusively.

The detective simply replied, "He passed."

The first thing Mike did when he got out of the police station was call his wife.

"The detectives are done with us. How are you doing?"

"I'm okay," she said.

"How did you find out about it?"

"I got a call from my mother. I knew something was wrong right away when she called me by my name instead of calling me 'Sis.' She also told me that she had my brother on three way calling and he needed to tell me something.

"Knowing I'd be frantic, my brother said, 'Hey, Sis, first thing is Mike is okay.' As soon as he said that I jumped up and knew it was something bad. 'Mike was involved in a shooting a few minutes ago. I'm off duty today but one of my partners is working and he heard Mike's name mentioned on the news. He called me right away.'

"I asked if you were alright. He said, 'We don't have all the info yet; sounds like he got in a gunfight with a car lot employee or something like that. They are doing aggressive CPR on one person. We think it's possibly the bad guy. The reports are sketchy right now but I think Mike's okay.'

"As soon as my brother told me that, I got sick to my stomach. I hung up and went upstairs to turn on the news. Our daughter saw the look on my face and knew something was wrong. She called me 'Mommy'; she's sixteen years old and called me Mommy. She asked, 'What's wrong, Mommy?'

"I told her, 'Dad's been in a shooting.' Immediately she burst into tears. I kept telling her you were alright. I didn't know for sure but I didn't want her to be upset. We turned the TV on and the first thing we saw was, 'Breaking News!' Then we saw an aerial view of your car.

There were those little yellow evidence things all over your car and the street. We thought those were all bullet holes in your car.

"Our daughter kept crying and saying, 'What will we do without Dad? He can't be dead. He drives me nuts but I love him.' I tried to reassure her but then you finally called from the police station."

"How's she doing now?"

"She's still upset but she knows you're alright."

"I was so scared, husband. I know that news reports never get things right the first time. But all I could think was that they might have thought you were the suspect and you were the one getting CPR. I called Pam to find out more and she didn't know anything either. You should call her. She didn't know anything until I told her. She sounded very upset. Let her know you're okay."

"I will. I'll call her right after we hang up. Did you call my mom?"

"Yes, I did. I called and said, 'First thing is Mike's okay but he's been in another shooting. Your mother just said, 'Oh no, not again.' Her voice was cracking and I could tell she was on the verge of crying.

"I told her that you were not shot but I think you killed a guy. You'd better call her."

"I will. I'll call Pam too. Can I come by and pick you up? I'm way too pumped to come home and sit on the couch. I'm going to grab a beer with the boys and unwind. You are very welcome to come along."

"No, I'm going to stay home with our daughter. You go with the guys but come home as soon as you can."

"I will," Mike promised.

"Then I called you and here we are. Well, Pam, that's about it. It's over."

Pam didn't know whether to laugh or cry. "Thank God."

The investigation by the prosecutor's office seemed to drag on forever. The word finally came down that no charges would be filed.

Mike, Byron, Gary and Savant could come to the police station and pick up their gear.

Once the investigation was complete they learned a few things about it:

The backpack Roque was initially wearing was unzipped and under the front passenger seat. It contained a 9mm pistol and a Mack 10. That's what Roque had been trying to grab.

Both of Mike's rounds hit Roque. One of them entered his left armpit, traveling through both lungs and his heart and came out the other side.

One of the informants Mike and Byron had been using on the case had been trying to work both sides. Byron and Mike had arrested him on his own outstanding bond and he was still in jail when the shooting occurred.

Once the informant heard about the confrontation he got hold of the detectives and tried to work out a deal for himself. He told the detective that he would testify in court that Byron and Mike planted the guns on Roque if the police would let him out of jail.

That little plot failed miserably. Roque's wife had already described the guns he had been carrying around to detectives so they knew what to look for, but they still had to go that extra mile and make sure.

With the investigation over and all involved cleared of any wrongdoing, it was time to once again focus on the living.

Pam's cases were still piling up and, as much as Pam and Mike could have used a break from the daily grind, life goes on.

Mike and Pam are still working together. She's still getting them out of jail and he's still putting them back in.

Hell of a way to make a living!

Aftermath

Politicking

Admittedly, Mike and Pam are not politicians. They are quite happy doing what they do: Pam bails people out of jail and when they skip Mike puts them back in jail. They've devoted their lives to their respective professions. However, they are very concerned that due to current bail trends, it may not be long before all bond agents and bounty hunters are quickly out of business.

For the first time, in 1997, an Indiana-based company enabled incarcerated inmates to post their own bails at the jail or court with a credit card. Since then, thirty other states have followed suit.

For several years in Washington State, Thurston County has allowed inmates to post their own bails directly with the jail or court. Auburn, Enumclaw and Wilkeson Courts in King County have since begun the same practice as well.

So, what's wrong with that? Pam and Mike believe plenty.

First, to become a bail agent in Washington State, one has to gain many credentials. Agents have to have clean police records, undergo background checks with the Federal and State governments, pass State tests, become licensed with the State and relicense every year—

all of which takes a lot of time and money. No such requirements are demanded of court clerks or jail guards.

Both Pam and Mike cry foul. If court clerks and jail personnel are doing the same job as bail agents, they should be licensed by the State and held to the same standards as bond agents. To give preferential treatment to one group and not the other is unfair, unethical and should be stopped.

Second, bail agents perform vital roles that court clerks and jail guards *can't* do:

> • Bonding companies will monitor defendants' whereabouts while they are out on bail and their cases are pending. If defendants commit new crimes while out on bail, bond agents usually know about it. State law says bond agents can return defendants to custody if public safety is at risk.
>
> • By returning defendants to custody, bond agents "produce" them in court to ensure justice is served. Though bond agents make no presumptions about guilt or innocence—that's up to the judge and jury to decide—bond agents return defendants to court so their guilt or innocence can be determined.
>
> • In a very real way, bond agents help reduce crime and promote public safety. Fugitives know that the police don't have the time or the manpower to specifically look for them—but bond agents do. By making all their own arrests, bond agents work with the police to get dangerous criminals off the streets.

With courts setting bail and, for instance, with a $1,000 bail bond or $100 cash, defendants are posting their own cash at the jail. The real problem with this is if defendants don't go to court, the court keeps the bail money. Courts financially benefit when defendants fail to appear. No one, to Pam and Mike's knowledge, specifically goes out to look for these individuals to return them to custody.

Pam has been in the bail business more than a quarter of a century. She learned from experience that defendants who aren't carefully monitored by bail agents and quickly apprehended after they jump bail often re-offend. In some areas, not surprisingly, the crime rate has already doubled and will only continue to escalate.

In 1978 Oregon outlawed bail agents and allowed defendants to post their own bails at the jail or court. What wasn't anticipated was that the crime rate would skyrocket. With no one designated to arrest fugitives after they jump bail, there are currently more than 26,000 felony warrants in one county in Oregon alone. This figure does not include misdemeanor warrants, which could easily totally in the thousands. Oregon, where crime has gotten so rampant, is ranked the eleventh highest in the nation for overall crime and is considering changing the law to allow bail agents again.

Pam and Mike's main concern is the victims who don't get their days in court. What about public safety?

In Pam and Mike's opinions, bail agents and bounty hunters have little known but vital roles in the justice system. Bypassing them merely to add funds to the court treasury is a serious and costly mistake.

Pam and Mike believe public safety is in jeopardy. They strongly feel new legislation is needed to outlaw this dangerous trend and to keep bail bond agents and bounty hunters in their separate, distinct roles in the criminal justice system before it's too late.

Pam's Acknowledgments

Linda Shank, thank you for having the courage to do it right and for being there when I needed you the most. You taught me everything I know about the bail bond business. May you be forever remembered for your great love, inner strength and personal integrity.

Mom and Dad, thank you for making my dreams come true and for your continuing love and support.

Brenda, you were the first one to read the rough draft. Had you been less than enthusiastic, the outcome could have been much different. Thanks for your excellent advice.

Dawn, you encouraged me to pursue my dream of publication. Thanks for being as special as you are and for doing what you do.

Val Dumond, an accomplished writer and publisher in your own right, if it weren't for you, this manuscript would probably be in a dark closet somewhere gathering dust. You helped give it life.

Joan Dunphy, Publisher of New Horizon Press, you took a chance on Mike and I, because you thought we had something important to say.

If it weren't for all of you, *Betrayal, Murder and Greed* would never have become a reality.

Mike's Acknowledgments

First and foremost I have to thank Pam Phree, who's worked with me for more years than I can count. She came to me and asked for my help in fulfilling her dream of writing this book. Now that it's done I must give her credit for making me accomplish something I could have never dreamed of. Kudos to you, Pam. You always try to bring out the best in those around you.

I need to thank my wife and daughter for trying to teach me about commas, quotation marks and a bunch of other weird stuff that's necessary for writing.

Last of all I must pay tribute to all the partners I've had in my life. That goes for both police and bounty hunting partners. Those are the guys who made sure I'm still around today. And since this is about bounty hunting, I have to give a special thanks to Mark Straub and Chris Dausch. Thanks guys.